WASHINGTON *Rollercoaster*

by

SONDRA GOTLIEB

Doubleday Canada Limited, Toronto

Canadian Cataloguing in Publication Data

Gotlieb, Sondra, 1936-
    Washington rollercoaster

ISBN 0-385-25254-4

1. Gotlieb, Sondra, 1936-   -Biography.
2. Ambassadors' wives–Canada–Biography.
3. Ambassadors' wives–United States–Biography.
4. Washington (D.C.)–Social life and customs.I. Title

PS8563.0838Z53   1990   973.927'092'4   C89-095371-6
PR9199.3.G6Z47   1990

Design: Styles Design
Jacket photos: courtesy Sondra Gotlieb
Washington Capitol photo: Joe Sohm/Masterfile
Typesetting: Southam Business Information
    and Communications Group Inc.
Printed and bound in the USA

Published in Canada by
    Doubleday Canada Limited
    105 Bond Street
    Toronto, Ontario
    M5B 1Y3

Care has been taken to trace ownership of copyright material in this book.
The publishers will gladly receive any information that will enable them to
rectify errors or omissions affecting references or credit lines in subsequent
editions.

CONTENTS

To Rebecca, Marc and Rachel

1/The Twinkling Hostess

"THE GLITTERING EMBASSY does not exist in Washington today, as it did in the 60s and 70s," wrote Sally Quinn in 1987. "The embassies that have always been powerful and influential are the British, the French and the Italian, depending on who the ambassadors are. Occasionally other nations' embassies will rise to prominence: Canada's under Allan Gotlieb and his wife, Sondra."

"The Gotliebs," she continued in her *Washington Post Magazine* article, "almost single-handedly managed to resurrect the Golden Days. During the first four years of the Reagan administration they were able to pull in most of the members of the administration, the Congress, the hot diplomats and the press. They instinctively knew how to put together a powerful Washington crowd, unlike so many who just keep passing down their outdated guest lists from one ambassador to another."

According to *Vanity Fair*, I was "Washington's twinkling hostess."

I had many ambitions in life, but being a hostess was never one of them, "twinkling" or otherwise. When I was sixteen, I longed to be a Winnipeg Blue Bombers Football Princess. My mother dissuaded me from entering the contest because, as she said delicately, "You have a little more baby fat than the rest of the contestants."

I wanted to marry, which I did; have children, which I have; and write, which I do. Like the rest of my female friends, I also wanted an absorbing job. Giving parties was never considered either absorbing or a job. In their eyes and mine, a hostess was not a serious person. A hostess was a relic from another generation, a social climber, a nouveau billionaire's wife in New York or Texas. But today even the super-rich wife will tell *W* magazine or *Town & Country* that she spends her days counselling at drug clinics and that the only reason she gives parties is to raise money for charity.

So when I first arrived in Washington I made a point of telling people that I had been a writer, a journalist, and a novelist long before I became an ambassador's wife. I even bragged about being the first woman in twenty years to win the Stephen Leacock Award for Humour. But I soon discovered that I was boring everyone.

In political Washington you are identified by your job. And the only job I had in my first two years was that of ambassador's wife and hostess. When I eventually began to write satirical columns in the *Washington Post*, Meg Greenfield, the Editorial Page editor and *Newsweek* columnist, described me as "author and wife of the Canadian Ambassador." But since my columns, in part, made fun about things that happened at our embassy and other Washington parties, the word *hostess* still stuck to me.

My mother believed that inviting strangers for dinner was "pushy," especially if they came from a headier social scale than her own. Mother was a hostess all right, but she wouldn't have dreamed of asking anyone who wasn't a close friend or family. The nearest she came to inviting a celebrity to her house was the night she invited my high-school principal for dinner. The evening made my father so uneasy he couldn't sleep afterwards. "I don't need that kind of excitement," he complained.

I have more than a touch of my father in my character. I don't sleep on nights after parties and I always whined to my husband about the social overload of embassy entertaining. "Don't you think it's pushy," I'd say, "to ask strangers for dinner?" He'd answer, "That's the job; that's what an ambassador's wife is supposed to do."

When I was asked to speak in public or on television or radio, they always wanted me to talk about hostessing. If I switched the subject to acid rain, to other U.S.-Canadian problems, or to the Washington political game, my audience would listen politely, and then someone would ask, "Do you use place mats or table cloths?" In the papers I was "columnist and hostess" or "humorist and hostess" or, in less favourable articles, just "hostess" or "ambassador's wife." So that word *hostess* has stuck. I'm convinced I can't take it away. Even if I returned to Winnipeg and devoted myself entirely to curling, the headlines would read, "Sondra Gotlieb, member of the winning ladies' team at Manitoba Bonspiel and well-known hostess."

I was astounded and bewildered at my success as a hostess because I didn't like being one. *Vanity Fair* said, "The Canadian Embassy in Washington is the only social hot spot on Embassy Row. Those who wouldn't be caught dead at an embassy affair will always go to the Gotliebs' certain of meeting someone they know or need to know." It was mystifying.

Two parties given at our embassy within a week of each other illustrate the "Golden Days" Kennedy-style parties that we were supposed to have recreated during the Reagan administration. They took place in December 1985, one year after the largest political landslide in U.S. history ushered in Reagan's second-term administration and what was expected to be the flowering of the Reagan Golden Age. One of the events was in honour of Walter and Lenore Annenberg and the other was in honour of ourselves.

Our guests at the two events included White House officials, senators, Republicans and Democrats, intellectuals (or rather think-tank persons, the word *intellectual* being considered pejorative during the Reagan administration), movie people and famous names who came into Washington on private planes from New York and California. Some were good friends of each other, some were secret enemies, some are dead and some became part of the walking wounded of Washington. A few, such as the Stevenses, the Bradlees, the Bradens and the Krafts, were hold-overs from the Kennedy days.

The first of the two parties, a buffet lunch in honour of the Annenbergs, occurred during the weekend of the Kennedy Honors ceremonies. The Kennedy Honors, which always occurs on a Sunday night in the first week of December, celebrates distinguished Americans' contributions to the performing arts. Such artists as Lucille Ball, Isaac Stern, Ray Charles and Virgil Thomson were given awards in the presence of President Reagan and Mrs. Reagan during an elaborate and glamorous production orchestrated by George Stevens at the Kennedy Center. It was Hollywood on the Potomac, as social and business people from all over the United States paid as much as $1,500 a ticket to attend this coveted annual weekend in order to mingle with the President, cabinet officials, ranking senators and congressmen, as well as Hollywood stars.

Official Washington always turned out in great numbers because cabinet secretaries and senators and congressmen from the heartland of America were keen to meet Hollywood celebrities. An ambassador did not usually attend the Kennedy Honors because of the prohibitive cost unless, exceptionally, he and his wife (I don't recall any women ambassadors) were asked as guests, as we were a few times. Beyond the spectacular main event there were always private lunches and dinners from Saturday to Monday on the weekend of the affair.

Walter and Lenore "Lee" Annenberg, members of the influential kitchen cabinet and close friends of the President, had invited us the previous year to a weekend at Sunnylands, their winter home in Palm Springs. We had come to know and like them when Lee was Chief of Protocol in the first year of the Reagan administration. We knew they were coming to Washington for the Kennedy Honors event.

About a month before the Kennedy Honors, I called Lee in Palm Springs to ask if we could have a luncheon in their honour. We had in mind reciprocating their hospitality by having a small party. But the Washington law was that parties are expandable, and this was especially true during the Kennedy Honors weekend. Whenever we gave a party for someone, American or Canadian, we always asked them if there was anyone special they would like us to invite. Lee responded to my request for suggestions by mentioning that a lot of the President's California friends were flying in with her and that it might be a good idea to include some of the visitors along with our own Washington list.

A media baron is always a powerful drawing-card in the administration, and this was especially so in the case of Walter Annenberg and Lee, the President's close friends. Certain people whom Allan needed to know better in the White House might come because of them.

Allan and I always gave White House and administration officials, senators and congressmen first priority on our guest list even if we might have preferred to ask some friends or neighbours who had no interest in foreign policy or politics. We accepted the principle that a diplomat is not doing his job when his invitation lists reflect only his or his wife's personal social preferences. Washingtonians see diplomatic parties as fishing ponds and if some of the guests they want to catch are difficult fish, they expect the hostess to know the bait. The fact is that an embassy's business is to promote the good of its country, whether it be by increasing the sale of light-armoured trucks or by finding out what's going to happen during arms-control talks. Social occasions may offer the best opportunity to lobby for a foreign country's interest. Hence we regarded it as axiomatic that embassy parties were extensions of work and that was why guest lists and seating plans took on a primary importance.

But we also accepted another and more important principle: a guest who does not have an enjoyable or interesting evening will not dine a second time at your table.

That week of the two events was one of the most difficult I had experienced in Washington. Two large parties so close together made the selection of guests especially complicated. Obviously we didn't want repetitions. Luckily many of the lunch guests had come from New York, California or Texas just for the Kennedy Honors, and so for the Annenbergs we found ourselves inviting

Bob Hope, a large portion of the Reagan kitchen cabinet, industrialists and multimillionaires. We mixed them with some high officials such as the Chief Justice of the Supreme Court and the White House Chief of Staff – not our usual Washington combination.

The dinner we were giving later that same week was in honour of our fifth year in Washington. For this second event we decided to concentrate on other Washingtonians we had come to know well and liked – cabinet and other officials and politically influential individuals.

Looking back at those prominent in public life who attended our parties in that particular season, I can now see that they were a very special group, special in more ways than anyone then knew or could even have guessed.

Among them were those on the political stage to whom fortune has been benign: George Shultz and Caspar Weinberger of the Reagan cabinet were there. So were Katharine Graham and Ben Bradlee of the *Washington Post*; Warren Phillips, publisher of the *Wall Street Journal*; David Brinkley and Barbara Walters; *Vanity Fair* editor Tina Brown; Federal Reserve Chief Paul Volcker and labour chief Lane Kirkland; Estée Lauder and her son Ron, whom Pierre Trudeau, a couple of years earlier, had called the Pentagon Pipsqueak and who subsequently ran for mayor of New York.

But there were others who dined at our table that season, most at the height of their very great power, for whom fortune had other things in mind. Top White House aide Michael Deaver was one of them. He had recently left the White House for a career in lobbying and public relations. There was Donald Regan, newly appointed White House Chief of Staff. There were the high White House National Security officials Robert "Bud" McFarlane and Admiral John Poindexter, CIA chief William Casey and Attorney General Ed Meese.

This was before the Iran-Contra frenzy, before the independent prosecutor hit on the Reagan team, and before the first indictments.

When I look back on the events of that period, I think of them as the meals of the walking wounded-to-be. We had survived a full posting of four years – and, in the view of many, had flourished in the most complex and power-driven town in the world. We wanted to celebrate. We had no inkling that suffering and disaster would occur within less than a year for many of our guests, and, in a different way, for ourselves.

Within a few months we were the subject of headlines and articles in the *Washington Post*, the *Toronto Star*, the *New York Times*, *Newsweek*, and other journals that were far less gushy than the *Vanity Fair* article about the "twinkling hostess." They occurred after a dinner we gave for Prime Minister Mulroney, when I was reported to have slapped my social secretary, Connie Connor, in front of the company including Vice President George Bush: "Embassy wife turns heads with Slap Heard in Two Continents"; "Slap echoes around continent."

In a way I was bemused at my sudden political importance – "continental" reverberations no less – but I wasn't so amused by some of the newspaper stories. One *Washington Post* article, published several weeks after the incident, warned readers about "A Big Chill for Canada." It pronounced that we had closed shop because of the slap embarrassment and also hinted that my husband was going to be fired because of what was becoming known as the Michael Deaver affair. Legends like this continued for more than a year, even though several thousand people managed to break bread with us during the period of our "chill."

My "slap flap", and the contract signed by Allan on behalf of the Canadian Government with Michael Deaver's public-relations firm, bought us a seat on the Washington rollercoaster, a wild ride taken by so many people in this book. The "slap flap" had a relatively short media life, to the disappointment of some who said it would be written on my tombstone instead of "twinkling hostess", but the dramatic Deaver affair and attempts to drag my husband and me into it resonated for a couple of years in the U.S. and Canadian press, as the prosecution of Deaver for perjury slowly worked its way through the U.S. legal system.

This book is about our adventure in the United States, a country whose difference from my own is greater than I would ever have believed. It is about our adventure in Washington, a town whose customs and politics have to be experienced or witnessed first-hand to be understood. It is about the trials of running a large embassy residence and entertaining people whose names and jobs, according to my mother's credo, would make my behaviour beyond "pushy." It was an unfamiliar and overwhelmingly public way of life. My years were exciting, exhausting, exhilarating and saddening.

2/My Life As a Saleswoman

"DO Y'ALL HAVE to wear national dress?" a Southern lady asked me at a lunch given by a senator's wife in the Senate dining room. Those lunches followed a tried and true recipe. Take two wives of foreign envoys, mix them with a wife of a visiting constituent and add a new "wife of" from the executive branch. Once we have been ushered to the table, the senator's wife tells us about her surprise. The surprise is not that the famous bean soup in the Senate dining room is mediocre and that beer and hard liquor are banned. The surprise is that her husband, flanked by his outriders, will arrive for a moment during our meal so that we wives can have our pictures taken with him. He rushes into the dining room, pauses, poses, smiles at the camera. His wife then gives him a grateful glance as he takes his place at another table with his peers.

The question about Canada's national dress was put to me by a constituent's wife who had settled for a while in Washington. I was wearing my dull brown suit and a blouse with a stringy bow, and she probably thought that was it.

"We don't have a national dress in Canada," I replied stiffly. Realizing that I had chosen the outfit of my own free will, she tried to extricate herself.

"Well, the other ambassadors' wives wear national dress or beautiful clothes made by their native designers. I've been asked to lovely fashion shows at the French, British and Italian embassies. I'm going to the Japanese today. They're having a tea ceremony with the modelling."

So that's how our fashion extravaganza started. I was goaded by a clothes-crazy Kentuckian or Georgian into becoming a saleswoman for my country. (She also made me much more self-conscious about my own clothes.) Not only did I learn to hawk clothes from the Embassy Residence, but we set up a permanent if metaphorical pushcart selling everything from Canadian foods and holiday resorts for American conventioneers, to race-horses, weapon systems, artistic productions, movies, ballets, circuses, orchestras, plays and, not least of all, light-armoured trucks from Ontario. We touted our significant individuals – writers, performers, promoters, bankers – and offered to sell them to America at breakfasts, lunches, teas, cocktails, dinners and midnight buffets.

Although the birth of our fashion promotion came from a barbed remark, it grew into a gala fashion show that was written up in the *New York Times* by Bernadine Morris, their premier fashion commentator.

Between the remark and the result we used craftiness, chutzpah and haute strategic planning to make it come true. Beverly Rockett, friend, photographer and then fashion editor of the Canadian publication *City Woman*, volunteered to organize the show from the Canadian end. Patrick Gossage, the press attaché at the embassy, threw in his resources. But Ms. Morris, who was charming, told me that the *New York Times* would only cover our fashion show if it were an evening social event. "We really want to see a few insiders, you know, Washington politicians at the fashion show. We're not interested in ladies' lunches."

Which meant part of my job was to get powerful Washington out for the New York fashion press.

"Senators and cabinet secretaries don't go to fashion shows," I was told categorically by those who know such things in Washington. "Have a ladies' lunch instead."

But the *New York Times* did not want a ladies' lunch. And I was informed that the Canadian designers who had been chosen to show their clothes at the Embassy Residence wanted pictures and publicity in the *New York Times*. So I decided to lie – perhaps it was more a sin of omission. I told Connie Connor, my social secretary, to put the word "gala" on the invitation to dinner, and leave out the word "fashion." Which meant those Washington insiders so necessary to the *New York Times* would not know until it was too late that the "gala" event was a Canadian fashion show. If they knew, they would not come. If they didn't come, there would be no coverage in the *Times*. I "forgot" to tell Allan that we forgot to put "fashion show" on the dinner invitation.

By this time, Beverly, up in Canada, was already making commitments. She decided to organize, with the help of the Quebec government, a large buffet lunch to be followed by a fashion show so that the Canadian designers could have their clothes modelled in front of chief executive officers from major American department stores as well as such of the fashion press as could be mustered. The lunch was to be at the Residence – the same day as the sit-down dinner gala extravaganza for one hundred and fifty Washington insiders.

The black-tie gala dinner would have to be served on the patio and around the pool, because we had no room for one hundred and fifty seated guests inside, not counting the waiters and the extra kitchen help – never mind the models, the hairdressers, the clothes dressers and designers. It had been raining all week, and, although we had put up a partial tent, I was worried that the guests sitting around the pool, like General Alexander Haig, who had just resigned as Secretary of State, William Casey, the Director of the CIA, Lawrence Eagleburger, Undersecretary of State, FBI chief William Webster, Ben Bradlee and their wives, were all going to be soaked along with Ms. Morris of the *New York Times*. I didn't even want to think what would happen to the sixteen models and the sixty outfits.

Glen Bullard, our maintenance man, told me that in the twenty-seven years he had been with the Canadian Embassy in Washington, there had never been one hundred fifty people for a sit-down dinner, indoors or out. "Mrs. Gotlieb, the White House can seat only one hundred twenty five." Glen said the kitchen was so small (the following year the government gave us permission to enlarge it) that the waiters and the food would have to "flow" from the garage. "Which means we're going to have a rat problem," he announced with relish. (He loved this kind of crisis.) "The rats will come from the sewers and run over the platters of food sitting in the garage. We need a bigger kitchen. This one hasn't been enlarged since 1947. Don't blame me if we get a call from the D.C. Board of Health."

I knew we had a space problem and a rain problem, but the rats added an element of nightmare to our fashion gala. I decided not to think about the rats. But I was still worried what the political types would do as they gossiped about strategic arms control and then the beautiful Canadian models suddenly appeared during the stuffed avocado. (We thought we'd slip the fashion show in between the avocado and the roast veal. If we waited until after dinner the guests would race out before the fashion show.)

There was also the problem of the chef. The problem was this: we didn't have one. This was at the time when Ibrahim, our first chef, had left and our new chef, Yves Safarti, had not yet arrived from France. Lucky Roosevelt, who had succeeded Lee Annenberg as Chief of Protocol at the State Department, had recommended a caterer but the guest list kept expanding after she was hired and I was nervous about her ability to cook for so many people.

"Can you serve dinner to a hundred and fifty people, maybe more?" I asked.

"No problems. Leave it to me. I'll make strubbles for dessert."

"But can you make enough strubbles?" I asked. Not quite sure of her ethnic background, I thought this might be a national dish.

"I make cake with the strubbles, there'll be plenty." Then I realized that "strubbles" were strawberries.

This was about three days before the event. Glen showed me a large diagram with arrows, hundreds of them, chasing each other around.

"This is our critical path if we have to go indoors because of rain."

"But what about the buyers' lunch?" I asked. "Do we have time to clear the chairs and clean the house before a hundred and fifty black-tie guests come in for dinner?"

"I don't know," Glen answered. "The show after lunch is supposed to last an hour."

I stared at the busy little arrows. Some of them were paths for the models, others for the waiters.

"What about the dinner guests?" I asked.

"The guests will have to eat standing up," Glen said sadly.

"If they eat standing up, they won't see the fashion show," I pointed out.

"I know," Glen admitted, "but we have no alternative."

I explained the situation to Beverly, who said, "It's not going to rain that day."

I decided not to tell her about the rats. Or that I had to go to a lunch given by an important cabinet wife that day and had only half an hour to attend the buyers' lunch. (Allan was lunching with the *Los Angeles Times,* trying to get a sympathetic editorial about our acid-rain quarrel with the United States.) Worst of all, Beverly didn't tell me about all the angry Canadian designers who had been left out of the fashion extravaganza in Washington. (I was not on the selection board.)

Our basement had become a storage room for furs and clothes and a dressing room for the models – the men, including Allan, were warned not to go downstairs.

After what seemed like forty days and nights of rain, the sun broke out on the day of the fashion show. We had reached Mount Ararat – we could hold the dinner outside and actually have room for our invited guests.

That evening I remember sitting near Larry Eagleburger and General Haig, neither of whom noticed the elegant black Haute Canada promotion cards on the table. They were deep in conversation about their difficulties with Ronald Reagan. Haig was telling Eagleburger that he had had no access to the President while he had been Secretary of State. "I simply don't understand the man," Haig was saying, when the drum roll announced the first of the sixty outfits (I think the furs came first). The two men looked up as three beautiful Canadian models swished by the swimming pool and fast-paced music filled the air.

"What the hell is happening?" Eagleburger asked.

"It's a fashion show," I explained.

"I'm leaving," he said, heaving himself out of the chair.

"No you're not." I pushed him down. General Haig was amused, and William Casey mumbled something I couldn't quite hear, but then he often did that.

"We're selling Canadian fashion. Give us twenty minutes and then you can talk politics," I said.

They relaxed and looked at the models. I had pulled a fast one and it worked. That night many Washingtonians told me it was one of the smoothest-running events of that kind they had ever experienced. After the fashion show the "insiders," the Powerful Jobs, as well as the models, danced until after midnight. And the Canadian fashion designers got mountains of publicity in the American fashion journals.

Later I was horrified to hear that some of the Canadian fashion people said I had deliberately starved the models. As if they didn't starve themselves enough. According to our scenario, the models were supposed to join the guests for dinner after they had modelled the clothes. By this time the guests would be eating their strubbles. The caterer had been warned that the models would need food later than the rest of the guests. She may have run out of food, or perhaps the waiters didn't want to be bothered bringing the twelve women a three-course meal after everyone else was finished. Waiters, at a large function like that, are a law unto themselves. Too many people, too little room, too much confusion and too full a day for the staff.

One or two Canadian fashion types who had their clothes shown at the embassy blamed me personally for the unfed models. They told various Canadian magazines, who printed their complaint, that Sondra Gotlieb, the big snob, the ambassador's wife, had given specific orders not to feed the models at the tables with the invited guests.

This was unfair press reporting. I did learn, however, that you're damned if you do and you're damned if you don't. If an ambassador's wife wants to avoid bad publicity, the wise choice would be to keep the Embassy Residence as a private fiefdom for herself. She should use it as bridge club for her pals instead of organizing promotional events for her country. But if you stick your neck out, there's always someone there with a bazooka ready to fire. My advice to all wives of men in public office who don't want criticism is to watch the soaps in the morning, play cards in the afternoon and never plan promotional parties that actually get publicity.

One farcical event followed another when we got lost on the Potomac the following day. At 8:30 A.M. Allan and I and a couple of the models went to Alexandria, Virginia, to sail up the river in a launch to greet the *Bluenose II*, a replica of the famous fishing vessel from Nova Scotia, which was taking part, if I remember correctly, in a Red Cross Waterfront Festival. A yacht carrying city leaders, festival organizers, ourselves and the models left the pier at nine o'clock to meet the *Bluenose*. The rendezvous was to be within a half an hour. There were six Coast Guard captains aboard the launch. After a lot of whispering among the naval personnel, one of them turned to Allan and said that the *Bluenose* "was lost." It was a bit odd, losing the *Bluenose* on the mild, ambling Potomac River. Didn't the vessel sail the wild Atlantic Ocean? After two hours the six captains still couldn't find the *Bluenose*, and Allan began to panic because he had a lunch with the *Wall Street Journal* in Washington. Binoculars were passed around with much concern and mutterings about the *Bluenose* not having radar. A sense of shame pervaded the yacht, even to the bar, where they stopped serving Bloody Marys. I felt I was in the middle of a farce worthy of Gilbert and Sullivan. At 11:30 A.M. the *Bluenose* was sighted at last, and everyone boarded the ship except us because Allan was late for his lunch. We had to be rescued by a passing motorboat, which putted us back to Washington. I arrived back at the Residence in time to greet the workmen who had come to take down the tent from the night before.

The fashion extravaganza was not the first time our sales efforts had got free publicity in the *New York Times*. Earlier, in January 1983, the Canadian chef Tony Roldan, now deceased, and Jim White, food editor of the *Toronto Star*, came to Washington to promote their book, *The Best of Canada*. They asked us if they could take over the Residence kitchen for a couple of days to prepare for an eight-course meal whose purpose would be to promote themselves and Canadian food. We thought it was a wonderful idea and invited thirty "notables," members of the media like William Safire, the *New York Times* columnist, Jim Lehrer, of PBS, and columnist Rowland Evans, and various officials such as the chairman of the President's Council of Economic Advisers, Martin Feldstein, and Richard Burt, assistant undersecretary of State, and of course their wives. Allan toasted the company: "We are going to eat what the chic eat in Canada – it's the kind of food on which our cognoscenti dine," he said tongue in cheek, or rather in the Winnipeg goldeye. When Jim Lehrer looked at it on his plate, he said, "It's not gold, it's red, and it's a damned catfish." Lehrer is from Texas where the catfish grow. It was an irreverent, gay evening. Kay Evans, then editor of the *Washington Journalism Review*, said of the New Brunswick fiddleheads, "Delicious, but I thought it was pasta." Thomas Enders, former American ambassador to Canada and at the time assistant secretary for Inter-American Affairs, told her, "Everyone eats fiddleheads in Canada except for New Brunswickers." As a main course there were Muscovy duck hamburgers from Brome Lake. And that was when we had Alberta Vodka for the first time. The next day the food evening received marvellous publicity in the *New York Times* and many other U.S. newspapers, but it resulted in an ominous Canadian whine.

The day of the party, Jim Coutts, who had just resigned as principal secretary to Prime Minister Trudeau and was teaching at the University of North Carolina, rang us up in Washington and asked us for dinner. Naturally we asked him to come as a last-minute guest for the Taste of Canada event. For some reason Jim's chubby face appealed to the *New York Times* photographer and there was a large picture of him and Allan helping themselves to Canadian caviar in the front section of the newspaper. A few days later Allan received a *New York Times* clipping of the event from an enraged Flora MacDonald, who thought Allan was favouring a Liberal with too much fancy food. "Allan – I always appreciated the subtlety of your non-partisan loyalties."

Flora had been the Conservative Foreign Minister when Allan was undersecretary of State for Foreign Affairs. She had never made any bones about her loathing for him. (He wasn't wild about her either.) Somehow this innocent but highly successful food promotion, with Jim Coutts's picture in the *New York Times*, made Flora think that Allan was cooking up a Liberal mess of potage. Her message was clear: if the Conservatives won the 1984 election, Flora MacDonald would do her best to get a hook and pull the Gotliebs off the Washington stage.

On the cultural side, when visiting Canadian artists came, we would have lunches or dinners in their honour, inviting guests from cultural rather than political Washington.

Our first such party was for Donald Sutherland. He is a fellow of the American Film Institute, and a retrospective of his films was being held in Washington. Although at the time we knew him only by name, we thought it would be a good idea for the Canadian ambassador to give a party in his honour. He was touched. It was the first time a Canadian ambassador had taken notice of his achievements. And for us it was a triumph: we had found our first famous ethnic Canadian in the United States. (More were to follow: Norman Jewison, Hume Cronyn, Peter Jennings, the late Lorne Greene, Christopher Plummer, Margot Kidder, Lorne Michaels, Garth Drabinsky. Show-business folk were quite amenable to being recognized as Canadians.)

I was nervous about having a famous actor as a houseguest. It turned out that Donald was equally nervous, fearing both diplomatic protocol and dreariness. So we twitched and fussed together sympathetically. Forty or fifty people were coming for dinner, and Allan and I had been busy every night that week. At this early stage the flower arranging remained in my domain. I was overwhelmed with seating arrangements and phone calls from people who hadn't been invited. Donald, who had been observing all this, decided to help by arranging the flowers. I remember lying down on the drawing room sofa watching a member of *The Dirty Dozen* (he played the maniacal tank commander) carefully match the different coloured irises in vases. I felt that we should put a sign on each bouquet, "Flowers by Donald Sutherland."

That party was our first Hollywood-on-the-Potomac effort – Norman Jewison, whom we had not yet met, happened at the same time to be shooting a film, *Best Friends*, in Washington with Burt Reynolds and Goldie Hawn. Classifying the Jewisons in our ethnic category, we invited them to dinner as well. Donald, on the afternoon of the party, asked if he could invite his friend Goldie Hawn. "Why not?" I said. She wanted to bring her Parisian boyfriend, but he had no shoes other than Reeboks. "Would that be proper dress for an embassy?" Donald asked.

Many otherwise self-confident souls become intimidated by the word *embassy*. For some, visiting an embassy is like attending the funeral of an acquaintance who belonged to an unfamiliar religion. They worry about blundering through mournful and awkward rites. Sometimes there was reason to fear. I have attended too many dinners at other embassies that were protocol-ridden, ritualistic and joyless. In Washington we tried to eschew the funeral.

After we had provided assurances that there were no embassy rules against Reeboks, Goldie's boyfriend arrived splendidly dressed in a dinner jacket, black tie and running shoes. At that time we had no social secretary working in the evenings. Goldie Hawn was left standing at the door with no one to greet her and refused to come in until a friend of mine, Polly Kraft, managed to persuade her to enter the crowd. I learned from that experience how important it was to have a social secretary at the door. Then Goldie Hawn, Donald Sutherland and the boyfriend sat beside each other at a round table, preparing a kind of defence-line against the Washington crowd – senators, Secretaries of Commerce and Agriculture and White House persons. Thankfully, all went well.

At the party Norman Jewison casually asked us if we would like to watch him film *Best Friends*. This was an invitation I had been waiting for all my life. I had never seen a film being made and cancelled my appointments for a week so I could spend my time on location. I even convinced Allan to come for the first day. Norman explained that the location site lacked glamour. Jewison's people had searched for the ugliest group of middle-class condominiums to be found in the United States. Happily for us, they had found what they wanted in Tysons Corners, about twenty minutes from our embassy, which we visited a couple of days later with the Jewisons. It was bitterly cold for Washington, and within five minutes I realized that I would be spending the week in a parking lot adjacent to buildings resembling a high-rise prison. The cameras were focussed on a Chevrolet in the parking lot. Jewison and a bunch of technicians in down jackets and balaclavas kept crawling over the car with booms, cameras and cables. Allan and I, standing up and frozen, wondered what was so interesting about the car. After a while Jewison came up and told us that the two dim figures in the front seat of the Chevrolet were Burt Reynolds and Goldie Hawn. If he hadn't told us, we wouldn't have known. Allan said, shivering, when Jewison left, "You sure you want to spend your week staring at a car?" We stayed on one more hour. That was my first and last experience being on a movie location. Later Norm took us to Burt Reynolds' trailer (which was warm), and Reynolds described the dinner he had had alone with the Reagans the night before.

"The President and I stood on the Truman Balcony facing the Washington Monument. We stared at the monument together for a few minutes, in total silence. It was very moving. Here I was alone with the President. We were equals. Both of us knew we had made it to the top."

Besides Donald Sutherland, some of the other visiting Canadian artists, writers and groups for whom we had lunches or dinners included Robertson Davies, much admired by those who read fiction in Washington, Alice Munro, Mordecai Richler, Kate Reid, Christopher Plummer, the Vancouver sculptor Bill Reid, the Canadian Brass, Le Cirque du Soleil (a huge success) and every Stratford, Toronto, Montreal, Winnipeg or Ottawa production that came to town. If a cast, corps de ballet or orchestra were involved, we would have late-night buffets after the performance. Unfortunately Washington goes to bed early. Inevitably, by the time the cast arrived, the Washington political types would have already eaten and disappeared. I always counted on two shifts at midnight buffets.

We found very quickly that while political Washington can cope with Gilbert and Sullivan and the occasional Shakespeare play, it stays away from anything avant-garde. We learned that when we held a buffet dinner and a showing of the prize-winning French-Canadian film *The Decline of the American Empire* at Jack Valenti's prestigious American Film Institute to enhance the Canadian presence in the film world. Neither Allan nor I had seen the film, but someone from the embassy said it had to do with sophisticated French-Canadian life on the shores of the St. Lawrence. I was pleased.

"It's time we gave Washington a sophisticated movie," I told Allan. "Americans are fed up with our lumberjack image."

So we had a great gathering of the political elite of Washington: senators, congressmen, cabinet members and media types. Some of the politicians thought we would be showing some kind of anti-American film, but I reassured them by telling them it was about sophisticated life in Quebec. The film was a little more sophisticated than we had bargained for. It was a talky film, mostly about the wild and crazy sex lives of professors from the Université de Montréal – the heroine being an aficionado of sadomasochism. Our guests sat stony-faced through the movie and most of them left without thanking us. Only newscaster David Brinkley spoke. "That's the worst movie I've ever seen in my life."

To give the film a little credit, maybe we had the wrong guest list. Or maybe there is no right guest list in Washington for *The Decline of the American Empire*.

Six years after we had arrived we were still selling Canadian achievements. But I didn't know about the horses until 1987. Gretchen Posten, formerly Rosalynn Carter's social secretary, who runs a successful public relations firm in Washington, called me about the International Horse Show dinner.

First she told me that in the past few years it had been held in one of the big embassies – the British, the Italian or the French, I've forgotten which. The next thing she said was, "There are Canadian horses running in the event. Don't you think it's Canada's turn?" And the third statement was most significant. "The Horse Show people will pay for everything – waiters, food, wine, flowers and even the tent. And all you have to do is sit by the sidelines and enjoy yourself. Basically we're renting an embassy." By this time I knew renting an embassy was a normal practice in Washington. But I was worried by the word *tent*.

The dinner was supposed to take place in late November, and Gretchen realized that the Canadians, unlike the other embassy residences, had no room to sit 125 people indoors. She figured a heated tent adjacent to the house would solve the problem. I had my doubts. We had had tents before in late spring and there had always been a chill factor. This was a very cold November, and I told her we would need a very warm tent. She assured me the tent people were experts. The horse show was considered a premier Washington event and, since Canadian horses were running, there was no good reason to refuse.

I told Glen Bullard, our maintenance man, that the Horse Show people were going to help supervise the erection of the tent. With Glen, it's all or nothing. "Fine with me," he said. "I hope they know what they're doing, because I'm not going to butt in."

Everything went as Gretchen had said. There was a lavish budget, not paid for by the Canadian taxpayer, which covered the elegant and expensive flower arrangements and the food, wine and service. They offered to bring in a caterer but Theodora Bataclan and Christian Le Pièce our excellent butler and chef, put their feet down. They didn't want strangers fooling in their kitchen.

Instead of suffering from my usual attack of anxiety, I was

relaxed. This party was "arranged"; it had nothing to do with me. Two-thirds of the guest list had even been supplied by the Horse Show people. All I had to do was put on a fancy dress and smile at the guests. About 6:30 P.M. I went downstairs in my evening gown to look over the splendour. Waiters were scurrying about organizing their stations, the tent was filled with the flowering trees, little grass walks, huge urns of marigolds and primroses, elaborately set tables with favours, place cards and tall thin vases so as not to obscure the eye-level view filled with drooping mauve and white French lilacs and tulips. Very expensive in winter. The billowing white tent matched the flowers.

But why was the tent billowing? Ice seemed to be forming about the heaters that were blowing cold breezes among the napkins and greenery. The political minister at our embassy, Paul Heinbecker, had come a little early and he read the thermometer. "It's about 40 degrees in the tent. I think they put in air conditioners instead of heaters. Get Glen Bullard." I rang Glen at home, and he raced to the Residence.

"I knew the tent wouldn't work," he said triumphantly. "They should have had heaters on full in the tent for at least a couple of days." He had watched from a distance, but had decided not to interfere. Then he disappeared, saying he would fetch and find some supplementary heaters – "Although I don't know where I'm going to find them at 7:30 at night." He did find them, but they were too few and too late.

Some of the guests had flown in from Hawaii and more than a few women were wearing strapless gowns to show off their tans. It was too late to do anything except turn off the air conditioners. Shortly after the guests had been seated, I heard a kind of drumming and the tables began to gently rock. This was because the guests were stamping their feet from the cold. Theodora had already brought out overcoats and all my sweaters for the shivering women, who gratefully threw them over their Givenchys and Ungaros; but we didn't have any galoshes. I told Theodora to fetch all of Allan's socks, "even the ones in the laundry room," and pass them around. My husband rose, went to the microphone and announced to the guests, "Ladies and gentlemen, waiters will come by shortly with a basket of socks. Feel free to help yourselves."

A contingent of Polish riders were the first to reach into the basket, and some of the women pulled them over their open-toed evening shoes. At the same time, our Tibetan terrier, Sweet Pea, was so excited by the event that he humped the leg of the Russian ambassador, Yuri Dubinin. Ambassador Dubinin, in the new mode of the smiling Soviets à la Gorbachev, pretended he was enjoying Sweet Pea's embrace. Allan, after several tries, was unable to unclamp the dog from the ambassador's leg. Then Allan grabbed a lamb chop off the plate of Senator David Durenberger, and the dog dropped the Soviet leg and went for the American chop. Towards the end of the evening the guests were in a pretty good humour, so Allan didn't utter a word as he watched the Polish riders march out our front door wearing his socks. In all, twenty pairs were distributed and only four were returned.

We were not the only ones to use the Canadian Embassy for sales purposes. Others took over our embassy to sell *their* causes or charities, since in Washington local charities, from the Washington Opera to the Diabetes Foundation, often use embassies as free locations for their fund-raising festivities.

Within a few months of the arrival of an ambassador of a good-sized embassy, he will be besieged by requests from perhaps a couple of dozen charitable organizations to use his embassy for balls, dinners, picnics, midnight suppers and tea parties. The more grandiose the embassy, the more it will be sought after. The British Embassy, which is the largest in Washington, was constantly being "rented out," as were the other big plants, the Italian and the French. As far as I know the embassies do not charge rent, and some of us even paid for the food and service at these functions. When ambassadors huddled together at official gatherings in Washington, their most popular theme was a complaint about how much of their time, as well as space, was being used to accommodate the organizers of the disease- or charity-of-the-week.

Traditionally, the number-one embassy in Washington is the

British. The British come first because they have the largest and most elegantly decorated embassy and they also invite Americans to dine with royalty – the Queen, Prince Philip, the Prince and Princess of Wales, as well as various British dukes and duchesses who might be visiting Washington. Mrs. Reagan wasn't the only person in the city entranced by British nobility. Wherever a British duke went, so went the American cabinet, the Senate, and the press. Those of us in smaller establishments had to fight a little harder for attention.

Surveys in the Style section of the *Washington Post* tended to put the French ambassador, who also lived in a very grand style, pretty high up in the pecking order. The Italian ambassador, Reynaldo Petregani, who appeared to have a lock on his diplomatic post (he was there when we arrived, and stayed on after we left), came second in the Most Popular Embassy of the Year award. He and his wife entertained Frank Sinatra, Perry Como, favourites of the Reagan years, as well as ex-wives of American industrialists, such as Charlotte Ford, who were of Italian origin.

Third on the list were usually ourselves and the Swedish Embassy, tied. However, *Vanity Fair* and other journals also described the Canadian Embassy as "the hottest" embassy in Washington, because of our habit of inviting mostly political and media figures to our dinners.

Even though we possessed a relatively small embassy Residence, we did our share of entertaining for local charities, sometimes with amusing results.

Jean French Smith, the wife of the Attorney General of the United States, William French Smith, was president of the Washington Opera Ball Committee, and it was her duty to ask various embassies to give dinners before the balls. I agreed to her request and she told me, shortly before the dinner, that some of Mrs. Reagan's California friends would be coming.

One of the legendary personalities of Washington was Mrs. Gwendolyn Cafritz, who used to be a famous Washington hostess, a rival of Pearl Mesta in the years following the war. I had thought she was long dead until I read her name on our list of dinner guests, all of whom had donated money to the opera.

I asked Jean if this was the famous Mrs. Cafritz.

"Impossible," said Jean, who was new to Washington. "Didn't she die a long time ago?"

Jean was wrong. Mrs. Cafritz was alive. She entered our embassy leaning heavily on a cane and a gentleman of about fifty. A glowering, dark gypsy-like woman, she muttered "I hate embassy parties" to Allan as he greeted her at the door. She seated herself, with the help of her companion, on a sofa far away from the rest of the guests.

"Give me champagne," she said to the waiter passing drinks. I nodded and he went to the kitchen and opened a bottle.

"Who are these people?" she muttered, gesturing with her cane at our guests. Since I didn't know most of them, I wasn't much help.

"The food at embassy parties is always terrible," she announced. I had heard this before from Sally Quinn, so I took it to be a traditional Washington remark.

Her companion seemed to know her well, but was a little edgy about Mrs. Cafritz's behaviour. "Just leave her alone and I think she'll be all right," he advised.

We went in to dinner. Allan had seated Mrs. Cafritz beside himself, Senator Mark Hatfield, and a Californian friend of Mrs. Reagan named Virginia Milner. Mrs. Milner was a blonde, bubbly, enthusiastic lady who was thrilled to be in Washington and going to the Opera Ball. She chatted happily to everyone around the table.

As Mrs. Milner talked, Allan heard Mrs. Cafritz muttering. Then the muttering grew more distinct.

"Why doesn't that woman shut up?" Mrs. Cafritz hissed.

This was heard clearly by everyone and ignored by everyone.

Mrs. Milner went on to chat gaily, describing her delight at being in Washington and at our dinner.

"Who is this woman and why doesn't she shut up?" Mrs. Cafritz hissed again.

The remark was definitely directed at Mrs. Milner. Senator Hatfield, Allan, and the others at the table sank into an embarrassed, painful silence. What were the men supposed to do in the face of gratuitous rudeness by one woman to another? Mrs. Milner ignored Mrs. Cafritz once again and bravely went on chatting.

"Who are you and why don't you shut up?" was hissed yet again across the table.

Then Mrs. Milner turned to Mrs. Cafritz and said, "Mrs. Cafritz, I'm Virginia Milner from California and have been an admirer of yours for a long time. I've heard so much about you as a famous hostess. It gives me such pleasure to be able to meet you at last."

Mrs. Cafritz was stunned and utterly silenced by this gallant turning of the other cheek. She said no further word and when coffee was passed around left without saying goodbye, accompanied by her somewhat vexed companion. She died about five years later, a sad and bitter recluse.

There are limits to how many charitable fundraisers an embassy can lend itself to, but it is not politic to say no when a wife of a Powerful Job asks you to help out.

Susan Baker, an extremely devout Christian who works with the homeless and takes on many charitable causes, is the wife of James Baker, now Secretary of State but during the first four years of the Reagan administration Chief of Staff to the Reagan White House.

Not long after our arrival, she wrote Allan a personal, handwritten letter asking him if the Canadian Embassy would give a dinner to raise funds to celebrate Hispanic Mental Health Week. The cause was remote from our country's concerns. But Susan Baker was the wife of a Powerful Man, and Allan decided we might gain some brownie points if we participated. He helped convince himself by thinking it wouldn't be a bad idea to show that Canada was sensitive to the Hispanic dimension of American life. Both the dinner and the ball afterwards were to be organized by a prominent Washington public relations firm. Being new in Washington, we knew nothing of public relations firms. Pat

Thomas, our first social secretary, did. "This one has a terrible reputation," she said, presciently.

We received our guest list, made up place cards, and set the table for about thirty-two people. By the time the chef was ready to serve dinner, half the people had not arrived and those who had arrived had names that didn't correspond to the names we had been given for the place cards. Chaos reigned. Some people spoke only Spanish, others thought they were at the Mexican Embassy. One man asked us what Canada had to do with Hispanic mental health, as well he might.

We had this in common with our guests. We didn't know them, they didn't know us, and none of the guests knew each other.

It was now getting late, and I sat people down as best I could. During the main course the doorbell rang and about twenty strangers stood at the door. "We were invited to dinner at the Canadian Embassy," they said. Their names mostly corresponded to the ones we had been given. It was difficult to disturb those who should have been at the Mexican Embassy but were already seated at our tables.

We set up an extra bread line in the living room. But the guests were outraged. "We donated a lot of money to this charity, and we expect to be seated properly." I didn't blame them, but I hadn't organized the event.

Eventually everyone was fed one way or the other and we all went to the ball.

It was a mob scene. After wandering aimlessly for half an hour in the grand halls of the OAS building among people we did not know, we spotted Susan Baker and her husband from a distance. We waved – they looked dazed. We fled.

3/How We Got to Washington

WE THOUGHT WE had organized our departure for Washington, back in 1981, fairly efficiently. Our furniture had been put in storage in Ottawa except for two hundred or so of my husband's prints and paintings, six majolica flower stands, a dozen antique porcelain slop-pails, two antique bird cages, one vintage Hungarian phonograph machine with a large pink horn, a number of antique green-glass Portuguese door knobs, Allan's collection of turn-of-the-century enamel cigarette boxes and art nouveau silver photograph frames – all of which had been sent on ahead to Washington. Allan, as they say in French, *adore acheter*. Our suitcases were in the hold of the aircraft taking us to Washington. They were mostly filled with my dirty laundry. I had just finished a ten-day promotional tour in Canada for my new novel, *First Lady, Last Lady*, and had had no time to do the laundry. But we picked up some unexpected baggage at the last minute.

The night before our departure we dined at the American Embassy in Ottawa, where the new U.S. Ambassador, Paul Robinson, gave us the traditional going-away party. Paul had no political experience except perhaps in Chicago, where he had raised a lot of money for the Reagan campaign. Before his ambassadorial reward – Canada – insurance had been his field. The dinner was going very well until dessert, when he raised his glass and said that he and Martha, his wife, had picked out a special going-away present for us. The company as well as the waiters were startled when Paul removed from a nearby cabinet two large service plates, engraved in gold with the American eagle surrounded by the words *E Pluribus Unum* on the blue porcelain rims, and handed one to each of us.

During our early morning flight to Washington the next day, I clutched the two plates in my arms, wondering what to do with this U.S. government property, feeling like a shoplifter. Since we have failed in our attempts to pass them off to a couple of other U.S. ambassadors, the plates are still in our china cabinet today.

Shortly after take-off from Ottawa's airport on December 1, the pilot announced that we had to return to Ottawa because the plane's landing gear was frozen and couldn't be raised. An ominous sign. While the apparatus was thawing I began for the first time to worry about being an ambassador's wife. I hadn't thought much about it before because I was too preoccupied with completing and later promoting my novel. Never having been an ambassador's wife, I hadn't any notion of what the job entailed. In all my life I had spent only two days in Washington and very little in the rest of the United States. As I sat in the aircraft waiting for another take-off, I began to review my early life to see what might constitute useful preparation.

I knew the difference between a good meal and a bad one and how to make up an interesting menu. I had written cookbooks and restaurant guides and had had a variety of gastronomic adventures.

I also knew how *not* to give a party. I did *not* want to subject my Washington guests to the kind of deadly diplomatic parties we had had to attend in Ottawa during the almost five years when Allan was undersecretary of state for External Affairs.

Because Allan was occupying the top diplomatic post in Ottawa, we had been besieged with invitations from the diplomatic corps. Allan had decided that it was his duty to attend one party at every embassy in Ottawa.

At first I thought it would be fun to go to an embassy dinner. What could be more civilized – amusing guests, good food, fine wine, and nothing for me to do except enjoy myself? This rarely happened. The worst vice of diplomats is that they entertain only themselves. Too often we would take up an invitation and discover that we were the only Canadians present. The formal table would be lined with ambassadors and their wives from Portugal, Poland, Mexico, Brazil and Czechoslovakia. It was a weird and daunting spectacle. It was as if the diplomats were living on an isolated luxury island, keeping themselves as remote from the natives as possible. They didn't seem to realize or want to accept that their job was to cultivate the people of the country to which they were accredited, indeed to influence that country's leaders in favour of their own national interest. No, in Ottawa they entertained principally each other. I was to see this phenomenon in many embassies in Washington too. It appears to be a global vice. Presumably the phrase "the diplomatic set" comes from this kind of inbreeding.

Of course there were exceptions in Ottawa. Thomas Enders, who was the U.S. ambassador to Canada in the late 1970s, and his wife, Gaetana, knew how to throw a party. People would fly across the country and from the United States to attend because the Enderses always had a good guest list – politicians, artists, writers, journalists, top businessmen and government officials. During my twenty years in Ottawa they were one of very few diplomatic couples who showed real flair in promoting their country's interests.

In those instances when Canadians were entertained, diplomats in Ottawa had a tendency to invite "embassy rats" – rich idle people who asked ambassadors to parties in order to be asked back to the embassy. These people had little or nothing to do with foreign relations or helping the diplomat's country. I was later to meet a lot of "embassy rats" in Washington.

As we flew across snow-covered fields, I recalled the least inspiring dinner we had attended in the past few years in Ottawa. The embassy of the Democratic Republic of Vietnam (that is, the Communist regime) had been calling Allan's office twice a month for several years begging us to come for dinner. "Sondra," he said, "we have to bite the biscuit. Let's go and get it over with."

The Vietnamese had bought a substantial house on one of the finest streets in the city. As we walked towards the front door, two Vietnamese, dressed in grey suits with Ho Chi Minh collars, barred our way, led us to a lower level at the side and ushered us through the cellar door. They spoke only Vietnamese. We followed them through the basement, past the furnace room and some other dark chambers piled with old Kentucky Fried Chicken buckets, until we reached the cellar stairs and climbed up to the light. "I suppose they're used to being underground because they lived in tunnels during the war," Allan said. I wondered about the chicken buckets.

We were now in a reception room, above ground, decorated in typical Asian Communist style: large imitation velvet sofas protected with lace antimacassars. We stood silently with the two men for some time. (Allan had told me that the Vietnamese did not allow their diplomats to bring their wives to Canada and some half dozen "political officers" had given the External Affairs Department this house as their home address.) It was a hot and humid summer evening and the four of us were sweating. The house of course had no air-conditioning. I could see the dining room from where I was standing. The table was all ready, set with large platters of fried minced fish salads and a variety of minced mystery meats. It looked as though the platters had been there a long time because a lot of flies were hovering over the food. Was there not a refrigerator in the house? Salmonella poisoning crossed my mind. Were we in Ottawa or Hanoi?

Eventually the ambassador and eight more men appeared. The ambassador had a translator who spoke a little English and French.

After the awkward formal greetings Allan pointed to a flowering plant, an oleander standing in a corner.

"Extraordinary," he said, desperate for something to say. "How did you get a plant like that to bloom in such a dark place?" It took about five minutes for the translator to explain this significant remark to the Vietnamese ambassador, who did not respond. I knew why. The plant was plastic.

We went to the table, beer was poured and the dubious food was spooned onto our plates. The eight Vietnamese diplomats were a silent lot in their grey outfits, but the waiter, also a

Vietnamese, was very different from his countrymen. He was wearing a vividly coloured Hawaiian shirt, which stopped just above his belly button. Fat and jolly, he talked nonstop in Vietnamese and roared with laughter every time he smashed a fly against the wall with his fist in between passing the food. When we left, he triumphantly pointed out the fly remnants squashed on the wall to his boss, the ambassador, and ourselves.

Allan said in the car, "At least it was different from the Swiss."

I decided, before we landed in Washington, that I would entertain the natives, the Americans, and not "the diplomatic set." My husband, after all, had been appointed ambassador to the United States, not ambassador to the representatives of Finland or Bulgaria.

What other lessons could I draw from the past? Well, Ottawa, like Washington, is a town with only one major industry – government. During most of my years in Ottawa, Canada was governed by the Liberal Party, but at the very start of Allan's career in the public service John Diefenbaker was Prime Minister. I was then a "wife of" a Foreign Service Officer 1 (the lowest rank in the service), had just turned twenty, and was not yet pregnant with my first child. Allan's first job in External Affairs had to do with specialized agencies of the United Nations and with refugees. It was a big step down from his former position as a Fellow of Wadham College, Oxford. After five years at Oxford as a graduate student and then as a professor, he had decided that he wanted to come home and join the foreign ministry. He was twenty-eight years old and idealistic, and his friends at Oxford were astounded when he gave up his coveted position. Allan's father, a businessman from Winnipeg, hated the idea of the public service. "It's for postmen," he told Allan. But Allan was fascinated with international law and foreign policy and went against the advice of family and friends.

I had no job and never dreamed of working. We lived in a small one-bedroom apartment, and, having nothing to do, I used to sleep late every morning. I never used to get up and make my husband breakfast, and he would not prepare his own. Allan, feeling peckish, would descend to the cafeteria in the East Block on Parliament Hill around 10:30 each morning and buy a jelly buster to eat at his desk. The middle-aged woman who was his first boss, and could determine whether or not he would be promoted, disapproved of Allan eating jelly busters on government time. One of the first of the handful of women officers in the Canadian diplomatic service, she was known for the severity of her outlook. After silently witnessing three months of this jelly buster routine, she asked Allan to step into her office.

"Mr. Gotlieb," she said, "why don't you have a proper hot breakfast in the morning, before you come to work, with cereal and eggs?"

My husband replied, "Because I'm not hungry in the mornings."

She stared at him and said, "I wonder."

My husband, taken aback, replied, "Wonder about what?"

"I suspect," she said, "that eating breakfast at work is a sign of a disorderly mind. You'll never make anything of yourself in the Department" (as it was then and is still reverentially called). Clearly she believed that a balanced hot breakfast, cooked at home by the officer's wife, would provide him with a less interrupted day, the better for clear thinking on matters of foreign policy.

But I continued to sleep late and Allan continued to eat jelly busters throughout his career as he rose to become the under-secretary of state for External Affairs.

What I loved most of all during the following years was cooking and reading about food. It was almost a genetic trait. In Winnipeg my mother was known as Fanny the Feeder. My father believed "the better the cook the better the person" and that good cooking and moral goodness were equivalent. Nothing made my mother happier than rushing home from a tea party to release the knob on the pressure cooker. She adored cooking and everyone she knew praised her culinary abilities. She was "fulfilled." And the women's movement wasn't around then to tell her differently.

I developed my own interest in cooking during our time in

Geneva, where Allan was posted in 1960 as second secretary attached to the Canadian Permanent Mission to the United Nations. We took a lesser Cunard across the Atlantic, then a boat train, and yet another, and then a train from Paris to Geneva. This wouldn't have been so bad except we were travelling with our children, nine months and twenty-three months, both in diapers, seasick and off their circadian rhythms. They hadn't slept for thirty-eight hours by the time we got on the overnight express to Geneva. I lay on one bunk with the girl and Mr. Second Secretary lay on the other bunk with the boy. They thrashed and drooled until five in the morning, and then we all fell into a deep sleep. We woke awash in wet diapers, to the sound of the porter yelling "Genève, Genève." Allan stuck his unshaven head out of the window and stared at his boss, who was there to meet us. His boss yelled, "You have two minutes to get off the train, unless you want to go to Berne." We passed sodden babies, seven suitcases and packages of paper diapers through the windows, threw our coats over our pyjamas and followed the rest of the goods through the window.

It was while in Geneva that I discovered France's greatest contribution to Western culture, the *Guide Michelin*, and spent almost all my time searching out restaurants. My gastronomic instincts, nurtured in Winnipeg, were refined and educated in the French and Swiss countryside. I discovered that there were fifty varieties of edible mushrooms instead of one, and I frequented butcher boutiques in Geneva where vases of seasonal flowers decorated the marble counters and meats were cut and displayed like jewels from Cartier. When I had my third child, the hospital served me wine and beer to increase my milk.

My older children learned to eat mussels, snails and *quenelles de brochet*, food I had never seen or heard of before. Geneva, the city of Calvin, did not evoke for me any austere Christianity. It taught me another religion; I knelt before the altar of total oral satisfaction.

When Allan was promoted to first secretary and a member of the Canadian delegation to the Eighteen-Nation Disarmament Conference in Geneva, we began to entertain delegates and "disarmers," as we called them, and even many Genèvois. But my fascination with food and eating did not carry over to entertaining. I saw it as part of Allan's job and not especially as a challenge to me.

When we eventually returned to Ottawa in 1964 I cast around for new directions. My father believed that "when you marry a daughter, a hump is off your back." To his joy, after a ten-day courtship, I had married at the age of eighteen and was convinced that I had accomplished my life's work. But after fifteen years of marriage, and with three children all in full-time schooling, I became increasingly restless and conscious that a lot of my friends were being "fulfilled" by working and earning money, or attending classes at university.

I had already tried charity work, but the committee meetings were tedious – usually tight-lipped altercations about such things as the accuracy of minutes of the last meeting. I was the cause of the only exciting moment in my committee work, when I told my co-workers that I had lost all the receipts collected from our door-to-door solicitations. Understandably I was not asked to serve on the committee again.

Instead I went back to school to get a university education. Before marrying I had failed my first year at the University of Manitoba and fifteen years later thought it was time for self-improvement in Ontario. Unhappily, during the subsequent three years of history of philosophy, baroque painting, one hundred Great Books, French literature and courses in Dante's *Inferno* and *Paradiso*, I held fast to my early pattern and failed again.

Although I was disappointed and felt a failure, I didn't mind because Allan had enough degrees for the pair of us: B.A., Berkeley, highest honours; Harvard Law, magna cum laude; B.C.L., Oxon., Vinerian Scholar, first among firsts. Subsequently everyone in our family got lots of degrees. One high-school graduate in their midst is a trifling thing.

At home in Ottawa we shared a disputed hedge with a couple who owned a small publishing firm, Oberon Press, which they operated from their house next door. Not knowing what to do with myself, I began to write about what I liked best, food. I decided, along with my neighbours, to write Canada's first coast-to-coast restaurant guide, *Where to Eat in Canada*, and wrote many of the restaurant reviews for the first two editions. I received $60 per review, which partly reimbursed me for the cost of the meal. Writing those reviews was my apprenticeship; that's how I learned to write sentences.

A couple of years later – I was then in my mid-thirties – I started my first paying job as a freelance radio broadcaster.

It came about because of an interview I had done with a country singer, Stompin' Tom Connors. Stompin' Tom had not yet hit the big time. Later, at his zenith, he played Nashville and every town in Canada. During a drive in the country to pick apples with another couple, I heard his songs on the car radio: "I'm Bud the Spud from P.E.I.," "Big Joe Mufferaw" and "Sudbury on a Saturday Night." We decided that he had star quality, even though at that time he was playing only to country audiences.

Allan, who was working his way upwards in the public service, was getting fed up with my search for myself and convinced me that an interview with Stompin' Tom would procure me a career in radio. We found him singing at a local hotel and bar in Kemptville, Ontario, before a small audience well into its beer. Tom's specialty, apart from his compositions about local heroes, was the manner in which he accompanied his songs, his foot stomping rhythmically on a wooden plank. Although Tom looked like Clint Eastwood, his audience was inattentive. While Tom stomped and sang, a drunk came over to a table where his sixty-year-old wife was having a rye and ginger and socked her in the mouth. Her tooth came out. About a third of the audience rose and began a little violence of their own, while the wife lay bleeding on the floor holding on to her husband's leg, yelling, "Leave him alone."

During all this Tom sang and stomped, not missing a beat. When the show was over I went up to him and told him a lie. I told him I interviewed singers for a network radio show on the CBC and wanted an hour's interview. He was ready to do it immediately, but I didn't have a tape recorder with me. In fact, I had never used a tape recorder, had no job with the CBC and was ignorant of any network program that would be interested in Stompin' Tom.

About a week later I borrowed an old Ewer recording machine, museum quality, and one Saturday afternoon Allan drove me out to Kemptville for the prearranged interview. I had not yet approached the CBC or any other radio station. Allan stayed in the Chevrolet while I went up to the hotel room with the heavy recording machine. It was a small room, above the ladies' entrance to the bar, which he shared with his manager. They were stretched out on twin beds, cowboy boots off, cowboy hats on, smoking cigarettes, and when I walked in they doffed their hats, struggled with their boots, and Tom scooted the manager out. He looked through the window down at Allan waiting in the car and asked me if he was my boyfriend.

"No," I said, "he's a driver from the CBC."

"That Chevy belongs to the CBC?" he asked, none too impressed.

The interview would have gone better if I had known how to work the Ewer. I even committed the cliché of forgetting to plug it in, which he immediately noticed. If it hadn't been for Stompin' Tom's deft handling of the machine, I would have been stuck. We were in the stuffy bedroom smelling of Brut and boots for a couple of hours. When I decided I had no more questions to ask, Tom then paid me a compliment and asked me to go out with him that evening. He had previously asked me if I had a boyfriend and I said, truthfully, no.

"If that CBC driver would take us to Ottawa, we could go dancing and maybe take in a restaurant." Tom travelled in a large signature van with his manager and musical accoutrements. "I don't like driving a date around in that bus."

I was tempted but hesitant. Allan had been eager for me to make good in radio, but I wasn't sure if he'd keep himself to himself while he drove us around the few dance spots in Ottawa. How far would Allan go to procure his wife a job? I decided against it and told Tom I already had a date that night and was leaving for Toronto on Monday for a big interview with Anne Murray.

I sold the interview to the local CBC station for $30. As a result, a couple of months later the producer asked me to read country newspapers on the radio once a week. Apparently he thought I was from a small country town. I read catchy excerpts from such newspapers as the *Kemptville Times*, the *Renfrew Star*, the *Carp Weekly*. I would cut out what I considered the most absorbing items for the listeners, describing malformed gourds or the mayor's complaints about the infrequent visits of the mobile library van. Mac, the professional radio announcer, and I would do a dramatic reading – my high voice alternating with his mellow tones. This technique was supposed to pep up the program. There appeared to be few listeners, although a woman from Carp called in occasionally – to say that Mac read better.

In the meantime I began writing *The Gourmet's Canada*, a gastronomic guide to the best food in Canada. The book described where to eat if you are fussy and broke, what to eat in each region and how to cook it. I discussed Canadian gastronomy from a historical, geographical and gourmet's standpoint, visited cheese makers in Ontario, exotic fruit shops in Vancouver, fish and chip stands in the Maritimes, and consumed everything from cods' tongues to loganberry wine.

Occasionally my free-loading arrangements didn't work out; a friend of a friend found me wandering with a suitcase around Yonge and Bloor in Toronto looking for a cheap hotel – she took me in for a couple of days. I stayed with fishermen in Newfoundland and shared an apartment with a young madame in Vancouver – the best food source I had met so far. We went down to Hastings Street at midnight to eat fried fish at a diner called the Only. The chef, a small but fearless Chinese, climbing in and out of his steaming vats of oil, produced the best fish I ate in all of Canada. We returned (not with the chef) to the apartment, which was furnished with pornographic books, except for a volume of *The Wisdom of Maimonides* and one bed.

The Gourmet's Canada sold exceptionally well and became a

book-club choice. My name became associated with food. The CBC removed me from the country-newspaper spot and made me Recipe Lady.

This was a dizzying period in my life; more people listened to my recipes than to my newspaper readings. I actually had an audience for about a year. People rang up the studio and asked if I would repeat my interpretation of Mrs. Sokolov's honeyed nuts or Quebec-style beans in lard.

But I come from a family that believes in the power of pessimism. "God will get even," my father would say. "Never be too sure of yourself." As Recipe Lady I forgot my father's warning. There was that fateful day when I was feeling too secure. I joked around with the announcer, passed around the honeyed nuts to the technicians and read out a recipe for Ukrainian-style dill pickles to my listeners. The following week my listeners rang the studio to say their Ukrainian-style dill pickles had blown up in the basement. Even though the pickles in my basement were quiescent, the station manager fired me.

This gave me an opportunity for another unusual and better-paying, temporary culinary job. I asked to be in-house restaurant spy for Cara Foods in Toronto. J. Boyd Matchett, a Cara executive, correctly believed that their best restaurants were losing money because the food was poor. He asked me to spend a few weeks in the big city, eating, and then make a written report about both the food and the service. In theory it was a good idea, but in practice my presence created fear, quarrels among the executives and a near walk-out of the restaurant staff. I came to feel the problem was at the top of the company building, rather than in the restaurant kitchens.

I would go to the restaurants around eight o'clock and order an expensive dinner. This was during the 1960s, and the sight of a woman eating lobster soufflé and Chateaubriand alone on a Saturday night attracted the attention of the room. The waiters were attentive but curious about my note taking. By the time I made my third appearance at the same restaurant they all knew I was the Restaurant Spy. When I complained that the Black Forest cake tasted of the artificial stabilizers that keep the whipped cream from looking droopy, one of the chefs had a tantrum. It wasn't his fault, he said. He had been ordered to use them by headquarters so the cakes would look freshly baked for the next day's dinner.

Pretty soon everyone on staff told me his or her troubles. The waiters considered the kitchen staff as the enemy. To get even with the waiters who would not share their tips, the enemy refused to make the Béarnaise sauce that was supposed to go with the Chateaubriand, hoping that the waiters would get angry customers who would refuse to tip. The chefs complained that there was no room for creativity – they didn't buy their own produce and had to obey the computer recipes slavishly. "Who can make a lobster soufflé with one egg white?" one of them complained. But most of all the staff complained about me, the Spy, whom they suspected of writing mean things about them in my notebook. I was told to forget about the report; Cara paid me off and I returned to Ottawa.

After *The Gourmet's Canada,* I wrote another cook and travel book, *Cross-Canada Cooking,* and began to engage in every kind of freelance journalism except political; my subjects ranged from ethnic folk festivals to expensive fat farms. I soon came to realize that the act of writing interested me more than the subject of food.

But living in Ottawa in the early 1970s as the wife of a mandarin was a definite disadvantage. (By now Allan was deputy minister of Manpower and Immigration.) I discovered that the only kind of writing newspapers and magazines wanted from Ottawa-based writers was political gossip or commentary. And that was the one thing I could not do because of my husband's job.

About three years after our return from Geneva, Allan was made legal adviser to the External Affairs Department and assistant undersecretary of state. His work brought him into contact with a man who was vitally interested in constitutional issues and international law, the new Minister of Justice, Pierre Trudeau.

Allan admired Trudeau's intellect and antiseparatist stand and began advising him on constitutional and foreign affairs. Trudeau became a frequent visitor to our house. It was at our home, at one of our small dinners, late in 1968, that he decided to run for Prime Minister.

Allan was deeply impressed with Trudeau, but disliked partisan politics. At a crucial point when Trudeau seemed to be backing off his decision to run, one of Trudeau's advisers, Marc Lalonde, urged Allan, whose persuasive abilities are world-class, to go to Trudeau and convince him not to back out. Allan refused. I couldn't understand why and remonstrated with him. "I'm a nonpartisan public servant," he said. "That's a task for a politician." Allan has held this view all his life and consistently declined to mix in Liberal or Conservative party politics. A leading Liberal later asked him to run for election and, again, Allan refused. When Pierre Trudeau won the election in 1968, he offered Allan the choice of four deputy ministerships. Allan chose to be deputy minister of Communications. He was interested in domestic policy as much as in foreign affairs – telecommunications, satellites and microchips seemed to be the stuff of the future.

Allan's rising prominence as a close aide of Trudeau resulted in even less freedom in my choice of journalistic topics. I did write one rather daring article at that time about political wives and their difficulties. They spilled their hearts out, but I had to promise them total anonymity. *Chatelaine* magazine published it reluctantly; the editors wanted real names.

Bored with food, and unable and unwilling to write about political Ottawa, I had only one other choice as a writer: fiction. Fantasy did not appeal to me. I was comfortable only with what I knew and had experienced, so this led me to autobiographical fiction. My first novel, *True Confections*, started out as short stories about growing up in Winnipeg; the tale of my arranged marriage was only one of the stories. But a friend of mine read the manuscript and was amazed that such an archaic rite could occur in Winnipeg during the 1950s. It was only then, twenty years after the fact, that I realized my marriage was peculiar. I revamped my book into a largely autobiographical novel about our arranged marriage and began a long and difficult – but ultimately successful – search for a publisher.

There were times when my husband was accused of conflict of interest because of my writing. When *True Confections* was published, we had a book party in our Rockcliffe house to which we invited everyone we knew. Standard book-promotion procedure. It is unusual for everyone invited to come to book-promotion parties except in Ottawa, where social life was a still pond. Put some wine on the kitchen counter, a ham in the dining room, mail out a few postcards, preferably bought at the National Gallery, and presto, one is a hostess in Ottawa. Given the local social pace, we had a large turnout. The guests included Soviet Ambassador Alexei Yakovlev, who lived next door (now high in the Politburo and one of the chief advisers of Gorbachev), cabinet ministers who were friends, other friends who were public servants, members of Parliament, press, book-store owners, and the U.S. ambassador, Tom Enders, who was also our neighbour. I basted a ham. My publishers provided the wine.

Doug Fisher, the columnist, was appalled. He wrote an article that cited an obscure but horrid review of my book and accused my husband of using the enormous power and influence of his office to get the great Power Folk in Ottawa to come to a party for trash written by his wife. The "trash" later won the Stephen Leacock Award for Humour. Mr. Fisher never acknowledged that fact. He used the power of his "office" – that of a nationally syndicated columnist – to try to discredit the efforts of a woman trying to make a career for herself. I could never understand the animus he showed towards me and my husband, of which there were to be further examples after we went to Washington.

These experiences and an innate lack of interest dissuaded me from analysing the public utterances or private behaviour of Ottawa politicians. Tempting offers came from magazines and newspapers. But I was convinced that my commentary on politicians and policies would adversely affect my husband's career. A public servant was supposed to be loyal to whatever government was in power. If I exposed my views in print, Allan's reputation for objectivity could be destroyed; I would be considered his mouthpiece. The unwritten rule about wives of top officials who write about politics did not seem to apply to the wife of Canada's ambassador to the United Nations, Michele Landsberg, who was to write a controversial column for the *Globe and Mail* during her husband's term of office. However, a politician who read something unpleasant about himself written by a public servant or his wife would certainly remember. The husband should be prepared to slither about in the slow lane of his public-service career.

During my writing years in Ottawa, I gave a party two or three times a year – *sans* chef, butlers, place cards and sometimes *sans* chairs and tables. Curiously, I came to be considered a hostess by Ottawa's modest standards. I believed in Jane Austen's phrase, "Everything happens at parties." I detested parties that were drawn from only one group, in Ottawa usually politicians or officialdom. Such gatherings became little more than paranoid huddles. The one rule we always followed was to mix people as much as possible, so we used to draw together cabinet officers, bureaucrats, politicians from all parties, journalists, diplomats and academics. This was thought of as an unusual and rather daring thing to do in Ottawa.

One element above all gave our parties a heightened interest. That element was the emergence of Pierre Trudeau as an important political personality on the Ottawa scene. Well before he became Prime Minister, and before he was Minister of Justice, I noticed from his presence at our parties that he had a magnetic effect on the rest of the guests. He would stand silently in a remote corner of the room and within five minutes there would be a dozen people around him. I've never seen anyone who was not yet famous have this same charismatic quality.

In May 1970, shortly after Pierre Trudeau named Allan deputy minister of Communications, he had come to a party we gave to celebrate the naming of the first Canadian communications satellite, Anik. The Prime Minister's date was Margaret Sinclair. I believe the party was her first public launching. Margaret was twenty-one and the most ravishing woman I had ever seen, with or without the Prime Minister. She looked like a black-haired

Marilyn Monroe, sensual and trembly, so beautiful that I noticed even the most polite at our party gaped at her when they thought she was looking in the other direction. Margaret wore a thigh-high lace-knit minidress and spent most of the evening touching fingers with Leonard Cohen, the poet-singer and icon of the sixties, who, along with Marshall McLuhan, had been a member of a literary committee selected by the Department of Communications to choose the satellite's name. Someone had brought a beautiful Asian woman who spent the evening in a trance, touching fingers with the P.M. and other guests such as Roy Faibish, Patrick Watson and Scott Symons. The public servants edged around but never entered into the zen group. Scott Symons, perhaps Canada's first author to write about his homosexual experiences, brought his latest work in a specially made blue Birks box. He asked Mrs. Alfred Pick, a neighbour and a kindly representative of the conventional middle-class life led by most of us in Ottawa, to open the Birks box – or as he called it, his "book." It revealed photographs of penises Scott had known, described in Scott's elegiac prose. Mrs. Pick didn't flinch.

The next time I met Margaret she had become Margaret Trudeau. The Prime Minister and his wife had asked some of us to dinner at their residence at 24 Sussex Drive – a few public servants, several Ministers and some friends who had children the same age. The flautist Jean-Pierre Rampal was to give a concert before dinner. We all arrived grossly overdressed. I remember wearing for the first time an antique amethyst necklace given to me by my mother-in-law. Margaret wore a peasant skirt and carried a baby on her hip. We were told that she had prepared all the food herself; it was delicious. Margaret, by this time tired of official parties, had decided to give an informal neighbourly buffet. Most of the guests had never been in the Prime Minister's residence during Margaret's reign and were expecting place cards, prancing waiters and protocol; however, huge helpings of Russian caviar, which the Trudeaus had brought home from an official visit to Moscow, mollified the uneasy guests. Margaret seemed a little confused, but she had a warmth about her and was anxious for the party to be a success. The Prime Minister, as usual, was a little remote.

I saw very little of Margaret after she married the Prime Minister, though I had one memorable encounter with her after she had left him, but while she was still living part-time at 24 Sussex Drive. This was when she was jet-setting to London, Paris and New York. Margaret, Our Lady of the Concorde, had just published her first book, *Beyond Reason*, and had recommended my first novel, *True Confections*, to her publishers in the U.S. and U.K.

Soon after this a mutual friend, Grue Southam, who had just separated from her husband, rang me up and asked if she could bring Margaret for lunch. So I bought fresh oysters and made oyster stew for the three of us. Margaret, whom I had not seen for several years, talked about her present life and her anger at individuals and the press. She was self-absorbed, and self-destructive; this was her lowest-of-her-low period.

Margaret wasn't in control during that lunch, and I was thoughtless. Grue asked for martinis. Our liquor stock was low; all I had was a few dusty bottles, gifts from the Soviet bloc embassies, including a strange-smelling bottle of yellow Polish vodka with a blade of buffalo grass inside and a bottle of slivovitz from Yugoslavia. We were allowed to accept gifts from foreign governments as long as they could be consumed orally. I believe three Christmases had passed since we were given these bottles. I used to preserve plums in the slivovitz. Anyway, Margaret drank slivovitz and buffalo-grass vodka martinis with her oyster stew. It nearly killed her. She was sick and went upstairs to sleep in my son's room for about five hours. When my husband came home around eight that evening, he asked, "What's new?" and I pointed upstairs and said, "Margaret." It took a long time to explain.

"Oyster stew," he said despairingly, "with slivovitz and yellow vodka. How could you?"

Margaret came downstairs, refreshed and hungry. We ate hamburgers in the living room and discussed the international situation. Then she returned to her rooms at 24 Sussex.

Until that lunch I had encountered Margaret only as part of a group and my sympathy for her was limited. I had seen her simply as Trudeau's most beautiful date, then as a perverse princess and finally a publicity hound. After that day my attitude changed. I no longer saw her as the perverse princess, but as someone almost catastrophically confused by and overwhelmed by the exciting worlds she had lived in. Margaret did not know where to peg herself, or which orbit she lived in.

Although I was in the midst of writing my second novel, I knew that I wanted to change the orbit in which I lived. I was ready for at least a pinch of the excitement that Margaret had experienced. When I saw her, she was thinking of making an exit from her turbulent life in New York and London and returning to Ottawa. My feelings were just the opposite – I felt that a little turbulence in my life would not be amiss.

Allan was getting a little restless too, but on the whole was comfortable in his post as undersecretary. Appointed chief "sherpa" for the Ottawa Economic Summit in 1981, Allan began travelling around the world with Prime Minister Trudeau preparing for the conference, the first of its sort Canada was to host. As his work for the conference was ending, Allan was confident the government would appoint him high commissioner in London if he wanted it. Although Allan had always hankered to return to England and the London post was regarded as prestigious, he knew from his experience in international affairs that there was no real work for the Canadian high commissioner to do. "I don't want to spend my time going to Ye Olde Weavers' banquets. The post is all ceremony, no substance," he said. He believed that our relationship with the United Kingdom was at best nostalgic and that there were no real issues between the two countries. For a man like Allan who thrives on hard and difficult work, I knew that Washington was the only possible diplomatic job for him. Even I knew that seventy-five per cent of Canada's trade had to do with the United States, that acid rain was polluting Canada and that our relationship with the States was the core of our foreign policy.

If it had not been for my restlessness, Allan might have turned down the Prime Minister's offer to be ambassador in Washington. He had come to share my fears that we would become a stale, pale public-service couple. Moreover, he was fed up with bureaucratic wrangling and turf fights and wanted more independence. Having been an undergraduate at Berkeley and a student at Harvard Law School, he had always been attracted to Washington as a place to work. I played on his real fear of becoming an out-of-touch Ottawa bureaucrat and urged him to leave – even though, for me, it meant becoming that creature so despised by serious women, a full-time hostess. But I had always planned my life around my husband's work. For the first fifteen years of my marriage I had not had a paying job, feeling too much emphasis on my "freedom" might threaten something enduring in our lives. Marriage and family had always come first. I was willing to go back to being an appendage wife or "wife of" so long as I had the opportunity of experiencing a new world. Just as I was ready to leave Ottawa, *Maclean's* magazine published a column I wrote about my admiration of women who place their loyalty to their husbands and families above their own careers. I wrote that women who appear to subordinate their personal fulfilment because they have no careers are made to feel half-human by the women's movement and the press. "Pushy wives and mothers are out," I said. "Assertive working women are in." I must have had some unconscious intimation that I would not be writing for quite a while. I was going over to the other side. I had ambivalent feelings about having to give tea parties for congressional wives instead of writing my third novel, but it was the only way I knew of getting out of Ottawa.

4/The Unpaid Manager of a Small Hotel

Why on earth would you want to become an ambassador?... Give Washington to the Belknaps.... Stephen and Moira can play bridge with the Congressmen and run after the Senators. That's what ambassadors do. All prestige and no power. High-class lobbyists. Let Moira give the tea parties and burst into tears when the wives don't show up.

From First Lady, Last Lady, a novel by Sondra Gotlieb

I WROTE THOSE words in 1978. I did not know then that they would come back to haunt me, that I was to become the despised Moira Belknap. I wrote without first-hand knowledge of high diplomatic life and learned only later how prescient I had been.

Just before our departure for Washington, the wife of the previous Canadian ambassador to the United States, Carol Towe, gave me a couple of clues about my future life.

"The butler at the residence is a little strange. I thought of firing him. But maybe he'll suit you better."

I wasn't quite sure what butlers did, so I kept quiet.

"Before I came to Washington," she added, "the embassy was actually using typed instead of handwritten place cards." Carol had been an ambassador's wife before and knew about place cards. Until she spoke, my mind had never dwelt upon them. Those were the only hints I had of what was in store.

The plane did make it to Washington, and we were met by a protocol officer and several members of the embassy staff who led us and our luggage straight past the customs officials and immigration lines. It was only then, with this "make-way-for-the-ambassador" procedure, that I realized that life was going to be different. No more passing suitcases through the windows and leaving the train in our pyjamas.

Our entrance into Washington was almost regal. Our chauffeur, Jacques Hèlie, was a Canadian who had been a driver with the embassy for more than twenty years and knew each ambassador's foibles, which thankfully he kept to himself. We were greeted at the door of the elegant official residence on Rock Creek Drive by Pat Thomas, the social secretary at the embassy; the enigmatic Spanish butler Rito, a sombre El Grecoesque figure in black; Ibrahim, the Turkish chef, over six feet tall and weighing more than 250 pounds; Noemi, the downstairs maid from Honduras who was pregnant; Thelma, the Filipino upstairs maid; and a little Portuguese man named Mario, who was described as a houseman. Pat Thomas tried to explain to me what each of them did, but it took me three years to figure out the duties of the houseman. Except for Thelma, the household staff spoke little English, and it was a mystery to me how they communicated with each other. Rito and Mario had related languages, but they loathed each other and never spoke. Noemi and Ibrahim worked well together in the kitchen with their innovative Turko-English-Spanish dialect. A Canadian film called *Quest for Fire*, which opened in Washington not long after we came, showed the beginning of speech in primitive man. It was a little like that at the Residence when I arrived in Washington.

Rito the butler's first act was to hand me a set of keys. I asked him what they were for.

"The downstairs storeroom," he said.

"What's in it?" I asked.

"Fifty cans of peas and two bottles of ketchup."

I asked about another key.

"That locks the thermostat so no one but Madame can touch it."

I made my first decision and told him not to give me any keys. Although I was too frightened to say anything then, I knew that we would not serve canned peas and ketchup to our guests. As for the other key, my idea of power was not being the only one allowed to fool with the thermostat. As a matter of principle, I stayed away from it during our stay in Washington.

The analogy of primitive man included ourselves. We had never lived in Washington, knew few people and for several months would feel like a Cro-Magnon couple who had been banished from our familiar cave and found ourselves settled near the first of an unknown tribe, the Washington power-seekers and cave-dwellers, whose customs and taboos were foreign to us. We had no understanding of the complexity of the political system or of the importance attached to social activity by the Reagan administration.

The departing British ambassador to the U.S., the extremely sophisticated Sir Nicholas "Nico" Henderson, gave Allan one hint about the byzantine nature of the political system: "If anyone tells you that he knows where a decision was made in this town, he's either a liar or a fool."

Allan said this was the only useful piece of advice he received during all the courtesy calls that diplomatic ritual required him to pay on his ambassadorial colleagues when he arrived.

During our early period of adjustment to Washington I would sit gloomily on the black leather furniture in the Residence's dark library and ask Allan, "What does an ambassador do? And where do I fit into all this?" Allan was playing everything by ear and was stumped for an answer.

My immediate concern had to do with the domestic problems of running a large embassy residence. I had always liked being alone in a house, and I was intimidated by so many people around me, no matter how helpful they were. The first thing I did when I opened my suitcase was hide away in drawers all my dirty underwear left over from my Canadian book tour. I was hoping to wash it late at night in the bathroom sink. My hiding places were discovered and three hours later my dirty laundry was cleaned, ironed and folded back in my secret drawers. This was the first time in my life anyone else had washed, let alone ironed, my panties. Despite this luxury my instinct was to return to Ottawa.

I had no idea how to supervise a staff. They were waiting for orders from their new patronne, but little information had been offered to me about their routine. For example, I had no idea who lived in or out of the house and whether they were supposed to be on duty during weekends. Of course I should have asked the butler, but I was reluctant to do so and anyway had already discovered that he didn't usually understand my questions.

Allan left for Brussels on my first weekend at the Residence and I woke early on a cold Sunday morning to a seemingly empty house. I went outside in my kimono to collect the newspapers. The door swung shut behind me and I heard the lock click. I ran around to the front door, also locked, and rang the bell. Nobody answered. I found myself on the front steps in my bathrobe, clutching the *New York Times* and the *Washington Post* to my bosom. A few men jogging across the street looked at me curiously. The houses nearby were large and unwelcoming, and I had no idea who lived in them. I knew the Canadian Chancery in Sheridan Circle was about a ten-minute walk down Massachusetts Avenue, but was reluctant to proceed there given my state of undress and the unusually cold weather. In Ottawa I wouldn't have worried too much about my predicament, but now I was an ambassador's wife and I assumed that more dignified behaviour was to be expected of me. Nevertheless I shuffled along in my slippers for a block down Massachusetts Avenue, holding the papers for warmth, hoping the guard at the Chancery would recognize the new ambassador's wife. Suddenly I heard a shout: the butler, who was fully dressed and had been watching from a window, ran after me and saved me and my country from shame.

The formal presentation of Allan's credentials to President Reagan took place ten days after we arrived. It was my first official event. I was very upset because my hair had shrunk – the result of a bad permanent. Also one of the maids had washed and shrunk the blouse I was supposed to wear with a brown suit. All my life I had done my best to avoid ironing and there I was ironing my blouse while Noemi the maid watched. She was willing to iron, but expected an order from Madame; I didn't know how to give one.

Lee Annenberg, then Chief of Protocol at the State Department, helped me get through the presentation of credentials ceremony with only minor embarrassment. The best part for me was speeding to the White House in a motorcade. It was only a little one, with rather run-down D.C. police cars fore and aft, but it was gratifying to run through a couple of red lights with the sirens going. Lee greeted us at the White House door and told us there was a gaggle of ambassadors waiting to present their credentials that day. Before we went to the Oval Office some anxious young men took us into another room and told us where to stand, how long to speak and when to shove off.

In the official Presentation of Credentials photograph, which was reproduced in the Canadian papers, my hair looked like corkscrews because of the permanent. And my brown suit was so unflattering that my brother didn't recognize me when he saw me on television. He told me later that he thought it was Mrs. Brezhnev standing beside the President. Actually only Mr. Ambassador (as the Americans called Allan) was supposed to have his picture taken with the President. I was told to move out of camera range, away from the fireplace where Allan and the President were standing. After the handshake with the President I backed into the camera crew. Some of the young men began to hiss at me, but the President graciously grabbed my wrist and insisted that I be in the picture too. Mrs. Reagan was not there. All I remember is flashing cameras and that the President was wearing a brown suit too.

Afterwards Lee told me not to worry about the frizzy permanent, for it would eventually come out. In the car I said, "Allan, I hope I didn't humiliate Canada." After so many years of marriage he knew that I get flustered easily and quoted a Newfoundland saying in my honour: "When she rises ups she gets confused."

Allan had another favourite comment for me in those first few weeks. "Assert your authority," he would say when he left for the Chancery in the morning, leaving me alone with Rito, Thelma, Ibrahim, Noemi, and Mario.

It was all very well for Allan to say that. He had been deputy minister of several large government departments including one with 25,000 employees. I had never been the boss of anyone except my cleaning lady in Ottawa, whom I never once contradicted in twenty years. I had arrived in Washington as an ignorant foreigner, used to a middle-class private way of life – little notes pinned on the fridge door and forgetting to put the sprinkler on.

I was also supposed to give orders to my social secretary and her assistant. What do you do with a secretary if you've never had one in your life? My social secretary, Pat Thomas, worked at the Chancery office, but had a direct line to me at the Residence. However, the telephone had five bewildering buttons. Press one, I would get a maid in the laundry room. Press a second and I could dial Disneyworld in Orlando, Florida. Press a third, I would overhear an argument in Tagalog; that was the staff's personal line – Thelma, the Filipino upstairs maid, was yelling at her ex-husband. Press a fourth and I would get a local line for making calls to people I barely knew and who usually had unlisted numbers anyway.

In Ottawa I had lived in a house with no servants and my children had been away at college for some time. I was used to privacy. But in Washington I was not living in my home. I was living in a place referred to by the Chancery officials as the O.R. At first I didn't know what those initials meant. Did we have an operating room somewhere in the embassy? I was enlightened by Allan, who told me the O.R. was the Official Residence.

I would wake up in the O.R. and go downstairs in my kimono to face Rito, sullen from the first fight in the morning with Mario, the idle houseman. Then I'd bump into a couple of political officers chatting in the drawing room, who had to come by to talk to Allan. There might be a procurement official waiting around to tell me I shouldn't have bought a dozen (very cheap) champagne glasses from Lord and Taylor because all champagne glasses must be ordered from headquarters in Ottawa. Occasionally there were outside workmen who wanted to come into my bathroom before I had time to get dressed. It was like living in a luxurious dormitory, or a small hotel. The O.R. was an institution belonging to the Canadian government. It was not a home. For the first year I was extremely unnerved by this lack of privacy and would whisper complaints into the telephone to Allan, who had escaped to the office, about "too many people around me all the time." I needed privacy, I said, or I would go out of my mind.

We finally laid down a set of rules that anyone who wanted to come and talk to me or repair something should call before their arrival. I also had Mario removed from the O.R. for a while in order to give Rito a chance to regain his nerve.

My normal retreat from so many people would have been into a kitchen. All the women in our family have loved to cook – but without anyone around them. My great-grandmother wouldn't let my grandmother in the kitchen because she wanted to be alone. When my grandmother had children, she wouldn't let my mother in the kitchen because she wanted to be alone. My mother wouldn't let me in the kitchen because she said I was a nuisance – she too wanted to be alone. I follow the family pattern. Cooking has always been my escape. At home there was nothing better I liked doing than closing myself in the kitchen, shutting out the children, turning on the radio, and trying out a new Julia Child recipe.

In Washington the kitchen was off limits to me. Officials in Ottawa think elaborate second kitchens in many Canadian embassies and consulates are acceptable budget items so that the wife of the ambassador can make toast or reheat coffee in the microwave all by herself. I considered this a futile expense for our O.R. In Washington I soon learned that I would never have the time or energy to use it. One kitchen per O.R. is sufficient.

This meant, however, that my hobby – my escape hatch – had disappeared.

Chefs hate Madame poking around in their kitchen, which in the O.R. belonged to the household staff. If I walked into the kitchen two maids, the chef and the odd chauffeur, with his mouth full, would jump up and ask if Madame wanted something. They would give me anything – tea upstairs on a tray, a steak in the middle of the afternoon – as long as I didn't disturb their private kitchen life. If we arrived home late at night and I wanted to heat up some soup, a maid would hear me and come running downstairs to find a pot. She knew where everything was supposed to go and I would certainly put a spoon in the wrong place.

Later, of course, when we were either entertaining or going out every night, the last thing I wanted to do was boil soup, let alone cook a meal. I tried to escape from the world by shutting myself in the upstairs sunroom, covering my eyes with a hot towel because the whites were tinged acid green. I wasn't suffering from jaundice, merely social overload.

My first test of strength in the kitchen had to do with Ibrahim, our Turkish chef. After about six weeks in Washington I realized that we'd been eating a lot of shishkebab. Ibrahim was good-natured but a little limited in his repertoire. I asked him if he could make a coulibiac for one of our first dinner parties; coulibiac is an elaborate dish, fresh salmon surrounded by a puff pastry.

"No problem, Madame," he said. "I can make anything. I cook for three hundred people when I work for King of Jordan."

He had mentioned his former employer, the King, several times, which had its desired effect on me. Nevertheless, I was a little worried about his capacity for cooking coulibiac, so I asked him if he would make a test coulibiac for Allan and myself the night before the dinner. That evening when we sat down, we were served shishkebab. I still didn't know how to work the telephones or deal with the paperwork coming across my desk, nor how to manage the quarrelling in the household between the servants and the difficulties in the office of my social secretary. Pat Thomas wanted to write out place cards by hand for our first dinner party, but for some reason no one in the Chancery would supply her with nib pens and black ink.

Tumult at the office, tumult at home. When Rito placed in front of me the shishkebab instead of the coulibiac, my eyes filled with tears. Allan asked, "Why are you crying?" I told him about the coulibiac. Apart from shaking hands with the chef on our first day, Allan had never spoken to him, or even gone into the kitchen.

"For God's sake," Allan said, "don't cry. Assert your authority."

"How?" I replied, thinking of the King of Jordan.

Allan rose, walked into the kitchen and backed the 250-pound Ibrahim into a wall.

"Where's the coulibiac?" Allan asked, stumbling over the word (he had never heard of a coulibiac before). Ibrahim muttered something unintelligible.

"When my wife asks for something, you make it," Allan said.

The next morning the two of us ate a huge test coulibiac for breakfast.

In this manner I discovered that unless the household and Chancery staff knew they would get hell from the ambassador, the "wife of" would get nothing at all. The ambassador was the boss and his word was respected. If the ambassador didn't care about things that worried his wife, nobody else would care either. But once word got around that the ambassador actively supported his wife in all her reasonable decisions (and my decisions, of course, were always reasonable), "wife of" got her way, sooner rather than later.

But Allan warned me I still hadn't got a grip on things when I had my second to-do with Ibrahim. I opened one of the refrigerators in the kitchen (a rather daring act for me at that time) and saw huge bags of frozen shrimp.

"What's this?" I said, "I want only fresh shrimp."

"No fresh shrimp in Washington," Ibrahim informed me.

"Nonsense," I said firmly. Someone had told me they sold fresh shrimp down by the wharf.

"No fresh shrimp down by the wharf, Madame."

I made Jacques Hèlie drive me and the silent Ibrahim to the wharf, where we saw shrimp piled high in front of the vendors. There were even fishing boats behind the stalls. I was triumphant. Ibrahim poked a few fish uninterestedly while I spoke to a vendor.

"Give me three pounds of fresh shrimp."

"Lady, we don't have fresh shrimp."

"What's that in front of me?"

"Defrosted shrimp. They freeze them on the boats in Carolina."

Ibrahim spoke only once on our way home. "No fresh shrimp in Washington, Madame."

Other early battles centred on redecoration. I knew that External Affairs in Ottawa employs decorators who are supposed to help furnish the residences owned by the Canadian government. Perhaps I was the only Canadian "wife of" who refused to let these decorators put their feet across my threshold.

I had seen their work in many Canadian embassy residences when Allan was undersecretary. No matter the country, no matter the style of the house, the decorators insisted on basic bland. As if Canada hasn't enough trouble fighting basic bland as its image. Their signature was wall-to-wall carpeting, neutral colours please, a ficus tree drooping in the corner (this inevitable tree was considered a decorating breakthrough), Sheraton-style furniture circa 1973 – brought in from Canada at great cost – and sofas made from strange nubby materials, usually oatmeal-coloured. A few pastel polyester cushions would be thrown around for colour contrast. The Canadian decorators had not the time, the desire or the taste to turn an embassy residence into anything other than a reproduction of a showroom designed for a department store catalogue.

I did get a warning from my husband about decorating: "Stay away from the Imelda Marcos image. Don't shop for the front pages."

With his words in my mind, and without the aid of the Canadian desecrator, gradually during our seven years I chose the colour for the walls, bought linens, curtains, rugs and furniture for the drawing room, library, sunrooms and bedrooms.

The drawing room of the Residence had a beautiful bow shape, and I wanted the curtains and rug to reflect its elegant curve. It was of course impossible to redecorate the drawing room in one swoop. Everything had to be done piecemeal because of the budget. One year there would be money in the budget for curtains but not a rug. The following year I would be told that there was something in the budget for recovering the sofa. Obviously starting from scratch would have been much easier than trying to match colours and materials to rugs and sofas that I knew would have to be replaced after three or four years. We covered up the white embassy rug in the drawing room with our

own Persian carpet. (Former ambassadors' dogs had all left their
territorial marks, and our dogs believed in keeping up the
tradition.) Allan hung his collection of Tissot prints in layers of
three and four in the dining room, which warmed up the
Operating Room considerably.

After years of past entertaining, we needed new table cloths. I
had heavy-duty red paisley cloths made for our round tables, and
they looked so good that Washington friends would call up and
ask if they could borrow them for their own parties. Our
porcelain slop bowls, antique door knobs, large horned phonograph machine, art nouveau silver frames, and turn-of-the-century
boxes and bird cages hid the Ramada Inn-style tables in the
drawing room and gave individuality, some would say eccen-
tricity, to the Residence. Allan discovered handsome mirrors as
well as hand-carved tables, hidden by piles of official documents,
in the Chancery offices and brought them to the Residence.
When we finally bought a rug for the drawing room I insisted that
it be smaller than the first in order to show the good oak floors
and that it imitate the bay shape of the room. I found it simpler
and cheaper to use Washington friends like Liz Stevens, whose
own house and those of other Washingtonians showed off her
talents. Liz called herself a "part-timer," but she knew where old
American wicker would be sturdily rewoven and had access to the
Design Center in Washington. Liz helped me choose a machine-
made rose rug with a handmade flowered border, which was
shipped from Hong Kong eight months later. The rug cost less
than the rug bought eighteen years before. If I saw an appealing
fabric in a window, I'd buy a few yards and throw it over a
particularly ugly table in the drawing room. Sometimes I didn't
bother using a seamstress; we just tucked the material underneath. Decorating embassies my way may be slapdash, but it
preserved individuality, fought the institutional look and cost
less.

In contrast, the U.S. government treats its embassies as show-
places. Lenore Annenberg and Wendy Luers, wife of the former
American ambassador to Czechoslovakia and Venezuela, and
now president of the Metropolitan Museum, organized private –

not government – funding to pay for the decoration of American embassies abroad. George Shultz, the Secretary of State, gave annual dinners in honour of the donors at the elegant State Department dining and reception rooms in order to encourage Americans to write cheques to pay for an antique quilt or a Sèvres vase, so that American embassy residences in foreign countries would be something to remember. The finest materials, antiques, paintings, objets d'art, particularly suited to the style and heritage of each residence, are chosen by curators and sophisticated decorators as well as the ambassadors' wives. The goal is to make these embassies a source of pride to all Americans.

As with redecorating, shopping for the O.R. might have been an engrossing experience, but somehow it ended up the least satisfying of my duties. Thankfully, I could count on the assistance of Glen Bullard, our maintenance official in the Chancery. Glen had been with the embassy "since the beginning" and would entertain me with stories about the foibles of my predecessors and their families. He pointed out the window box where someone's child had grown marijuana during the sixties, showed me the spot where an embassy dog had chewed the brand-new drawing room carpet and told me which ambassador's wife had maintained perfect discipline in the Residence with her exemplary English butler. "He was just like a lord, and he was the only servant she spoke to in the household. It was the silent treatment for the rest."

Glen made me laugh, and from the very start when I was confused, or angry, I would always call Glen, who, unlike me, understood the bureaucratic system though he shared my irritation with irrational rules. He was my hand-holder and helper in many crises. Once, during a very large party, there was terrible confusion among the waiters, and Glen stood in the kitchen, or rather the garage, barking out orders. "I don't want twelve trays at one table. I want one tray at twelve tables!" Glen loved emergencies during grand events.

When I made my first shopping foray for the Residence, to purchase a Mr. Coffee machine ($21.95), there were dark rumblings from shadowy administrators in the Chancery. Apparently I was supposed to ask an embassy procurement officer from the Chancery if there was money for a Mr. Coffee machine. If he wasn't on vacation and if there was money in that particular budget, he might then go out and buy something resembling what was needed – in a couple of months. Only he knew, or claimed to know, how much money I was allowed to spend on a Mr. Coffee machine. The embassy procurement officers were mostly ex-military people who bought office equipment in large quantities – not single coffee makers or upholstery for dining room chairs.

The sunroom downstairs needed new couches, and the embassy procurement officers gave me the good news that the sunroom decorating budget for the O.R. hadn't been depleted by our predecessor. I had been in Washington about two weeks and didn't know where to buy furniture. After the Mr. Coffee episode, the embassy procurement official told me to go and buy a sofa all by myself. He designated two discount warehouses in the wilds of Bethesda as suitable places from which to buy a sofa for the Canadian Residence. I went with Jacques Hèlie, my driver, who had been given only a sketchy idea where they were located. After a wild goose chase of three hours we found them barred and empty – gone bankrupt years before.

The Mr. Coffee incident and the bankrupt warehouses brought me to a new reality. I became aware of the anomalous position of the wife of an ambassador. I lived in the world of bureaucratic diplomacy: every embassy employee – the ambassador, the press attaché, the embassy procurer and the downstairs maid – had a job description and official classification. Butlers were not butlers: they were house managers, W.S.4.

But nobody knew what to do with that quaint, old-fashioned figure, the wife of the ambassador. She was the only person in the embassy without a job description. Yet somehow the "wife of" is supposed to assert her authority over those who are legitimately employed. There she is, this "wife of," this diplomatic remnant from the Congress of Vienna of 1815, powerless because she doesn't control the purse strings, ignorant because she doesn't understand bureaucracy, trying to find out from Chancery administrators – who may or may not tell her – how much money there is to upholster furniture or buy a rug, or at what salary she might employ a chef.

Yet it is clearly she who is supposed to hire and fire maids, social secretaries or butlers, as well as redecorate the embassy. I soon discovered that the wife of an ambassador is in fact the unpaid manager of a small hotel.

5/Putting Canada on the Map

DOMESTIC TRIALS WERE nothing compared to our ignorance of the capital. When we arrived in Washington we had no personal relationship with any members of the administration or Congress – the sort of contacts vital to any ambassador who wants to promote his country's interests. A number of Canadian journalists subsequently wrote with great conviction that we came from Ottawa with an elaborate social game-plan, designed by my husband and Pierre Trudeau and aimed at putting Canada on the Washington map.

Nothing could have been further from the truth. Allan told me that not a word was ever spoken between the two of them about what his goal was to be in Washington. There were no prior calculations about public diplomacy or a Canadian blitz on the Washington media. Allan had no political briefings. He knew well, from his previous job as undersecretary, that U.S.-Canadian relations were at an all-time low. The American government, business community and press had expressed over and over again their dislike for several of Trudeau's policies, especially the National Energy Policy and the foreign investment review activity.

Allan was also well aware that Pierre Trudeau had never been especially troubled about our economic difficulties with the United States. Trudeau always felt more at ease with the Commonwealth and European nations than he did with the Americans and tended to play down our relationship with the United States.

As the young wife of a public servant in Ottawa, I was, not to put too fine a point on it, terrified when I had the infrequent opportunity of talking to Prime Minister Trudeau. He had the sheen of power and celebrity combined with an unnervingly reticent conversational manner. I always noted in a crowd that people were mysteriously drawn to him. He always waited for them to make the first remark, and they would soon find out if he thought it was a foolish one.

In the United States, Pierre Trudeau's name was as well known as a first-rank movie star. Washington insiders told us, not long after our arrival, that although Trudeau was not well-liked by the Reagan White House, we should not underestimate his popularity and appeal in America as a whole. Everyone – even the most right-wing of the Reaganites – wanted to meet him, although some might occasionally make an ambivalent remark while accepting an invitation to a dinner in his honour. Trudeau was a star, a drawing-card, and everyone from the most prominent senator to my hairdresser would ask about him – and Margaret. As a writer and wife of an ambassador, I found him far more approachable than in earlier years, and always an undemanding guest. Perhaps he sensed my greater confidence as he would gossip easily with me about the U.S. and the various guests at our parties.

The first time Prime Minister Trudeau came to Washington during our stay there, he told us that he had asked Margot Kidder to the dinner we were planning for him. He asked me to sit her next to him. The rest of the guest list – and the seating – he left to us. Margot, like many of Pierre's dates, looked upon him as possible marriage material, but at the dinner he played his usual flirtatious but aloof game with women. He seemed bemused, not annoyed, at the hot attack Margot mounted against Michael Deaver over Reagan's attitude towards nuclear disarmament. After dinner, a former congressman, Stuart Symington, stood by the piano and sang Cole Porter songs from the 1930s, to Pierre Trudeau's delight. Then there was a kind of spontaneous dance – rare in political Washington.

Although seldom engaging in social chit-chat, Trudeau loved parties and staying up late. Later, when he was in Washington to see Reagan about arms control and his peace initiative, we had been asked the same day as his visit to a dinner dance at the Madison Hotel, given by Buffy and Bill Cafritz (nephew of Gwendolyn). When I told her we would be joining the Prime Minister at a small dinner Vice President Bush was giving for him at the exclusive Alibi Club, Buffy said, half jokingly, "Come after and bring him along!"

I mentioned the Cafritz dance to Trudeau later and was not surprised when the idea appealed to him. He created a minor sensation walking into the dance with his date Lacey Newhouse, a beautiful blonde from Texas, and old friend of the Bushes. Although he had spent a large part of a tense day preparing for and meeting with Ronald Reagan – the high point of his peace mission – Trudeau was in good form on the dance floor.

Before we left for Washington, Allan didn't expect much advice from the Prime Minister – and he already knew the limitations of the briefings given by the people in his own department. Washington was Allan's responsibility and it was left to him to shape our diplomacy in Washington. After all, he had been the undersecretary. It was Allan himself who only a few years before had agreed to establish the U.S. Bureau in External Affairs where previously the United States had been treated only as part of the Americas. Very few of the officers in the bureau had even served in the United States. No previous ambassador gave Allan any personal insight into the workings of the United States' political system.

Canada doesn't provide charm schools for wives of ambassadors. There are no briefings about the trials of managing embassies and giving dinner parties. Canadian diplomats and their families who are posted to "high risk" countries where medical and domestic facilities are poor are given language courses and briefings on native customs, safety and health care.

The United States is hardly a "high risk" country. But few in government were able to give us any help in understanding how the U.S. system was changing and what these changes could mean for Canada. For that we had to wait until we got to Washington. We could only find out about the radical changes since Watergate by on-the-job training.

When Allan met the new British ambassador, Sir Oliver Wright, he told Allan that he had discovered, on his arrival, that his schedule was filled for the next three months. Allan was astonished because when we arrived our schedule had been empty except for the Presentation of Credentials and a ball in Palm Beach, Florida. People in Washington were not interested in Canadians unless they had such names as Wayne Gretzky or Pierre or Margaret Trudeau.

Two people in Washington became crucial to our entrée into the capital's political society, and no two people could have been less alike or lived in such different worlds. Their only common denominator was their deaths in the same year. I doubt if they ever met. One was Joe Kraft, the late syndicated columnist, and the other an elderly eccentric named Peggy LeBaron, a former Ziegfeld Follies girl and wife of a member of Herbert Hoover's cabinet, who had contacts with the wives of the cabinet officers of the Reagan administration.

I met Joseph Kraft at a party in Ottawa given by the writers Richard and Sandra Gwyn in the summer of 1981 while he was in Canada covering President Reagan's first official visit outside America. During our first weeks in Washington I saw Joe Kraft again with his wife, Polly, at a small dinner given by Tom and Gaetana Enders. Joe Kraft, a highly informed, hard-working journalist nurtured in the New York–Washington axis, had been an observer of changing administrations in Washington since the Kennedy period and a friend of many leading political figures. His intellect was far-ranging, and he was one of the few columnists we met, during our whole period in Washington, who wanted to hear about and discuss Canadian problems and policies. The great majority of columnists who were interested in foreign policy had fixed their vision permanently towards the Middle East, Central

America and the Soviet bloc. Polly Kraft, a hostess as well as a professional painter, kindly and somewhat impulsively asked us to several dinners, where we dimly began to figure out the Washington system, or What Every Ambassador and His Wife Should Know.

The significance of Washington social life and how it could be used as a tool to advance Canada's interests began to dawn on us only after we observed the patterns of the powerful at parties. We soon noticed that the presence of the press at these events served as a magnet for high officials and congressional figures – and of course the press wanted to be with them. Leaking to the press, we discovered, was one of the Reagan administration's standard ways of making and communicating government policy. It was a practice constantly indulged in by individual administration players, each aiming to get his own position out or discredit that of his rivals. We also discovered that congressmen and especially their staffers had been doing this for years.

I remember coming home with Allan from one of the parties; he was puzzled, but intrigued. "Do you know what Joe said, when I asked him what the Reagan administration is interested in? 'Social climbing and parties.' "

It took me two years to understand what Joe Kraft meant by that remark.

At that time I believed in the cliché phrases we had seen in Canada and in much of the U.S. press about the Reagan administration's hard-line foreign policies, about the right-wing kitchen cabinet from California, which controlled the President's mind, about the Ayn Rand followers in the White House, the influence of the Heritage Foundation and of the American Rifle Association, and so on. What had all these ideological obsessions to do with social climbing? And what were these mysterious high social peaks that Nancy Reagan, if not her husband, wanted to climb in Washington, never mind New York, California and Texas? In Canada I was more used to socialists than socialites. It was very bewildering.

The second week after our arrival, my social secretary, Pat Thomas, gleefully told me, "We've struck gold. Peggy LeBaron asked you to lunch. She wants you to be a member of International Club #1, which is good, but the lunch invitation is even better. I heard she was giving a lunch for the Attorney General's wife, and I suggested she invite you."

I had no idea that social secretaries could do that sort of thing. Needless to say I didn't know a Peggy LeBaron, or the wife of the Attorney General. But Pat, a former Winnipegger like myself but wise in the ways of Washington, wasn't shy in organizing my first social steps. Before I left for lunch Pat added, "Peggy promised me she'd give you a good seat." I was glad she told me, because I wouldn't have known what a good seat was. That lunch was the first time I met the wives of the new cabinet officers. Few of them were from Washington, and it was only much later that I learned they were as bewildered as I was.

Peggy LeBaron, in her eighties at the time, had a widow's hump, a trembling gait and wore a huge coloured bow in her hair. She was as ambitious and aggressive as an aspiring Junior Leaguer. Why did Peggy go to so much trouble for ambassadors' wives? In Washington, I soon learned, a favour received might mean a favour returned. Ambassadors' wives have swimming pools – Peggy loved to swim. Ambassadors' wives have cars with chauffeurs – Peggy didn't drive; she needed lifts to take her to the lunches and teas she organized. Ambassadors' wives had the facilities to give lunches and teas in honour of her very large International Club #1. And she and her ninety-year-old Hoover-cabinet husband might get an invitation to a dinner.

Approximately sixty women attended that lunch, all wives of high administration officials, senators and congressmen. After lunch Peggy made each of us stand up and introduce ourselves by declaring our husband's job. I was seated next to the wife of the Secretary of Energy and the wife of the Secretary of the Navy. I think we were the last of the "wives of" to introduce ourselves. All I can remember is that phrase "I am the wife of" going up and down the tables, until it was my turn, and, flustered, I introduced myself as the wife of Canada. Some of these women had jobs of their own, but Peggy, typical of many in Washington, felt their prestige came from their husbands' positions. She ran single-handedly the most important International Club in Washington, and before the new cabinet wives had even arrived to take up residence in the city she had called them at their homes in various states inviting them to be members. Like myself, they joined out of curiosity, ignorance and loneliness.

"Your husband has a better chance of meeting the top men, if you know the wife," the Australian ambassador's wife confided to me when Allan and I paid a joint courtesy call on the couple. The problem was that foreign policy was not a high priority of the Reagan administration in its early years, nor of Congress. Officials in the new White House had no interest in meeting the 150 or so ambassadors stationed in Washington. While Allan was having considerable success in getting appointments with some of the cabinet officers, the White House was virtually a closed shop to diplomats. The unpopularity of Prime Minister Trudeau and his policies among those closest to Reagan obviously did not help.

The Reagan team's wives had their own problems. They either came from the generation of nonworking wives or their husbands' jobs had such a high profile that any paid activity they might take on was sure to be criticized in the press. Many of them were lonely, on unfamiliar terrain in the capital city and anxious to meet people. The easiest way to do so was at luncheons that Peggy gave in their honour. The wives of the Reagan cabinet were new stars. Everyone wanted to meet them. It was Peggy LeBaron who introduced me to the wives of the Meese-Baker-Deaver triumvirate, which ran the White House during the first four years of the Reagan administration. It was through Peggy that I also met Jean French Smith, the wife of the Attorney General, who was the President's long-standing friend and legal adviser, as well as many congressional wives.

Nothing ever deterred Peggy from her goals – including introducing senators and cabinet officials to wives of ambassadors they did not wish to meet. Peggy would take us to lunch at the National Press Club, drag us up to the podium as Senator Charles Percy or Donald Regan (then Secretary of Treasury) finished his speech, then plant us so that we blocked his getaway path, forcing him to acknowledge her and us. She knew that we would go home and tell our husbands we had actually touched the flesh of men who may not have returned our husbands' calls. Once, Peggy took the wife of the Japanese ambassador and me to the Women's Republican Club for lunch to listen to Mac Baldrige, the Secretary of Commerce, whom I had not yet met. We were the only ambassadorial wives present. Mac told the Republican women how foreign countries like Canada and Japan were using unfair trade tactics towards the United States because they practised the sin of hidden subsidies. Mac was unaware of the presence of the wives of the representatives of these notorious foreign countries.

Peggy never listened to the speeches. She was very frail and it took most of her energy to edge and nudge us towards the speaker as he was winding up. By the time Mac had finished, Peggy had us well up front and plucked at his sleeve as he started to leave. Mac said, without looking around, "Not now, Peggy, I'm late for an appointment."

Peggy held me in an iron grip with her other hand (the wife of the Japanese ambassador stood meekly beside her) and said, "You can't go until you meet the wives of the Canadian and Japanese ambassadors. After all, Japan and Canada are our best friends."

I would have done anything to become the Invisible Woman. Mac stared at us, embarrassed, and said, "Don't believe everything I say."

Unlike the reclusive Carter administration, the Reaganites liked social activities and brought with them from California a zest for parties, glitz and glamour. Although the permanent powers in Washington are by and large Democrats, they were sick of the austere Carter regime – Washingtonians resented the cola cans, paper cups and absence of liquor at the few White House receptions to which they were invited – and wanted to meet and mix with the Reagan crowd. The Carter administration had a reputation for stinginess. Americans were furious when Jimmy Carter sold the presidential yacht, *The Sequoia*, and Mrs. Carter was criticized for not buying a new dress for the presidential inauguration balls. The inaugural dresses worn by the First Ladies are traditionally worn once and then given to the Smithsonian Institution.

On one occasion Jimmy Carter asked a cabinet secretary and his wife to dinner; it would be just the four of them. The cabinet officer gladly accepted with one warning. "Mr. President," he said, "you know my wife and I usually have a vodka martini before dinner." He was aware of the Carters' ban on hard alcohol at the White House. President Carter told him he would have his vodka martinis. The President was as good as his word. The cabinet member and his wife were served martinis at the White House, and the Carters sipped water. A few days after the dinner, an envelope, sent by hand from the White House, arrived at the office of the cabinet member. It contained a bill, for four vodka martinis – $12.50. Our friend, the member of Carter's cabinet, wrote out a personal cheque to the Carters, and then had the bill framed to put up on his office wall.

Given this kind of austere behaviour, it became easier to understand why during the first years of the new Reagan administration the mood of the city was "let's party."

We arrived just as the two groups – the new administration and the permanent people – were beginning to be aware of each other in social Washington.

When I first arrived in Washington I had been advised by another diplomatic wife to "beware of embassy rats." These are people who usually call you up within the first weeks of your arrival and ask you out to concerts and balls in order to get on your invitation list. As delightful as some of these people are, they have little to do with the goals of one's country. If an ambassador wastes money and time entertaining the "rats", he will get the reputation of being frivolous, lazy and not interested in substance.

It is a given in Washington that the substantive people – cabinet officials, congressional warlords, anyone who is important that week in Washington – tend, with some exceptions, to disdain embassy parties. And usually with good reason. We had been in

Washington only two weeks when we learned why embassy parties are often looked upon as trials of endurance.

An attractive and experienced ambassadorial couple from a minor European embassy kindly asked us to dinner because we were new. That dinner proved to be a lesson in what not to do if one wants to give a successful party in Washington.

The invitation said black tie and mentioned that a concert was to be performed before the dinner. The party was in honour of Senator Strom Thurmond, the highly influential chairman of the Judiciary Committee in the Senate who was then almost eighty years old, and his wife, Nancy, a former beauty queen, who was forty years younger than her husband.

(I remember attending much later a dinner and movie given in honour of the Thurmonds by Jack Valenti, the powerful president of the American Motion Picture Association. After dinner Jack Valenti rose and toasted Nancy Thurmond's graciousness and civility. Senator Thurmond rose slowly to respond and said, "Jack, I'm glad you toasted Nancy on her civility and refrained from mentioning my senility.")

The other guests of honour were Senator Charles Percy, who was chairman of the Foreign Relations Committee, and his wife Loraine.

There must have been about seventy people crowded into the old chancery – all unfamiliar to me and dressed far more fashionably than I was used to in Ottawa or Toronto. We sat in gold chairs while the ambassador's wife sang lieder to the accompaniment of her husband, who was an accomplished concert pianist. The wife, however, was not so accomplished an artist. She gestured and grimaced her way through complex pieces by Wolf and Schumann. Her exaggerated mannerisms and voice, often off pitch, began to cause a tittering through the audience. And she went on, encore after encore, prying reluctant requests from the audience.

Finally the ambassador's wife got off the stage and the crowd trampled upstairs, where there was a large buffet of lobsters and salads. We helped ourselves as best we could in the pushing, crowded food line, and then were shown our seats at different tables. Husbands and wives never sit at the same table in Washington, unlike at so many dinners I have attended in Canada.

My dinner companion on my right, who looked about ninety and who I thought I heard being introduced as a member of the cabinet or the White House, seemed in a state of outrage.

"Look at that," he said. "They've got them separated from the rest of us."

I looked where the finger was pointing and saw the host and hostess sitting at the same round table, which was raised on a dais. With them were the two senatorial guests of honour, their wives and one other couple. This special group looked down upon the rest of us guests.

"It's bad taste," he said. "The guests of honour and the hosts shouldn't sit separated off like that. Higher than everyone else. It's literally putting everyone else below the salt."

This was the first but not the last time I heard criticism of seating arrangements in Washington. I have seen prominent people, at large affairs, check out their place card at the table, then surreptitiously shift the cards if the seating was not to their liking.

I didn't think I was below the salt, because I was sitting next to a member of the White House or cabinet. I asked him which it was. "I was in the cabinet," he said, "with Eisenhower. Fred there," he said, motioning to my companion on the other side, "was in the Coolidge White House." He chuckled and explained. "In America, honey, we keep our titles. Once a Mr. Secretary, always a Mr. Secretary."

The other gentleman, who seemed even older, didn't say much except to pronounce the lobster uncooked.

When I left that party I vowed I would never separate the important guests in such a manner, would never have a concert before dinner and would always invite people who were part of contemporary political affairs. Later I discovered that most of the people at that dinner were charming locals who had lots of money and had entertained the ambassador and his wife.

Within a few months our obscure status in Washington began to change radically, as a result of public attention, although we each received it for different reasons. It is a truism that publicity is a Pandora's box. But in a highly competitive city like Washington the right kind of publicity can lead to invitations, access, requests to speak or appear on talk shows and other opportunities. Washington is crowded with public-relations firms earning large sums by devising ways for their clients' names to be mentioned in the press. Conglomerates and private individuals, embassies and politicians routinely employ these firms, many of whom are responsible for organizing parties and getting "names" to come to them. The Canadian Embassy has, of course, always had a press section, but the publicity we personally received did not originate from any embassy plot or from a public-relations firm.

My first public baptism occurred in February 1982 and had to do with my being a sort of hermaphrodite, an ambassador's wife and a writer. About a month after our arrival Donnie Radcliffe, a prominent social writer in the influential Style section of the *Washington Post*, mentioned in her social column that the new Canadian ambassador's wife was a novelist. That created enough interest for Chris Wallace on NBC's *Today Show* to interview me about *First Lady, Last Lady*, which had not been published or distributed in the United States. My first reaction was that of a writer – to regret that my book, which was getting all this marvellous publicity, was not available in U.S. bookstores.

But the *Today Show* interview had a serendipitous result – curiosity about us as an ambassadorial couple in Washington.

Shortly after I appeared on the show, we gave a dinner party in honour of Mark MacGuigan, at that time Canada's External Affairs Minister. Although it ought to have been easy to get a good turnout in honour of a Minister of External Affairs, this was not the Washington way. At a dinner in honour of the Turkish Foreign Minister I had been astonished that not one senior member of the administration was present. Allan was shocked. "Imagine," he said to me after the dinner, "here's a country that borders on the Soviet Union, is a stalwart member of NATO, a moderate influence in the Arab world, and occupies one of the finest embassies in Washington, and yet no powerful American political official could be bothered to attend an official dinner in honour of its Foreign Minister. What are we up against?"

We had an added problem. As Mark MacGuigan was coming to Washington on a private visit, there was no need, according to the rules of protocol, for important officials to attend a dinner in his honour. And, of course, at that time we didn't know anyone important in Washington. Despite these drawbacks, Allan made a list of some of the most powerful officials in Washington whom he thought our Minister of External Affairs should meet and had Pat Thomas call their social secretaries. The list included Secretary of State Alexander Haig; Secretary of Defense Caspar Weinberger; Ben Bradlee, editor of the *Washington Post*, and his wife, Sally Quinn; Jeane Kirkpatrick, who was U.S. ambassador to the UN; Walter Stoessel, Deputy Head of the State Department; the Krafts; Hélène Von Damm (Paul Robinson had told us that she was very important in the White House); Arms Control chief Walter Rostow; and writer and broadcaster Elizabeth Drew. We had been in Washington some six weeks when we asked our guests. Two weeks later, four days before the party was to take place, Allan thought he would have to cancel it because most of the important guests had not yet responded. I don't know whether it was because of the *Today Show*, or some kind of social secretaries' tom-tom, but our first major acceptance came from Caspar Weinberger four days before the party. A few minutes later, Alexander Haig accepted. We were particularly well pleased because it was, by then, well known that the two men did not get on. Then everyone else accepted, which makes me, to this day, suspicious of Washington phone lines.

The party was small, some twenty-four people, but it flustered our butler, who apparently wasn't comfortable with sit-down dinners of that size. On the day of the party, while Pat and I agonized over the seating plan for the four tables of six, Rito waited until all the handwritten escort cards had been finished and sorted out by Pat and the delicate seating arrangements worked out. To this day I can't explain how escort cards work except I know that if there's any kind of change, the seating goes flooey. Then Rito told us that the Residence didn't own four round tables. We managed to rent them at five o'clock that same afternoon. It then began to snow heavily, which in Washington means total paralysis. I was sure the guests would all be late or not come at all. The primroses I had bought for the tables were drooping, and all you could see were the elastic bands holding the stems together.

Pat Thomas was a wonderful social secretary, but she was not working at night because her little girl was very ill. At most embassies a social secretary usually greets the dinner guests, shows them into the drawing room and then helps them find their places at the tables. I learned that later on.

At 7:30 P.M., Glen Bullard told me that some television people were outside and wanted to come in. I knew nothing about television people, and Allan, who had just arrived from meetings, was in the bathtub. I put on my new long dress, went downstairs and dithered until Patrick Gossage, the embassy's senior press attaché, arrived and made some kind of decision.

It was fortunate that I was downstairs because fifteen minutes before the party was to begin Secretary of Defense Weinberger walked in. I didn't recognize him and said, "I'm your hostess, but I'm new here; would you tell me your name?" Weinberger laughed, introduced himself and said he had heard I was a writer and told me he used to do book reviews on television. A scholarly man, he didn't fit into my preconceived image of a fire-eating right-wing American Secretary of Defense. I managed to get word upstairs to Allan that Caspar Weinberger had arrived, and he came bounding downstairs, still tying his black tie. Most of the guests arrived before the appointed hour of eight o'clock. The Secretary of Defense and the Secretary of State were accompanied, as was always the case, by Secret Service men with earplugs, and as snow was predicted they had brought out a four-wheel drive earlier in the day. The Secret Service, again following routine, had checked the embassy site in the afternoon and noted for security reasons where their great men were being seated.

Alexander Haig, a handsome man with high cheekbones who

looked as if he has some Tartar blood, arrived shortly after the Secretary of Defense. Haig was genial despite the growing rumours around town about trouble between him, the President and Caspar Weinberger. Jeane Kirkpatrick, intense and formidable, made only one remark to me that evening. When the spun-sugar maple-syrup bombe was passed around she said, "That looks like a very Third World dessert." I wondered whether she thought Canada was part of the Third World.

Elizabeth Drew noticed the presence of Helene Von Damm. "Nancy Reagan doesn't talk to the hired help," was her comment about Ms. Von Damm's status. Ms. Von Damm was subsequently made chief of White House personnel and later ambassador to Austria. Drew, who covers the White House beat for *The New Yorker*, knew what she was talking about. During her sojourn in Austria, Ms. Von Damm left her first husband for a younger man, who owned the famous Sacher hotel. The boulevard press in Austria became fascinated with her personal life, and she rather liked the idea of being followed by cameras. Evidently she became the subject of some ridicule in Austria and Nancy Reagan had her fired. Helene Von Damm later wrote a book which included some nasty barbs directed at Mrs. Reagan.

We were unaware at that time of the significance of Weinberger, Ben Bradlee and Haig being together at a relatively small dinner. This was a rare combination of powers in Washington, whether at an embassy party or any other event. Weinberger and Bradlee took advantage of it. Two years later Ben Bradlee told me that he knew then for the first time that Haig was going to be fired because of the derisive way Weinberger spoke of him at our party. One must assume under such circumstances that whatever Weinberger said to Bradlee had to have been deliberate, that he was prepared to see the *Washington Post* publish stories about Haig's failings. When the Bradlees left they said, "We generally don't go to embassy parties because they are so boring. But the next time you have one, ask us again." We had impressed the *Washington Post*, which, in some circles in Washington, is considered better than impressing the Secretary of State or Defense. A couple of days later, Stephanie Mansfield called up and said she had been asked to interview me for the Style section of the *Washington Post*.

The interview appeared on the top of the front page of the Style section on 10 February, about ten weeks after our arrival. It was entitled "Sondra Gotlieb Drops in: The Canadian Ambassador's Wife and the Hard Knocks School of Diplomacy." I was described as "deliciously offbeat" and the article was replete with revealing quotes from my books, including the one where the heroine in *First Lady, Last Lady* refuses to go to Washington as wife of the Canadian ambassador because it's "all prestige and no power."

Stephanie Mansfield, one of the *Washington Post*'s skilled destroyers of reputations, had not believed I was a real writer until she read my books and then – as she told me – liked them. This raised me a notch in her eyes.

The *Post* garnished the page with a huge picture of me, a rather unflattering stomach shot, but the interview was exceptionally sympathetic, although I was certainly indiscreet for an ambassador's wife. I told Stephanie, for example, how much it upset me when I read an article in the *New York Times* about Countess Ulla Wachmeister, the wife of the Swedish ambassador to the United States, who had made her own dining table centrepiece by growing grass on styrofoam tennis balls as a theme for a party she had given in honour of Bjorn Borg. I knew that I was incapable of growing my own grass for unusual party centrepieces; I told Stephanie how insecure I felt when I read about those grass balls.

In the interview I also spoke about how I was intimidated by the servants and how nervous and fearful I was about my role as ambassador's wife. I even said, "English women are the pits."

The day the interview appeared, the phone began to ring and did not stop for a couple of weeks. Everyone from cabinet wives to strangers, from lobbyists to the British ambassador's wife, said they wanted to meet me or congratulate me on the interview. The publicity was worth gold and put us at a stroke on the Washington map. Invitations, interesting and not so interesting, flowed in, and I received requests for interviews from the *New York Times*,

People magazine, many other American newspapers and magazines and, of course, the Canadian press. The *Post* article was reprinted in the *Los Angeles Times* and in newspapers all over the U.S. Strangers wrote to me from such places as Waco, Texas, to say, "I always thought ambassadors' wives were stuffy and remote. It's nice to know you've got a sense of humour and worry about making mistakes."

Even so, I had my first taste of blood from a member of the city's colony of hit women – freelance writers, mainly, who live on the social edges of Washington. A member of the press section at our embassy advised me to give an interview to a woman named Joy Billington for a California paper. Our staff member assured me that Joy was a pal and wanted to do a sympathetic piece. As soon as Ms. Billington came in I sensed hostility, but since she was supposed to be a pal I ignored my intuition. She asked me what the Canadian ambassador's wife might use as a party centrepiece. I made a poor joke. "How about a bashed stuffed baby Canadian seal?" Then, recognizing that this was in bad taste, I said, "That's off the record of course." She printed it in a California paper. The next time I saw her was at a White House dinner, standing in the press scrum watching the guests file in. Foolishly, I became angry and accused her of printing something that I had said was off the record. She called our embassy the following morning and said she was going to sue me for my behaviour. I never heard from her again, but it was my first taste in the United States of the press as an enemy. Fortunately, her piece was not widely reprinted.

About the same time, Allan began to receive publicity in the American and Canadian press for different reasons. He was attacking the Americans. He was deliberately trying to alter the image that American business had of Canada. There were at that time serious economic differences between the Trudeau government and the Reagan administration over Canada's energy and investment policies. At the same time the mood of Congress was becoming protectionist and there were increasing calls for retaliation against Canada. An outbreak of nasty articles about

Canada's energy policies occurred in major newspapers across the country.

The *New York Sunday Times* published a prominent counter-attack by Allan entitled "Freezing in the Dark Is Not Our Style." Allan believed that American businessmen and the press were being heavily influenced by the Reagan administration's hostile attitude towards many of Pierre Trudeau's policies. He felt the only way to deal with unfair publicity was to answer back, publicly. Allan now began to be referred to as the "Outspoken Diplomat." He became news just as the Iranian or Nicaraguan Ambassadors regularly did, because he publicly lambasted the Americans for their misunderstanding of Canada, for protectionism in the Congress and for refusing to tackle the acid-rain problem. "Getting the U.S. to pay attention to Canada," he said, "is like preaching temperance on a troop ship."

Allan became the undiplomatic diplomat and the press adored it. He felt that there was not much to lose by being so outspoken because the relationship between the two countries could not have been worse. Later, when we went to Dallas in the spring of 1982 to attend various ceremonies, the lead editorial in the *Dallas Times* that day accused Canada of being socialistic, collectivist, interventionist and practically communist. This gave Allan a wonderful opportunity to answer back, and local T.V. crews followed him around while we ate barbecue and tried on ten-gallon hats. The *New York Times* interviewed both of us, and a quote of mine, "For some reason, a glaze passes over people's faces when you say Canada – maybe we should invade South Dakota or something," was repeated on their front page and in most of the U.S. press. Suddenly we had a high profile in both countries. We were, according to the press, "Putting Canada on the Map." Public diplomacy was considered rather un-Canadian, but it fascinated Washington and attracted attention; we began to gain entrée into circles where Allan could actually make contact with people who could help improve the situation between the two countries.

By the spring of 1982 Allan still had virtually no contact with the White House. The State Department didn't let on, or possibly didn't know, how much President Reagan disliked Pierre Trudeau and his policies. Allan knew that Trudeau thought of Reagan as an actor rather than a statesman and disapproved of his hostile attitude towards the Soviet Union. Later, when Allan had contact with those within the Reagan loop, Richard Darman, who worked for James Baker in the White House, told Allan that the Reaganites were sure Pierre Trudeau had called the President "an idiot" and, even if he hadn't, thought he was.

Allan's first clue about Reagan's personal feeling came from an unofficial source. Later that spring, at a salmon barbeque at our embassy, Allan sat next to Joan Clark, the wife of William Clark, who was a hard-line, right-wing National Security Adviser to the President until Michael Deaver and Nancy Reagan eased him out. Mrs. Clark, a quiet, modest woman of Czech origin, naturally hated the Soviets because of their rape of Czechoslovakia. She was polite, but at one point turned to Allan and commented on Trudeau's anti-American proclivities or something to that effect. No matter what Allan said, she seemed to remain firm in her belief. An ambassador can dismiss this sort of remark if it's pronounced by a right-wing Palm Beach society lady, but he has to take it seriously when it comes from the mouth of the wife of the President's National Security Adviser.

The first time anyone from the administration hinted that the situation should and could be improved was at a party in June 1982, given by Joan Braden, a well-known Washington hostess, and her husband, Tom, the television commentator. By this time our publicity was at a peak and we were even considered catches by "the Georgetown set" (the traditional "in" group in Washington whose members don't necessarily have to live in Georgetown). It was seven months after our arrival, and Joan and Tom threw a Washington "Power Party." The main "catch" was Michael Deaver, the open-sesame man to the President, and his wife, Carolyn. Until then Allan had seen nothing of Deaver. Joan's party included the old Georgetown establishment – the late Joe Alsop, former columnist and Washington observer since the Roosevelt era (as well as being a Roosevelt himself); Evangeline

Bruce, Washington hostess and widow of the famous diplomat David Bruce; Katharine Graham, publisher of the *Washington Post*; the British ambassador, Nico Henderson (the top diplomat, as seen in Washington); the Democratic establishment lawyer Robert Strauss; Jack Valenti, motion-picture chief lobbyist and formerly Chief of Staff to Lyndon Johnson; Bob Gray, the powerful Republican lobbyist for whom Joan worked; Larry Eagleburger, the brilliant assistant secretary of State; Senator Paul Laxalt, a "close-to" of President Reagan's; humorist Art Buchwald and other celebrities. There was a piano player in attendance, and after-dinner dancing on the terrace. I remember Carolyn Deaver perched on a delighted Joe Alsop's lap and Allan talking intensely to Michael Deaver.

That conversation was significant. It was the first time the Canadian ambassador felt that he was able to get through the iron gates the Reagan administration had closed against Canada. Deaver originated the conversation. He came up to Allan after dinner and told him that President Reagan had read an article written by Lubor Zink in the *National Review* that described Trudeau as a communist.

Allan said, "That's a lunatic idea."

Deaver said, be that as it may, the article had made a strong impression on Reagan and something should be done to ease the situation. "Why don't you invite Bill Clark and me to your embassy for lunch? I don't think this kind of thing should be going on between Canada and the U.S., between your guy and my guy."

Allan was flabbergasted, but appreciated the first attempt on the part of the Reagan administration to address a terrible problem. No one from the State Department had let on that the animosity was so profound.

6/Diplomats As Props

ONCE A DIPLOMAT'S wife accepts that she is an anachronism, a relic from the Congress of Vienna, it's then possible for her to enjoy her unpaid job. In fact her husband is himself often accused of being an anachronism. How often did I hear the question posed to Allan: does a country really need an ambassador when you can fax, telephone and commute from one capital to another? He either ignored the question or gave a serious answer that would cause "meglo" ("my eyes glaze over") syndrome in the unfortunate interlocutor. The necessity of effective ambassadors in the modern world was not a subject for me to discuss: I dealt with and liked the froth and shadow of important events.

The last foreign ambassador who was an intimate of the President of the United States was Lord Harlech, the British ambassador during the Kennedy era. Since that time no ambassador representing any country to the United States has had that kind of easy social access to the White House.

Nancy Reagan, who enjoyed absolute control over the guest list at the White House, was not interested in entertaining foreign diplomats unless they were accompanying or close to a member of the British royal family or had connections to European royalty. Nevertheless, for reasons of protocol, the entire diplomatic corps was invited to the White House from time to time.

It's a dull business entertaining 150 ambassadors and their wives. (Some of the ambassadors had more than one wife with them in Washington.) Many ambassadors in Washington seemed to have very little interest in the American political system and were even disapproving of it. A good ambassador to the United States should look upon himself, whether he likes to or not, as the chief lobbyist for his country. Many ambassadors, even if they did recognize this, felt that lobbying was a rather undignified task. There were many significant exceptions, but too many ambassadors lacked passion and engagement and declined to participate in the congressional fray. These diplomats stayed so aloof that their interest in the latest American political gossip, the dominant ingredient of conversation in Washington, was virtually nil. Which is why so many Americans found diplomats dull people to entertain and why most Presidents and First Ladies become glum when it is time to entertain the Washington diplomatic corps. The late Joseph Alsop, the immensely influential syndicated columnist, once said to me, "One diplomatic couple at dinner is sufficient. Any more is ruinous to the conversation."

The Reagans solved this problem by using us as props. The public relations advisers would call out the television cameras and the official White House photographer was always present so that the world could see that the international presence in Washington was being taken good care of by the President of the United States.

The ambassadors became actors without lines, part of the visual displays in a staged political event. The President did not discuss foreign policy matters – or anything, for that matter – with the individual ambassadors; they became background scenery for the President like the sandbagged fortresses between North and South Korea selected by Michael Deaver.

Occasionally I would be invited with Allan to these events and other times it was Mr. Ambassadors only. It usually took many hours of waiting to become a propaganda extra for the President. When the picture-taking part of the event was over, the President and Mrs. Reagan would vanish, with the cabinet officers and members of the administration quickly following suit – and the diplomats would be left happily talking to themselves. Who can blame the Reagans or the cabinet for not wanting to listen to diplomats enunciate the conventional wisdom of last week? These affairs tended to be nonevents, but at least one could write to the folks at home and brag about being invited to the White House.

The first time the Reagans entertained the foreign ambassadors, they planned to give a white-tie dinner at the White House. But with so many countries involved they had to hold two dinners, and so the countries were divided by alphabet. The ambassadors weren't told about this division, and when half the corps wasn't invited to the first dinner, a few thought they had been deliberately snubbed. We had just arrived in Washington and had received an invitation to the first dinner, and this annoyed some of our colleagues. It finally dawned upon us that we merited such extraordinary attention only because Canada starts with a C. The Cypriot and Cameroonian ambassadors had also received their invitations. Eventually, when the invitations for the second dinner were sent out, the ambassadors from Mexico down to Zambia were mollified to learn that the corps was not divided into "A" and "B" lists, but into "A to L" and "M to Z" lists.

At that first event I remember being seated at a round table hosted by Larry Eagleburger, then Assistant Secretary of State for European Affairs. On either side of him were two wives of ambassadors from developing nations. Both wore unusual and attractive headdresses and elegant national dress. Inexplicably, both fell asleep at the table, their turbaned heads leaning very slightly on either side of Larry's shoulders. It was a delightful and peaceful sight.

That year of the white-tie dinners was never repeated; such events were too cumbersome and time-consuming. The next party for diplomats went to the opposite extreme. It was an indoor barbecue. There was much discussion beforehand about what to wear to such an event at the White House. Tie, no tie? Silk dresses, slacks or square-dance dresses? The President and Mrs. Reagan had dressed appropriately – Nancy Reagan wore a khaki skirt and simple white blouse with a gold necklace, and the President wore jeans – but some of us, confused by last year's dress code, had gone astray in ankle-length chiffon. The President and Mrs. Reagan did not stay for the indoor barbecue. The diplomats were nevertheless glad to pick up their plastic glasses, paper plates and cutlery at the buffet, and we didn't mind too much when the little plastic knives bent as we tried to cut the delicious barbecued beef. The White House must have decided it had gone too far with formality at the last event.

Then, in an odd kind of double reverse, the excellencies were asked about a year and a half later to a cocktail party at which the men had to wear white tie and the women long dresses. As at all White House affairs, each ambassador and his wife had the opportunity of having a colour photograph of themselves taken standing with the President and Mrs. Reagan. These photographs, dutifully inscribed, were generally displayed in a prominent place in each embassy residence. The picture taking occurred during the receiving line. The chef de protocol would introduce the ambassador, then his wife, to the Reagans and immediately thereafter an aide would gently slide the diplomatic couple in beside the President and his wife for the photo-op. Outside the White House on Pennsylvania Avenue, an enterprising photographer had erected life-sized cut-outs of the President and Mrs. Reagan so that tourists could have their pictures taken with the presidential couple as well. The living President and his wife were about as animated during the snapshot sessions as their cardboard duplicates on the street. They would look right through us. Only after the Free Trade deal with Canada was signed, six years after our arrival, did a glint of recognition come into their eyes as we filed by.

The 1985 version of the official White House entertainment of the diplomatic corps came in July, when Donald Regan was Chief of Staff. The entire diplomatic corps was invited to the White House at 4:00 P.M. to attend a short concert by the Boston Pops. The summer had been unbearably hot and humid even for Washington. Our dog had fleas, the grass was scorched, and there were stories in the local news about the old times when Washington was part of the malaria belt. Official Washington travelled only from air-conditioned offices to air-conditioned cars and into air-conditioned homes. Nobody voluntarily went outdoors to get a breath of jungle air.

We had all expected the White House invitation, which had been sent out long before, to be cancelled, not because of the weather, but because President Reagan was being operated on for cancer of the colon. No cancellation took place, however, and ambassadors in dark suits and wives in cocktail dresses (with sleeves, in expectation of air-conditioning) arrived promptly at four. There was a muted moan of dismay when the marine guards and assistant social secretaries led us outdoors to a row of seats placed in a special corner – the only corner of the White House lawn where there was no shade. At four o'clock the sun still shone brightly. No awning had been installed and shade trees appeared to be everywhere except over our heads. The Boston Pops were all ready in place and the musicians were sweating in silence. Time passed, diplomats and their wives began to fan themselves with the programs, murmuring louder and louder like a swarm of bumblebees. One of the wives from a European country declared dehydration or faintness, and a marine guard took her inside the White House while the rest of us looked on. But there was no sign of the Reagans.

Selwa "Lucky" Roosevelt, part of whose job as chief of protocol was to look after the diplomats, came very late, carrying a parasol. We stared enviously at the pretty ruffled thing. None of the diplomats' wives had brought garden-party hats to shade them from the sun. By this time many of the men had placed their programs on their bald pates and the women were dabbing at their dripping mascara. A kind of cloud of moisture settled over us – a climatic reaction, something to do with our drops of perspiration rising and making a rendezvous with the humidity in the air.

Vice President Bush, Barbara Bush and the Secretary of Defense, Caspar Weinberger, arrived and waited, somewhat impatiently, with us. They were getting fractious too. The Vice President rose, looking annoyed, and took off his jacket, revealing two large sweat spots on his shirt. Everyone cheered. The

Secretary of Defense removed his jacket, and then the ambassadors, to a man, rose and undressed. We "wives of" removed what
we could.

Finally Mrs. Reagan, preceded by Donald Regan, appeared.
Lucky Roosevelt jumped up and offered Mrs. Reagan her parasol,
but it was gracefully declined. Mrs. Reagan and Mr. Regan were
beaming as if they had a happy secret. This was perhaps the last
time Nancy Reagan and Donald Regan shared joy together. Less
than a year later Regan was pushed out of the White House by
Mrs. Reagan because of his handling of the Iran-Contra scandal.
That afternoon, however, they were mutually relieved because
the doctors had given them good news about the results of the
President's operation.

When the two of them had taken their places, the Boston Pops
struck up a medley of Broadway show tunes, and afterwards we
were invited inside the air-conditioned White House for a drink
while Mrs. Reagan presumably joined the President.

At this and other functions we attended at the White House,
including state dinners for Prime Minister Brian Mulroney, the
press always took their stance inside the White House. The guests
would run the gauntlet in front of flash and video cameras, while
the reporters would yell at them, addressing them by their first
names. "Love your dress, Liza" (Liza Minnelli). "How much
money do you really have, K?" (The Aga Khan.) After a state
dinner they would surge into the dining room with their sound
booms, and those guests who were not aware that their comments were being picked up sometimes found their private
remarks part of the five o'clock news. The President and Mrs.
Reagan didn't seem to mind the press swarm and usually
answered a couple of the questions before they went to bed or
briefly joined the crowd at an after-dinner reception.

Looking back at those functions, I recognize how hard the
Administration worked to try to provide some official, American-
style hospitality to the large unwieldy diplomatic corps of
Washington. The protocol officials didn't lack imagination.
Sometimes we were invited on the 4th of July to see the fireworks

on the Potomac from the top floor of the State Department. An immensely ambitious tour was laid on for the whole corps to attend the Bicentennial celebration of the Statue of Liberty in New York harbour. And there were other activities. But they all had one thing in common. They were not something to look forward to nor to enjoy. We sensed ourselves on such occasions to be a part of the American pageant, but not a very important part. We were witnesses, we were observers, we were a chorus, we were props. We were everything except ourselves.

It's hard, perhaps impossible to explain to those who are not diplomats why these formal representations were so unsatisfying during the Reagan years. Perhaps the best explanation may be that they were without soul.

7/Upstairs, Downstairs

ONE OF THE most demanding of my activities in managing our small hotel was looking after the reservations. That is, planning the parties and co-ordinating them with our social secretary, the chef and the butler, not to mention my husband, who had his own competing schedule.

The arduous task of putting together a harmonious guest list for our important parties was always left to the quietest day of the week when we thought ourselves to be most relaxed.

Every Sunday morning Allan and I used to go over our long program, a kind of scroll of twenty or more extra-length pages detailing all our official and social activities for the year. The embassy staff used to revise the program every Friday to accommodate the frequent changes in our schedule. We would pick dates for parties, diplomatic travels and speeches, decide on the events we needed or wanted to attend and argue and agonize over our guest lists.

A little later I wrote in the *Washington Post* about my confusion over the mysterious invitations that we'd receive. I described an anonymous invitation:

Who are Dr. and Mrs. Carbfut from the Global Institute, and why are they asking us to a ball, a gala or dinner at that home-away-from-homes, the Washington Hilton? Should I ask my social secretary to make inquiries? – She finds out that everybody from the President on down is on the list of patrons, but is not necessarily coming. She can't find out anything about the Global Institute, the Carbfuts or who will be sitting at our table. I put a "bring forward" note on the invitation. I didn't know about "bring forwards" until Washington. It means we shall forget about the invitation, all of us, except, of course, the Carbfuts.

For the first couple of months in Washington I was constantly on the phone to Pat Thomas, my social secretary, fussing about these strange invitations and the requests, letters and guest lists that came across my desk. Then Allan, Mr. Executive, showed me another way.

"When you get Pat's envelope with all the papers, don't call her back right away. Just write what you want on top of each paper and at the end of the day a messenger will take it to the Chancery so she can work on it the following morning. Why waste your time with all those stupid phone calls?"

I didn't know I was allowed to write comments on top of papers that came from the embassy. I had been treating them as if they were made of ancient papyrus.

I hated those Sunday mornings. During this ostensibly quiet period, dressed in our slippers and kimonos, it would take us a couple of hours to fuss and fight over what each of us considered high or low priority. For me low priority was any function where I would have to stand and mingle with those who would rather talk to the powerful, attend a late-night buffet after a concert or fly off to a ball. But for the first two years we decided that a conscientious ambassadorial couple should go everywhere and try everything. Allan, paraphrasing Goethe, commented on one event he attended. "Once a philosopher, twice a pervert."

After reorganizing the long-term program we would normally get ready for Sunday brunch. Sunday brunch was the time when official Washington was at its most relaxed and the media and Washington hostesses most loved to entertain. We always found such brunches the most worthwhile event of the week. For an ambassador it was a compliment to be invited. Political Washington and its hostesses discounted ambassadors except the British and the French or those who, from time to time, made some kind of scandalous or exciting news. Since ambassadors aren't supposed to make scandalous news, most of them are rarely invited to such affairs.

After reviewing the program and reading the humungous *Sunday New York Times* and *Washington Post*, my face and fingers dirtied with ink, we'd dress up or down, depending on the event. It was always a puzzle to know what to wear to these brunches and lunches. Sometimes the men were wearing ties and blazers, and the women Oscar de la Renta suits. Sometimes the men left their ties at home, and the women wore Yves St. Laurent slacks and triple-ply cashmere sweaters, made in Scotland, not Hong Kong. Inevitably I wore a suit to the slacks affair and a sweater to the Oscar de la Renta suit brunch.

One of the reasons I found our Sunday morning deliberations so difficult and exhausting was that long-term planning was not in my nature. I always disliked thinking about even my own holidays too far in advance. My father believed that if you try to manipulate the future, you tempt the Gods and will suffer for your hubris. I discovered from all these efforts that I was not a natural hostess. The only parties I really enjoyed giving were the last-minute kind, for eight or ten people sitting around a single round table. Then there was no time for the dread and anxiety that embassy entertainments always aroused in me. I was always sure no one would come, or if they did, it wouldn't be because of our fascinating selves or our interesting country, or that when they did arrive the guests wouldn't like each other, or the food, the flowers, the curtains, the vases or the sofas, and that they would certainly leave before coffee.

Initially I was hesitant even about initiating an embassy dinner. One of our first significant dinners was in honour of the Attorney General of the United States, Bill French Smith, and his wife, Jean. I had met Jean at the large luncheon organized by Peggy LeBaron in honour of the wives of the Reagan cabinet, where I noticed that she lowered her head in discreet amusement when Peggy gave a fulsome speech about the prestigious nature of International

Club #1. As I left, Jean Smith had caught my arm and asked me if I would send her a copy of one of my books. By coincidence Allan had a meeting with her husband that day over a rather sordid international matter. Two American bounty hunters had kidnapped a land developer, Sydney Jaffe, in Toronto and taken him by force back to Florida, where he was being prosecuted by the state for an alleged land swindle. Allan knew where his duty lay in protecting Canada's interests, but he wished that Mr. Jaffe had a more uplifting character.

This was February 1982 and we had given only a few parties. Pat Thomas said, "You ought to have a party in honour of the Attorney General and Mrs. Smith."

"But I've only spoken to her once and I never met him," I protested. "It's pushy," I said, reflecting my mother's upbringing. I was intimidated by the title, Attorney General of the United States. Pat may as well have suggested that I give a party in honour of Queen Elizabeth. Allan thought that Pat's idea was wonderful, but he delegated me to ask the wife of the Attorney General if we could give a dinner party in their honour. For the first time in my life I poured myself some Dutch courage, two ounces of scotch at three o'clock in the afternoon. Then I dialled the number of the Jefferson Hotel, where the Attorney General and his wife resided. Jean accepted with alacrity and we had one of the first parties that mixed Georgetown with members of the Reagan cabinet. Both sides seemed wary but pleased. Jean Smith became a close friend and now I feel free to phone her without a tumbler of scotch in my hand.

One of the things I learned early on was that an entertaining party evening in Washington does not involve entertainment. Washingtonians like to go to bed early, because they have to get up early for those dreadful events called breakfast meetings. If a guest stays past 10:30, your dinner becomes a historic evening.

When we began to give dinners, we thought it would be a wonderful idea to have some kind of entertainment after dinner. I remembered President Reagan's first visit to Canada in Ottawa. A gala show was put on for him by Pierre Trudeau at the National Arts Centre, the highlight of which, in my opinion, was comedian

Wife of public servant with cigar. *(Photo courtesy of Sondra Gotlieb)*

The recipe lady. *(Photo by Ted Grant)*

On the front hall stairs at the Official Residence with our
Tibetan terrier Archie. *(Photo courtesy of Sondra Gotlieb)*

The drawing room. (When I first arrived I called it a living-room. One of my first but not the worst of my *faux pas*.) *(Photo courtesy of Sondra Gotlieb)*

The dining-room, covered with Allan's Tissot prints. *(Photo by Guy DeLort)*

Relaxing on the garden terrace with Charles Wick, Chief of the US Information Agency, and his wife Mary Jane. *(Photo courtesy of Sondra Gotlieb)*

Christopher Plummer and Donald Sutherland, with a handsome devil in the middle. *(Photo courtesy of Sondra Gotlieb)*

Dinner in honour of Pierre Trudeau. Margot Kidder and Carolyn Deaver are next to Ben Bradlee of the *Washington Post*. *(Photo courtesy of Sondra Gotlieb)*

Letting Canadian hair down at our dinner party for Pierre Trudeau. *(Photo courtesy of Sondra Gotlieb)*

Pierre and Margot dancing. *(Photo courtesy of Sondra Gotlieb)*

With Dan Rather at a celebrity cook-off for a Washington charity. *(Photo by Paine & Waters Photography, Washington, D.C.)*

Houseguests at Katharine Graham's house in Martha's Vineyard. Edward Ney, now US ambassador to Canada, with Katharine Graham. *(Photo courtesy of Sondra Gotlieb)*

Candlestick Park in San Francisco. The ball never reached home plate. *(Photo by Dennis Desprois and courtesy of the San Francisco Giants)*

Secretary and Mrs. Shultz arrive at the Canadian Residence.
(Photo courtesy of Sondra Gotlieb)

Michael Deaver tickling the
ivories at the Residence.
*(Photo courtesy of Sondra
Gotlieb)*

First meeting with President Reagan. Notice my too-tight perm. *(Photo courtesy of the White House)*

Meeting Nancy Reagan with trepidation. *(Photo courtesy of the White House)*

At a small dinner party given by Vice President Bush in
honour of Michael Deaver when he resigned from the White
House. Guests included James Baker, centre, and Susan
Baker, second from right in the blue dress. The dinner was
held at the exclusive Wobbly Wasp Alibi Club. *(Photo
courtesy of the White House)*

Allan with Vice President Bush. *(Photo courtesy of the White
House)*

At the White House, greeting the Mulroneys with "pals".
(Photo courtesy of Sondra Gotlieb)

Allan with Bud McFarlane,
another victim of the
rollercoaster. *(Photo
courtesy of Sondra Gotlieb)*

With Henry Kissinger. *(Photo courtesy of Sondra Gotlieb)*

The Star Spangled Banner at the White House at the signing of the Canada-US Free Trade Bill. From left to right, President Reagan, Allan, US Trade Ambassador Clayton Yeutter, Secretary of the Treasury James Baker, Senator Robert Dole. *(Official White House photo)*

Connie Connor with Allan and me. (*Photo courtesy of Sondra Gotlieb*)

At the dinner for Brian Mulroney, March 19, 1986. Seated: Barbara Bush, Brian Mulroney, Barbara Walters. Note our butler Theodora Bataclan in the background at right. *(Photo courtesy of Sondra Gotlieb)*

Our children, Rebecca, Marc and Rachel, visiting us in Washington. *(Photo courtesy of Sondra Gotlieb)*

Our daughter Rebecca, with her husband, Keith Ham. *(Photo courtesy of Sondra Gotlieb)*

Dave Broadfoot's monologue on the difference between Canadians and Americans. It brought the house down.

When, a year later, we gave a large party in honour of Ken Taylor, Canada's former ambassador to Iran, "the hero of Teheran," we persuaded Dave Broadfoot to come to Washington and do his stuff for our sixty guests. This was planned as an after-dinner surprise; the guests had no warning. Dave Broadfoot and the Taylors were staying with us, and the former, a true comic artist, was extremely nervous. This was our first big dinner party in the garden, and I tried to conceal my anxieties and sympathize with him. We had fresh salmon flown in from New Brunswick, and Ibrahim flamed it in brandy over the buffet barbecue. I had shown Ibrahim a recipe for how native Indians in British Columbia barbecued salmon, but he disliked the concept.

"I flambé salmon in cognac, much better," he said. His salmon flambé was delicious, but the buffet line was inching along at about a rate of three people filling their plates every three minutes. We were experiencing buffet gridlock. A second flaming salmon table would have obviously speeded the process up. But I was still green. Anyway, I believed this kind of complicated logistical matter would have been taken care of by Rito, our butler. I had seen *Upstairs, Downstairs* and was now beginning to believe that I was Lady Margerie. Rito's strengths did not lie in the area of crowd management.

Luckily the weather was perfect, so people didn't seem to mind the delay. Dave Broadfoot was to perform in the dining room, where sixty chairs had been set up by Glen, who had also fussed with microphones, sound equipment and podiums. After dinner Allan stood up and announced the big surprise: Dave Broadfoot, our famous Canadian comedian, was going to perform in the dining room. Dave was not well known in the United States and the dinner had been delayed by the lack of salmon flambé tables. Senators, congressmen and administration officials rose and scrambled over the bushes into the street before they got caught in the dining room. About thirty people remained, including the waiters. Dave did a wonderful job – even though he saw some of the remaining people slipping out the front door during his act.

Political Washington hates late evenings, and after the Broadfoot episode we vowed to ban surprise concerts and comedians before, during or after dinner. What people like in Washington is conversation, or rather the exchange of political gossip, which for them constitutes conversation.

About eight months after our arrival, Rito, the butler, and Pat Thomas, our social secretary, told us they were leaving. Pat's little daughter in Texas was extremely ill, and although Pat didn't want to leave Washington, she knew it would be best if she joined her husband so they both could attend to their daughter's health.

Rito had been with the embassy a number of years and was very conscientious, but the maids made fun of his somewhat eccentric behaviour. This had created serious problems for me because the butler was responsible for supervising all the servants and all the arrangements in the Residence. It had been distressing to hear Rito announce at our first dinner party, an hour before the arrival of guests, that there weren't enough table cloths. And I soon ceased to be amused at the surprised look on his face when he glanced down as he passed the platters of food around the table and discovered there were no dinner plates. Rito eventually left of his own accord. I think he was undone by coping with our pace and wanted a quieter life.

We had many parties planned for the fall program, and I knew I had to find a butler and a social secretary quickly.

How does one find a butler in two weeks?

The butler is the pre-eminent person on the household staff. He is the senior servant, the supervisor, the person who has to calculate household accounts. He is responsible for counting and cleaning of the silver and china and the training of the other servants in their duties. If a maid didn't know how to iron, shine shoes or make a bed, the butler, in consultation with Madame, had to decide whether she was trainable. When the air-conditioning or heating broke down, it was the butler's responsibility to see that someone was called. The butler must hire reliable waiters for cocktail parties and dinners, and rent whatever extra chairs, glasses and tables are needed – which means he has to know the inventory of the household. If there are insufficient table cloths or wine stocks, it is his job to warn the ambassador's wife before a crisis occurs. Above all he must act in liaison with the chef. One can't give a party if the chef doesn't tell the butler what he's feeding the guests.

The butler controls the flow of traffic from the kitchen to the dining room and works with the chef in choosing the tureens, platters and serving dishes that will facilitate the passing of the food around by the waiters as well as suit the chef's creations. He should know how many waiters are needed for the number of people coming and how much to pay them. A butler has to set and serve at a formal table, and, as long as it is a talent of his, the buying and arranging of flowers are within his domain. A butler should not be too grand to vacuum carpets, clean the downstairs bathrooms and wash dishes, if necessary. If Madame has a complaint about the Residence or the servants, she is supposed to speak to the butler about it first. The butler, above all, must be honest.

Where could I find such a paragon? I knew by this time it would be foolish to call the Chancery – they would only put an ad in the paper. But I knew if I couldn't find a butler quickly, I couldn't do my job at all.

Shortly after our arrival we had paid a joint courtesy call on the ambassador from the EEC, and Madame EEC had told me something interesting. (Courtesy calls between ambassadors and their spouses are on the whole futile relics of old-fashioned diplomacy. But we did learn two or three practical things, usually about domestic staffing. We paid calls on about half a dozen of the hundred and fifty embassies in Washington and then became too active to continue with the rest.)

Madame EEC, who was a Belgian countess, told me that she had a wonderful Filipino maid who was better than any butler. "She's much better than the butler I had before," she said. "He wrote the telephone messages down in triplicate and didn't dirty his hands doing anything else."

Although I had only met the countess once, she invited us to their going-away reception just about the time Rito announced his departure. As soon as I reached her in the reception line I asked, without ceremony, "What's happened to that wonderful maid of yours?"

"She's desperate," was the whispered reply. "The ambassador who's taking our place doesn't seem to want a woman. And I can't afford to take her with me back to Belgium."

The next morning Theodora Bataclan came to the residence for an interview. I told her that we could not employ her husband, but that he could stay with her in the single room we then provided at the O.R. for the butler. She accepted my terms and I hired her immediately. Theodora, slender, shy with a wide smile and an acute intelligence, stayed with us as our butler for the duration of our post – over six years. Theodora had a reticent manner and never instigated a conversation unless an important household decision had to be made. Nevertheless, I soon began to feel secure enough to delegate many household duties to my new female butler. Her competence was such that she would never fluster, even when I told her three hundred were coming for cocktails instead of a hundred and fifty. Although I believe women are better than men at running households, ours was the only embassy in Washington that had a female butler.

As for replacing Pat Thomas, it turned out that finding a social secretary was complicated. We had to give the Canadian employees at the Chancery a first crack at the job. For various reasons none of the Canadian employees passed the social-secretary test, and we finally decided we really needed an American who knew the difference between the State Department and Congress and the White House, could make up a skeleton of a seating plan according to official Washington protocol and knew something about the network of social secretaries who control dates and events in the city.

By then Lee Annenberg had left, and she was replaced as chief of protocol at the State Department by Lucky Roosevelt. The protocol department at State employs many social secretaries or protocol assistants, and Lucky strongly recommended Connie Connor, who was leaving her job at the State Department.

Eventually we hired Connie, and she stayed on with us until our departure from Washington. Connie, of course, was the renowned "slapee."

To add to my consternation over staff changes, just after he had cooked a splendid dinner in honour of Prime Minister Trudeau, Ibrahim announced that he was leaving because he wanted to fulfil his dream, the dream of every chef. He was going to open up his own restaurant.

I hadn't the faintest idea how to hire a new chef. The officials in the Chancery told me that they would put an ad in the paper.

"What about salary?" I asked.

"It depends on their experience," they said, not giving me any figures.

But I wanted to know about my competition – all the other embassies in Washington.

It would have been folly to call the ambassadors' wives myself. They would naturally have suspected that I was going to steal their chefs. So I said to our Chancery officials, "Please call your peers in the other chanceries and find out what the chefs at the French, British, Italian and Swedish embassies are paid." After several weeks they gave me some figures about salaries.

"The Swede gets the least; the Italian, British and French are on the same level. We can probably match the British salary."

I went to the Swedish embassy for dinner and complimented Countess Wachmeister on her chef.

"He's such a darling," she said. "But of course our government provides him and his family with a beautiful house on our grounds. He gets two months' holiday, and the government pays for him to return to Sweden every year."

Ibrahim had to drive back and forth from his house, about an hour away from our residence, every day. I knew we didn't pay for his living expenses or vacations back to Turkey.

I went to the British Embassy for dinner, and the wife of the British ambassador told me she had *two chefs*, for whom they provided suites and free trips back to Britain. Subsequently I found out that the Italian and the French embassies also gave their chefs free living quarters and trips back home.

Now I knew why I was having a terrible time hiring a chef. A stream of incompetents had been wandering through the kitchen since Ibrahim left. There was the bald Bulgarian who had worked in hotel chains in Cairo, Egypt; Newport, Rhode Island; and Birmingham, England. He was fine the first day. We had a perfect piece of grilled halibut and lime sherbet for dessert.

"What will you make tomorrow?" I asked.

"Grilled rockfish and strawberry sherbet," he replied.

The grilled rockfish was delicious but the sherbet, like the one he had made before, was a little sweet. I asked him about his menu for his third day.

"Grilled salmon and raspberry sherbet."

"How about a chicken dish and something with apples for dessert," I asked.

"I don't cook chicken, I only cook fish," he answered. "That's what I did at the hotels. Work at the fish station. Another kind of chef makes chicken dishes."

After he left, Thelma, the upstairs maid, told me that he had walked in each morning with a new pint of sherbet from the Safeway.

A gifted amateur with press clippings wanted to become a professional chef on my time. He used to be a professor of theology but, according to the *Washington Post* food critic, his talents lay in the culinary rather than the religious field. I asked him to make a classic egg-white dessert, a floating island pudding, something I used to cook for my guests back in Ottawa.

All day long we could hear the banging of pots and pans in the kitchen, maids running up and down stairs to the kitchen, and whisperings. After eight hours I looked in. Every pot and pan in the kitchen had been put to use and the maids were trying to keep up with him washing each pot as he threw it aside. Finally Theodora, who knew how to cook very well herself, told us the truth.

"He's no good, Madame. He asked me how to heat up the egg

whites. And he used five dozen eggs and still doesn't know what to do."

We had others, including a chef who had worked in the Catskills in kosher hotels. When I vetoed his menu of knishes, brisket and noodle pudding as too heavy, he took umbrage and walked out. And there was a young American who had been recommended by the Jockey Club in Washington, but he had worked only in the meat station. "I don't do fish or desserts," he explained.

What I really wanted was a good Canadian chef, and I called Jamie Kennedy, a young and talented chef in Toronto, because I had been told he might be interested in coming to Washington. Jamie sounded intrigued, but I think he was discouraged because we didn't provide housing for chefs. Of course he had many other irons in the fire. Jamie did recommend several other Canadian chefs with whom I had long and inconclusive conversations; they all wanted salaries that were completely out of our orbit.

By this time the wife of the British ambassador trusted me not to pull a fast one. She gave me an application sent to her embassy by a twenty-one-year-old Frenchman who had had several years' training in the British Embassy in Paris. He came highly recommended by the head chef. The young man was anxious to live in the United States, and because of our diplomatic status we could bring him in without having to bother with American immigration procedures. I interviewed Yves Safarti while I was on vacation in Paris and hired him on the spot.

Despite his youth, Yves was an excellent chef. Guests like Robert Strauss talked for years about his potato pancakes. A year after he arrived he prepared everything – from *chaud froid* of chicken to delicate cream puffs and strawberry tarts – for our daughter's wedding reception and astonished Washington.

But at the beginning Yves was very sad. He didn't speak any English and moped around in his single little room in the O.R. Thelma told me she was afraid for his mind. Yves told me that Paris was much more fun than Washington, where there was no place to practise his hobby, disco-dancing. And of course he wanted to talk to someone besides me in his language.

A member of the embassy told me about a French-speaking Catholic church in Georgetown where all the French chefs gathered and indeed had parties in the basement on Sunday evenings. I asked Yves if he was interested. He seemed delighted and went off to see a few of his countrymen and colleagues. All went well for a few weeks until I was called downstairs by Theodora who said Yves had received a phone call and seemed disturbed. She could tell me no more since she didn't speak French and he didn't speak English or Tagalog. "What's wrong?" I said to Yves, in French.

"They called me from the church. They want me to sing in the choir."

"That's wonderful," I said. "You'll make friends. You won't be alone all the time."

"You don't understand." He shook his head vehemently. "My mother wouldn't like it. Je ne suis pas tellement religieux."

"So what?" I said. "You'll make some friends if you sing in the choir."

"Mais je suis même pas chrétien," he exploded. For a moment I thought Yves was Muslim, like Ibrahim, because he told me he had been born in Algeria.

"Je suis juif," he said angrily, "and I won't sing in the Catholic choir."

"Guess what?" I said. "I'm Jewish too. So let's forget about the whole business."

Since there was no French-speaking synagogue in Washington, I steered Yves to a network of Moroccan Jewish French-speaking hairdressers in Washington, which some of my new friends told me about, and he seemed to be content.

When we first arrived the staff quarters were small and meanly furnished. There was one large room that was supposed to belong to the butler, but nothing for a chef. The kitchen was the same age as the house, forty years old. When we gave large parties, the trays of food had to be laid out in the garage, attracting the ubiquitous D.C. rats. Eventually we had the kitchen enlarged and built a small apartment on the third floor for either a butler or a chef. The apartment helped us immensely in keeping a competent and loyal staff.

Although the kitchen was off limits, I did have to check the conscientious but youthful Yves, who was new to the Washington climate, about health hazards. On a typical August day, hot and humid as the Amazonian jungle, I discovered a huge vat of tepid creamed sweetbreads cooling on the back porch. It was a question of which would come first – the flies or the salmonella bacteria. I made the kitchen maid throw the whole thing out. (All chefs have to have a kitchen maid. Chefs I have known don't like washing pots or pans. At least those trained in French cooking schools don't.) Apart from the nauseating idea of serving creamed sweetbreads to human beings in a Washington August, I didn't want to kill my guests. I was learning how to assert my authority. I explained to Yves that if he didn't immediately refrigerate food in the hot climate, he would be fired.

I discovered that most professional chefs, even the good ones, have four faults:

1) They hate thinking up new dishes.
2) Either they make the meals too rich . . .
3) . . . or they become infatuated with designer cuisine – that is, three brussels sprouts, a pea pod and a raw scallop artistically arranged on a plate with a nasturtium flower.
4) They don't know how to put together a menu.

I spent many hours clipping recipes from *Gourmet* magazine and bought recipe books for Ibrahim, Yves, and our last chef, Christian Le Pièce, a Belgian who was with us for four years before our departure. Our turnover in chefs was far lower than at other embassies. Most embassy chefs stay one to two years and move on, move back home or start a restaurant of their own. After Ibrahim's restaurant failed he wanted to return, but by this time I had hired Yves. Yves eventually left because he thought he could get more money working for rich Americans.

I tried to sit down with the chefs every morning to go over the daily menus. Unfortunately, I was never in full control of our program; a telephone call from the office might announce that there were sixteen coming for lunch when I thought the day was empty. I could never predict what would happen during the week, so whatever I told the chef to do would inevitably have to be changed. All the chefs at first found this hard to adjust to, but eventually they learned to be flexible.

I explained to all of my chefs about cholesterol, about the new Washington horror of red meat and the aversion to anything swimming in butter or cream. When I sat down with the chef every day and went over the menus, the meals were balanced and light. But if I was too busy to meet with them, or was away, the chefs would revert. My guests would get butter, cream and oil, red meat and two kinds of potatoes, and buttercream for dessert. My last chef, Christian Le Pièce, was by far the best. Intelligent, with an equable temperament, he understood about diets and cholesterol and still could make a mean *tarte tatin*.

What do Powerful Jobs in Washington like to eat and drink? Powerful Jobs do not think about eating or drinking. The few gastronomes and oenophiles in the city live on a barren patch and are not looked upon by those who count as serious people. After all, this is the town of Richard Nixon, who liked cottage cheese with ketchup; the Carters, renowned for their austerity regime; and Nancy Reagan, size four, who is rumoured to live on clear soup, salad and one chocolate chip cookie a day. George Bush once said he has only fruit and coffee for breakfast. Republicans, cabinet members, senators and other Powerful Jobs who desperately want to appear on television are convinced they have to look slim.

Everybody in Washington gets up early and many go out for dinner almost every night. This means they hate sitting too long at the table. A separate course for salad was a thing they dreaded like the middle seat in an airplane, so I eliminated it. We settled on three courses only, with a little salad on the side. When trays were passed at our dinners, guests rarely took more than a forkful of red meat and then they messed it around on their plates. I often wished that just once I could have gluttons as guests.

Although fowl and veal were preferred because of anti-cholesterol propaganda, for some reason prudence vanished at dessert. Anything chocolate was always eaten, and although guests voiced virtuous approval if we gave them sherbet and fruit, I knew there were inward pangs of disappointment.

Most of the power-people who dined at our table in Washington didn't know if they were drinking Château Petrus or a Beaujolais. We served fine wines on important diplomatic occasions, and my husband wept at the sight of brimful glasses left on the tables. We were complimented on our wine just twice in seven years, once by the president of the AFL-CIO, Lane Kirkland, a genuine oenophile, and the second time by Michael Deaver, who admired a California white. However, the handwritten menus at our dinners always revealed the name of the wines being served. I have seen rather famous guests of honour pick up the menu card and look gratified that we were offering them a wine as worthy as themselves. I learned that important wines were necessary for important people. So far as I could discern, it was the appearance that counted, not the content.

Hard alcohol was generally shunned. A vodka martini, a vodka and tonic, anything white and innocuous-looking, was preferred to a revealing yellow scotch. Allan likes scotch and didn't mind who knew. Actually more people took whisky than I realized, because our liquor inventories usually showed a decided depletion of scotch. I knew George Shultz favoured Manhattans, so I made sure the butler knew how to mix one whenever he came. After dinner we usually got up for coffee, and then the brandy, liqueurs and Havana cigars were passed around. Perhaps one person in twenty would take a cognac, and the rest of the liqueurs were usually spurned. Paul Volcker adored the Havana cigars, but Alan Greenspan, his replacement as chairman of the Federal Reserve Board, shunned them.

Although Washingtonians were not interested in being members of the Chevalier de Tastevin Society, we had to have a wine cellar because of our heavy representational duties. We needed large quantities of decent wines very quickly when we arrived, since we found little in the basement. I became, willy-nilly, an amateur sommelier. But I took the business too seriously and the selection of a wine cellar became one of my more nightmarish activities. My vexations were the following:

1) How much money could we spend?
2) How much wine did we need for six months?
3) Foolishly I consulted too many wine guides, which usually gave conflicting advice on vintage and vineyard.
4) I knew nothing of California wines.
5) When I went to the local wine stores I irritated the owners, usually named Sam or Morris, by holding up my guidebooks in front of their noses.
6) Sam or Morris didn't seem to stock what Hugh Johnson or the *New York Times* recommended.

I ceased being a nuisance in the local wine stores when I met Mrs. Andrea Bronfman at one of our early receptions.

"I suppose Seagram's sells only whisky," I asked naively, "not wine."

Mrs. Bronfman explained that Seagram's owned many vineyards. Three weeks later I received a catalogue from the Chateau Estate Wine Company in New Jersey, a wholesale house that sold the wines from Seagram vineyards in France and United States to retail outlets.

Instead of continuing to irritate Sam and Morris, I pored over the Seagram's catalogue, holding my Hugh Johnson wine book in one hand and various wine columns in the other, checking vineyard labels and referring conflicts back to the catalogue. This took many afternoons. When I made my choices, I had to show them to Allan, who had an idea of how much we could spend. He would disagree with my choices and change everything, which irritated the secretary who had already phoned in my order. Twice a year for seven years we went through this lengthy and contentious wine-selection routine.

During one summer about halfway through our posting, we discovered that the temperature in our wine cellar was 80 degrees. Our wines were not being properly maintained by the old and faulty cooling system. The accountants in Ottawa headquarters decided that losing the wines would cost more than putting in an air conditioner. So we got a decent cooling system in the cellar.

We served American and French red and white wine, and occasionally some Canadian white. The reason was simple. We believed that maintaining a standard of excellence gave the best image of Canada, and most Canadian wines could not begin to compare to the quality of imported ones. I tried serving Canadian reds a couple of times. It was one of the few times the wine was noticed, but for the wrong reason.

I received a complaint from the Conservative Minister of Agriculture, John Wise, after we gave a dinner in his honour. We had invited his counterpart, the American Secretary of Agriculture, John Block, and members of the Canadian and U.S. Agriculture departments and their wives. We had served Ontario lamb, Manitoba wild rice, a Quebec maple-syrup mousse and American wines. I was rather pleased with the dinner. The chef had excelled himself and the visiting Ministers seemed particularly pleased. However, John Wise's thank-you note was a masterpiece of irony.

He acknowledged the beautiful flowers and the Canadian Club we had sent him, as well as the splendid dinner, and then added a sardonic P.S.: "I can only imagine the difficulties which your staff must have unsuccessfully gone through in Washington in trying to secure Canadian wine for the dinner. As a result, please find enclosed a Canadian equivalent of Chateauneuf du Pape – a bottle of Pinot Noir – the start of what I would hope to be a well-stocked Canadian selection in the Embassy's wine cellar."

I was the nonpaid member of Allan's "staff" who was so unsuccessful in securing Canadian wines.

I found it was impossible to push Canadian wine in the United States for the obvious reason that Californian wines were cheaper and better – not to mention the availability of superior French, Italian, German and other wines in Washington liquor stores. I told my husband that Canadians can drink Canadian wine if they want. But don't ask me to sell it. Sometimes patriotism can be taken to a point where it becomes a disadvantage to one's country. Why Canadians insist on making indifferent wine at a relatively high price in a world where there is a wine glut remains a mystery to me.

For a while I thought I was doing my patriotic duty serving Alberta vodka as an aperitif with Manitoba golden caviar. We had been given a sample case of the vodka and it was fine. Years passed and I proudly pointed out the Alberta vodka on the menu card to our guests. One day I went downstairs to the wine cellar and discovered there weren't any bottles left.

"Theodora," I said, "we're out of the Alberta vodka. Better order some more."

She gave me a blank look and then her wide smile. "I pour Smirnoff or Stolichnaya into the empty Alberta vodka bottles. Nobody knows the difference." So much for patriotic gastronomy.

I always made a point of offering Canadian dishes on important occasions. In writing my Canadian cookbooks I had researched a multitude of ways of using maple sugar and syrup, and when we had a large dinner in honour of Mila Mulroney we served a maple mousse cake decorated with a marzipan maple leaf. My recipe for *tourtière* with tomato was a winner at buffet dinners, and we often served New Brunswick sturgeon as well as golden Manitoba caviar with crêpes and sour cream. Other Canadian products included Winnipeg goldeye, New Brunswick sturgeon caviar and British Columbia smoked salmon.

The garden was another element in our entertaining. Previously, gardening had provided me with another escape from the world, along with cooking. Yet gardening in Washington did not give me much pleasure until the very last years of our posting.

Allan's escape was collecting prints, old books, enamel boxes, amost anything, really. Even if he didn't have the funds to buy, he escaped from Washington tensions by studying print catalogues, waxing the covers of his leather volumes, reframing his pictures and making not-so-secret visits during working hours to public and private art galleries.

In Ottawa I used to escape from worries by planting old French roses, growing basil and nasturtium from seeds, fussing over the

Madonna lilies, musing over flower catalogues and trying to find literate and sensible gardening books. I even set up a little light system in our basement to grow seedlings.

A garden, like a kitchen, really has to be one's own. But for me the garden in Washington was initially untouchable, just like the kitchen.

The sunniest part of the garden was planted with large flowering magenta-colored azalea and rhododendron bushes, silencing me with their showiness. A northerner like myself knew nothing about such flowers. I wasn't even sure if I liked them or not. The climate was so different from what I was used to that I hardly knew which bushes and plants would flourish in the damp hot summers of Washington. In Ottawa I used to haunt nurseries within a range of forty miles for unusual species and perennials. Now I decided to hold off and see what grew well in the District before I plunged in with my ideas. In addition, the procurement official at the embassy controlled the garden budget. He told me that garden funds "had to come from headquarters in Ottawa."

Mario, the houseman, who I was told was supposed to work in the garden, didn't know or care about flowers, grass or trees. His favourite task was hosing down the cement patio, and Glen Bullard and I would get a kick out of watching him watering while it rained. Glen loved big projects, and his gardening goal for the Residence was to replace the acre of patio stones, some of which, he rightly claimed, were coming loose especially because of Mario's assiduous watering. "Look," Glen would say, "he's loosening the stones again." But I didn't relish the idea of having my access to the garden blocked for a couple of summers by workmen replacing cement. We gently argued about this grand scheme for seven years. I left it to my successor to help Glen in this particular goal.

It took me about three years to figure out what grew well in Washington, and how much money there was in the garden budget for renovation and replanting. Many bushes, trees and plants, all new to me, had died and needed to be replaced. I decided that I disliked the showy azaleas, which had taken over the whole garden, and had stopped flowering in any case. Yves

Dupien, the gifted Chancery carpenter, built me bowers for climbing roses, which seemed to do well in Washington, and I added more clematis and roses to hide the large brick wall. The patio was grey cement and terribly hot in the summer. I tried to soften and cool its harsh hot appearance by putting out huge clay pots of white annuals or plants with silver foliage, which showed up well in the dark for evening parties. I chose Dusty Miller, petunias, dianthus, geraniums, anything I could find that would hold out during the long drought of Washington summers.

I am an informal gardener and am apt to put a sloppy butterfly bush where someone with a sense of space and design might put in a conical cedar. Plants and flowers interest me more than garden concepts. Naturally our garden, like most of the gardens in Washington, was set out for more formal kinds of plantings. My first task was to order vast amounts of spring bulbs from catalogues, and I stood over Mario, a farmer's son, and showed him how to plant tulip bulbs. I was sure I had ordered pink-and-white lily flowering tulip bulbs for the front, which were supposed to come up at the same time in the spring. Pink and white may not have been arresting, but I needed a safe match for the part of the O.R. that faced the world. Instead vast numbers of violent tango-red tulips rose up and clashed with corals and striped pink tulips. Georgetown ladies with their formal one-colour tulip gardens would arrive at the O.R. for lunch, commenting on my "interesting colour display."

During our fifth year, we had permission from headquarters to hire Jane Macleish, a landscape specialist, who drew a garden plan for the grounds, which of course we didn't have the funds to follow up on. But she gave me something invaluable – the telephone number of a firm that would sell us bulbs wholesale. Each spring and fall I would order bulbs and flowering plants, and go to the local nurseries and replace roses and look for interesting and unusual plants. I did my research at the Washington Arboretum. Of all my duties at the O.R., this was the one I enjoyed the most.

I cared about the flowers and bushes, but Allan is a grass person. Too bad for him. Every year the grass, without fail, would grow withered, brown and weedy while our neighbours' grass prospered. I read somewhere that the British ambassador had airlifted elephant dung to fertilize his grass. (The British had experienced gardeners, as well as a large indoor greenhouse.) Embassies in Washington are constantly asked to give dinners and receptions for local charities. Somehow we found ourselves giving a reception to raise money for the Washington Zoo. The head of the zoo was so grateful that he promised me free tiger dung as a thank-you gift to spread on our dying grass. Was tiger dung as good as elephant dung? He didn't know, but he told me that it was nice and fresh. I called up the arboretum and asked them about fresh tiger dung. Dried dung was good, they said, but I should put it down in the spring, not the fall. This was in September.

"Ask the zoo if they'll dry out the dung for you. Fresh tiger dung will burn the plants and the smell might annoy your neighbours."

Glen Bullard called the Washington Zoo to see if they would oblige us, but the zoo people weren't enthusiastic.

For seven years we tried, with Glen Bullard's willing support, to get an underground sprinkling system, standard for large houses in Washington. The sprinklers go on automatically at night, so that the grass and flower roots don't dry out during the day, when watered under hot sun. I believe the lack of such a system was the reason for our problem. An underground sprinkling system is now being planned for the Residence. The next ambassador's grass will be greener.

8/The Golden Days

ALTHOUGH AN EMBASSY party by its very nature is always impersonal, some of the guests for the two Kennedy-style parties we hosted in December 1985 had become our good friends. I never fooled myself, however. The attraction of our embassy had everything to do with whom we invited and nothing to do with my magnetic charm or my husband's power. Ambassadors have no power to exercise in Washington's political world, and any prestige they might garner emerges from the quality of their guest lists and their conversation, as well as their professional capabilities.

I use the word *quality* in the most superficial sense. In Washington "quality" people are powerful people. Qualities such as loyalty, wisdom, integrity and humour aren't always adjuncts of power. In Washington you are known by your job, or your access to Important Jobs, and people come for dinner to gather information, arrange a meeting or lobby for their interests.

I once sat next to Senator Paul Laxalt, a close friend of the President, and at that time a possible presidential candidate, at a Christmas party organized by a prominent Republican lobbyist. More than two hundred people sat through a long evening, ending with a floor show starring Attorney General Ed Meese disguised as Santa Claus. Some cabinet and White House wives attended Santa on the stage dressed as Santa's elves. The noise was unbearable, what with the number of guests in the room and the Marine band belting out "Silent Night" and other carols during dinner. Yet most people stayed on to see Santa give out joke presents to a few of the guests. The elf wives sang "Jingle Bells" and then each one of them read out a "funny" verse about each recipient of Santa's gifts. No one heard their feeble voices because of the roar of the crowd. Only the wives of the powerful were asked to be elves; yet I knew some of them felt like perfect fools. (One year I was asked to be an elf – a great privilege, given my husband's powerlessness. So I accepted.) The party was restricted to cabinet and White House officials, senators, congressmen, staffers and Republican fundraisers. We were the only ambassadorial couple invited.

Senator Laxalt, taking his seat beside me, looked exhausted. I could barely hear what he was saying because of the noise. It seemed that he had been out every night for several weeks: when he wasn't at a fundraiser or a party he was attending evening sessions at the Senate. I asked him why he bothered going to parties, especially a large, long-drawn-out affair like this one. "Honey," he said, "I've been chasing after a couple of fellows for six weeks and I knew both of them would be at this Christmas party. I've made three deals tonight." That's what parties are about in Washington – making political deals.

As you may remember from Chapter One, the first of the parties coincided with the Kennedy Honors weekend and was in honour of Lee and Walter Annenberg. At the outset of our planning for the Annenberg lunch we thought we'd ask eighteen or twenty, certainly not more than thirty-two. Thirty-two was the magic number in our residence for a seated meal, because that was how many we could comfortably fit in our dining room, using round tables and rented chairs. But I had not taken into account the number of people from other parts of the country floating around Washington with free time before the Kennedy Honors performance.

Lee, of course, knew far more of the visitors than I did. After we had invited thirty-two people, a mixture of Californians and Washingtonians, Lee would call up apologetically and say, "I don't think the Hopes are doing anything for lunch. Do you mind if we bring them?" Or, "Do you mind asking Don Regan?" Who would not want to have Bob Hope for lunch? As for Donald Regan, he had replaced Jim Baker as Chief of Staff of the White House and the press was calling him "the Prime Minister" because of his supposed total control of the White House. (That's what they said until the Iran-Contra hearings.) Allan had been able to make very little contact with him since he had switched from his post as Secretary of the Treasury. White House Chiefs of Staff dislike going to embassy parties. They are overworked, have no time for their families and their interest in foreign countries is minimal unless they think the President's crisis of the week is coming from that region. Most White House people, senators, congressmen and such think that a hundred and fifty ambassadors are too many for a town like Washington. They believe, like Tip O'Neill, that "all politics is local." Only about half a dozen ambassadors would be able to get their phone calls answered by the Chief of the White House Staff during crucial periods, and often the only time an ambassador could get to meet a Chief of Staff or a National Security Adviser, or whatever reclusive but Important Job he needed to talk to, was during a social occasion. The Regans did accept, not because of us, but because of the clout of the Annenberg name and their close relationship to the President.

Allan, who had a far more expansive approach to entertaining than I had, and never worried about such trifling things as space or overcrowding, was also adding names. He would say, "Now we can pay back the French ambassador." Or, "I'd like to ask Chief Justice Warren Burger and the new undersecretary of State." Or, "I'd like to have our newly arrived political counsellor and his wife."

The day before the lunch for the Annenbergs, Connie Connor, my social secretary, told me that over sixty people had accepted. Somehow we had to fit them inside the house. Also the variety was great – from Nancy Reagan's friend Mrs. Justin Dart, and Mrs. Edgar Bergen, to Meg Greenfield of the *Washington Post*, Ambassador Jeane Kirkpatrick, Senator Alan Simpson, and many other prominent people from various walks of life.

Connie asked, "How are we going to make up a seating plan?"

I said, "Forget it, it's too late, just steer the Annenbergs, the Regans, and the Chief Justice near Allan and me. I'll sit in the sunroom and Allan can take the dining room."

I knew the downstairs furniture would have to be removed to make space for all the tables and the long buffet. I had learned my buffet-gridlock lesson four years earlier at the salmon flambé party and had a plywood structure built by the embassy's accommodating carpenter, Yves Dupien. Because of its size, it had to be covered with three overlapping coloured cloths, a technique devised by our butler, Theodora Bataclan. Either one had a long buffet or various "food stations" would be placed throughout the house. Powerful people in Washington dislike standing in line for anything except a metal detector. A metal detector is gratifying because it means the President or Vice President is at the party too.

Furniture moving at the Residence had become almost routine. The day before a large party the maintenance men from the Chancery would come in and carry divans, sofas, dining room chairs, umbrella stands, wicker rocking chairs and easy chairs upstairs, and the bedrooms and hallway would look like an upscale, upstairs garage sale. Once, there was an attempt to move the grand piano into the garage, but at the last minute it was deemed not necessary.

I broke this last-minute news of thirty extra guests to Theodora, who had planned the waiters, the flowers (I used to do the flowers, but she did them better), the tables and the general planning, and to our newly hired chef from Belgium, Christian Le Pièce. The two of them took it in their stride. Christian and I decided that steak and kidney pie and hot caramelized apple pie (his mean *tarte tatin*) would be perfect, along with salads and Canadian whitefish caviar. The food was successful although, now that I think of it, we had two pies in one meal, something the health obsessives from Washington and California would usually avoid like yellow fever.

"So how are we going to sit sixty people *and* have room for a long buffet table?" I asked Theodora.

"No problem, Madame." It had become her (and my) favourite phrase. "We put the buffet table along the side of the dining room wall, and then we'll have room for extra tables for the guests to sit."

It is not easy greeting lunch guests when one hasn't met half of them before, but I had had four years' experience by the time of the Annenberg lunch. Actually, we didn't really greet them, because they all rolled on the same wave; a kind of telepathy must have passed through the guests about the precise moment for arrival. I never spoke to Bob Hope, because he was swept into the dining room, and I was in the drawing room, divided by the crowd. I felt like one of the soldiers he used to entertain in Korea and Vietnam, sitting far away in the bleachers. To add to the confusion, *Life* magazine, with a profusion of photographers, was taking pictures of the lunch. During the Bloody Mary hour before lunch, a sullen writer for *Life*, E. Graydon Carter, who was to play a part in our life later, would, from time to time, snarl at the crowd and try to gather the most celebrated faces together to smile for the photographer. I don't know why we allowed *Life* to come to our party. Perhaps the Embassy Public Affairs section thought it would be good promotion for Canada.

When we sat down, I was between Walter Annenberg, who said he liked eating pie for the main course and pie for dessert, and Don Regan, who looked over at Meg Greenfield of the *Washington Post* and said, "I want a word with her." By this time I knew about the remarkably cosy relationship between the administration and the press, especially at the beginning of the second Reagan administration. On the other side of Don Regan was a Mrs. Wilson, whose husband William was the U.S. ambassador to the Vatican. (Subsequently her husband also joined the walking wounded: it was reported that Mr. Wilson was asked to leave his post because he had started his very own diplomatic negotiations with the Libyan leader Moammar Qaddafi shortly before the U.S. bombed that country. It seems George Shultz decided that Ambassador Wilson was reaching beyond his ecclesiastic turf, even though Mrs. Wilson was a good friend of Mrs. Reagan.)

Just before the dessert, Connie Connor squeezed her way through the tables and whispered that Bob Hope was seated beside three men and looked glum. She suggested that we move a few people around at dessert. In addition, since the Chief of Staff of the White House had expressed a desire to the hostess that was not indecent or illegal, I thought his will should be done. At dessert I told Connie to move Bob Hope and a few others, and somehow she managed to remove Mrs. Wilson from Don Regan's side and replace her with Meg.

A high Reagan official who often attended dinners at our embassy was Robert "Bud" McFarlane, then National Security Adviser and later a sad participant in the Iran-Contra affair. There were at that time unsubstantiated rumours, which I deemed invented by certain members of the press corps, about Bud McFarlane having an "adulterous affair." I was already aware that these rumours were deeply upsetting to Bud and his wife, Jonda, to whom he was devoted. Sometimes the woman mentioned was a member of his staff and occasionally the chimera became a member of the press corps itself.

As soon as Meg Greenfield sat down beside Don Regan, he spoke to her of Bud McFarlane's "affair" and expressed himself deeply shocked about it. The Chief of Staff of the White House appeared to be spreading gossip about the National Security Adviser, his close colleague, to the Editorial Page editor of the *Washington Post*, whom Regan barely knew. It was widely believed at the time that Regan didn't like McFarlane's access to the President and was determined to destroy his credibility and get him out of the White House (which he did). I felt that as hostess I was being used for a sorry political purpose.

After coffee, the crowd retreated in the same fashion as they had entered, all in one swoop, to get themselves ready for the Kennedy Honor celebrations that evening. There were hairdressers, make-up specialists and masseuses on special call that Sunday afternoon and none of the ladies wanted to keep them waiting; anyway, we all needed a nap.

The second party, a black-tie dinner celebrating, as it said on the invitation, "Ambassador and Mrs. Gotlieb's 5th year in Washington," took place five days later. It was the kind of Kennedy-era party Sally Quinn lamented the loss of in Washington.

Like the first, it was a gathering of both the hard-line Republican right (for example, Ed Meese, the Attorney General; deputy National Security Adviser Admiral John Poindexter; the Secretary of Defense, Caspar Weinberger) and left liberal Georgetown (the Ben Bradlees, the George Stevenses, the Tom Bradens, and others).

It was also a chance for the media – Elizabeth Drew from the *New Yorker*; Tina Brown, the new editor of *Vanity Fair*; Barbara Walters of ABC – to mix with senators, congressmen and cabinet ministers from the Reagan administration, as well as others such as union chief Lane Kirkland.

The party was a gay, relaxed affair where politics were put aside and people with different approaches and philosophies of life were pleased to meet and mingle. They were bemused to find themselves in the same company.

The party was written up in the *Toronto Star* by a Canadian journalist who was one of the guests. Entitled "Meet Mr. and Mrs. Canada," it was a favourable piece. It was the last favourable piece about us in that newspaper.

Most ambassadors rarely stay more than four years in Washington, the plum of any diplomat's career. My husband had been appointed by Prime Minister Pierre Trudeau and had recently been reappointed by our new Prime Minister, Brian Mulroney. It seemed as if nothing could go wrong. We knew all the players, there was a love affair going on between the President and Brian Mulroney, and although many issues, such as acid rain and a multitude of trade problems, were still unresolved, we were looking forward to an interesting and busy couple of years. I had just published a book of my *Washington Post* columns, entitled *Wife Of*. What could go wrong?

As it turned out, our two parties in December 1985 marked a high point in our lives and our guests'. In the next two years many who were with us that season fell off the rollercoaster and suffered multiple injuries. By way of illustration, here is a reminder of what happened to five of our guests:

Carolyn Deaver. I was very fond of Carolyn Deaver, who, like me, had started off as a newcomer making her way through the Washington labyrinth. Nevertheless, because of their busy schedule (the Deavers were one of the most sought-after couples in Washington during the Reagan era) we saw them only several times a year.

When Michael left the White House, Carolyn was supremely happy because she expected to see far more of her husband. At the time, she looked forward to resuming a normal family life as well as to the higher income her husband's new occupation would surely bring. She would be able to choose her own occupation without the press hounding her and her employers for possible conflicts of interest. Realistically, she knew that their social desirability, the glamour in their lives, would diminish. She would be saying goodbye to those White House dinners where she used to meet Tom Selleck, Burt Reynolds, Princess Di and the New York social set. In Washington the Deavers were used to receiving about fifty invitations a week from people of all political hues, from embassies and from ambitious Georgetown hostesses. I remember Carolyn saying, "Now that Mike's out of the White House, I guess I better give my long dresses to the Goodwill Industries. Where will I wear them?" Carolyn had a wistful yet controlled manner. Her control was to carry her through a public and private nightmare which had two sources.

On the private side, unknown to everyone, Michael was already an alcoholic. Not even his wife or closest colleagues were aware of the problem for a very long time. On the public side, in April 1986 John Dingell, all-powerful chairman of the Energy and Commerce Committee in the House of Representatives, started a congressional investigation of Deaver's lobbying activities. Dingell, who represents Michigan and the automobile industry, was then notorious in Canada for his opposition to any legislation to curb acid rain.

Ed Meese had always wanted to be the Attorney General, even while he was part of the Meese-Baker-Deaver triumvirate at the

White House. Recently nominated to be Attorney General, he was close to the apex of his power. Ed and Ursula lived simply, and Ursula wasn't the least bit interested in clothes or decorating fashions, the cultural emblems of Mrs. Reagan and her friends. Unlike most of the people I knew in Washington, Ursula and Ed were indifferent to fancy trappings. The Meeses had had a tragic year because their son Scott had been killed in an automobile accident. Although they were not venal people, some two and a half years later Ed Meese was driven from office – tarred by accusations of "sleaze," shady dealings and financial favours to a friend – and threatened with indictments. His friend, Bob Wallach, later indicted and convicted in the Wedtech Scandal, was at a dinner we gave in honour of the Meeses when Meese was still Counsellor to the President. I believe that when we asked the Meeses if there was anyone special they wished us to ask, he was their sole request, apart from some visiting relatives.

Admiral John Poindexter was soon to be promoted from Deputy to National Security Adviser to replace his boss Robert McFarlane. His wife Linda, an outgoing lively woman, was about to become an Episcopalian priest. I found her outspoken and amusing and quite unafraid to make remarks about the dismal role of the wife in the Washington scene. Admiral Poindexter was quiet but easy to talk to. We sat Katharine Graham beside him at our Residence, the first occasion on which she had met him. Within two years, Admiral Poindexter became the key figure along with Oliver North in the Iran-Contra hearings and began to occupy a lot of space in Ms. Graham's front page. Could a fiction writer with the most leaping imagination have invented so improbable a development? Subsequently he was indicted, and tried to get President Reagan to testify at his trial.

Don Regan became the target of a press lynching for his role (or as it turned out later, his non-role) in the Iran-Contra affair. Mrs. Regan was a plump, forthright person with whom I once judged a doll contest for the Salvation Army. Our job was to make sure that all the dolls' clothes were home-made and award prizes to the most original concepts. The dolls were given away to the poor at Christmas. This was the old-fashioned idea of "wives of" duties in

Washington. Such an innocent activity seemed so out of context, almost absurd, when it was the Regans' moment to fall off the rollercoaster. After the negative publicity against Don Regan became intolerable and Mrs. Reagan forced him out of his job, he retaliated by writing a best-selling book, describing Mrs. Reagan's important role in the White House as the President's quarterback. The astrology part was the least of the revelations.

Bud McFarlane, the object of Don Regan's venom, was the National Security Adviser, the man who took the cake, bible and military equipment to the Iranians, and who later attempted suicide. He didn't have that self-important manner which so many Powerful Jobs in Washington seem to cultivate. Jonda, his attractive wife, was a school teacher and a frank and intelligent woman. She reminded me of my Ottawa pals. One day I turned on the local television news and was horrified to hear a tape of her voice, calling for an ambulance – she said she thought her husband had a heart attack. This was Bud's suicide attempt. Unbeknownst to her the para-medics sold the tape of her phone call to the media and her agonized request for an ambulance was repeated over the radio and television as a morbid entertainment.

Only time will tell if these five people, and others amongst our guests who suffered heavy injury, will recover completely. The rest of us had only minor bruises. We were the lucky ones.

9/Inspecting America

OUR TRAVELS IN the United States do not belong in the pages of *National Geographic* magazine. There were no visits to Yellowstone Park, the Grand Canyon, Big Sur or the Florida Everglades. National parks and sites famed for their beauty or historical significance were not part of our official agenda. I never visited Williamsburg, only a few hours away by car from Washington. Our inspection of America was of people rather than landscapes – we studied sociology, not geography.

Two kinds of trips are *de rigueur* for ambassadors to the United States. One is the speech trip – boosting and explaining the homeland – with speeches delivered to the American press, business executives and foreign relations or world affairs councils across the U.S.A. The other kind involves ambassadors' balls and charitable galas. Finally, it is important to attend the Republican and Democratic presidential conventions.

At first I went with Allan on his speech trips. I listened to him from the head table at formal banquets in Holiday Inns, J.W. Marriots, Westins and Sheratons across America. This kind of travelling has nothing to do with tourism. I began to complain. "Not fair," I said to Allan. "Instead of seeing any natural scenery, we meet lots of environmentalists in hotels in Colorado and Arizona." Allan explained to me that the environmentalists were against acid rain and acted as a helpful local American constituency in the Canadian cause. Good people though the environmentalists were, I continued to view his speech trips to them, or to any other group, egotistically. At least in Washington I was known as a hostess and, after a couple of years, as a writer. I had a role. But on the speech trips I was extraneous. I wasn't even "wife of."

"What's my function on these trips? The hosts are never sure who I am except they know I'm too old to be your bimbo," I pointed out to Allan. A couple of times I had overheard the welcoming officials, dismayed, whispering, "I think he's brought along the Mrs." Which meant that they had forgotten to put me on the program and would need extra space for me in the car as well as a front-row seat during Allan's speech. I was worse than "wife of" or "the Mrs." I was an unnecessary appendage of Allan, like a gall bladder.

On the speech trip a car would meet us at the airport and we'd see the landscape around the airport road on our way to the hotel. Allan never seemed to give his speeches in those chic little expensive hotels that were recommended to us by American friends who always knew the best places to stay. "What, you didn't stay at the Mansion on Turtle Creek in Dallas?" or, "You should have picked the Bel Aire in Los Angeles," these connoisseurs would say when we returned.

If we stayed in a city for one day or more, there would be a reception, usually at the top of the largest building in town. Our hosts were most anxious to have us look down at their city from the highest point available. As this place was always too far to walk to from our hotel and was only accessible by limousine, we rarely got to walk on the street. I began to feel that these reception areas were like decontamination centres – where the ambassador and "wife of" could be kept immune from the local germs. I still shudder when I recall such comments as, "We're having the party in the penthouse of the Ozone building. That's where you can really get a view of our city."

After a year of staring down at gridlocked freeways and trying to smile like Nancy Reagan during my husband's speeches, I rebelled. The rebellion took place in Scottsdale, Arizona, where Allan had been invited to speak. He assured me Scottsdale had no tall buildings. I would be able to walk around like a real tourist and skip the speech. From what I could see from the car going to the hotel, Scottsdale was a pretend cowboy town featuring shops selling cowboy boots for eastern tourists who would never wear them after leaving Scottsdale. Nevertheless, I was anxious to tour. But it was not possible. The motel where we were staying was constructed so that all the rooms faced a green square. If I wanted to leave the room, my only exit was through the square that was already rapidly filling up with people who had come to hear Allan speak and were whiling away the pre-lunchtime hour drinking piña coladas. My choice was to join the piña colada crowd or stay in the motel and watch daytime television. I chose the latter.

"Where's the Mrs.?" a few people asked. "Oh, she stayed at home this time," Allan replied. When everyone had gone, he snuck me out and we flew back to Washington. After that Allan and I made an agreement. If the trip was shorter than three days, I would stay behind.

Our first trip to California lasted about eight days and was a speech and hotel trip. San Francisco was at the end of the tour, and I was looking forward to it because I knew I could walk around and see the town. Allan was supposed to be meeting Jerry Brown, then governor of California, somewhere in the city. For an unfathomable reason (to me, at least) the consulate had booked us into a luxurious suite in the posh Clift hotel. It was huge and done in a Chinese style with lots of yellow couches and chairs. Before my walk I decided to wash out our eight days' worth of laundry. I put on one of those terrycloth robes that one is not supposed to steal from hotel rooms and shampooed (the shampoo is usually stronger than the soap supplied at luxury hotels) bras, socks, panties and stockings and hung them over the yellow chairs in the suite. I was feeling pretty good, and when there was a knock at the door, I was sure it was the hotel bringing us some complimentary fruit or champagne. I opened the door in my bare feet, wearing the terry robe, and found myself face to face with two Secret Service men, the hotel manager and Governor Jerry Brown.

"Who are you?" the Secret Service man said. "Where's Ambassador Gotlieb?"

Just then I saw my husband veer around the corner with his people. He hissed in my ear. "Don't you read the program? Our meeting is in this suite." Only then did it dawn on me why our accommodation was so fancy. "Get rid of the stockings dripping on the chairs."

As gracefully as I could, I swept the undies from the furniture and retreated to the bedroom. I was of course not introduced to the governor. Who knows, maybe he thought the Canadian ambassador travelled with his laundrywoman? About five minutes later Allan came into the bedroom a little shamefaced and said, "You'd better meet Jerry Brown. Get dressed and put on your high heels." Allan had noticed my bare feet and I guess he thought high heels might erase their memory from the governor's mind.

I put on my best suit, high heels, and entered the suite. Only two chairs were damp. I wished Governor Brown good luck in his Senate race (which he lost). I retreated again to the bedroom, where I remained for two hours, the length of the meeting. I was afraid to turn on the television because of the noise and had left my books in the other room. So I stared out the window, looking at the gridlocked traffic in San Francisco. If I had had my wits about me, I would have walked through the suite and out the door. But I was new at the job and my mind worked no better than a stunned ox.

Our other obligatory travelling was to the ambassadors' balls and charitable galas that are held in many major cities in America. For some reason the word *ambassador* has an appealing resonance to people of wealth, and especially to people of wealth outside Washington. An ambassador has instant status because of his title and accoutrements – chefs, butler, maids and large embassy residence. An ambassador can entertain in the style in which the rich expect (and the not-so-rich like) to be entertained. As well, many Americans with money think they might like to become an ambassador too. The occupation of ambassador is an acceptable alternative to being an investment banker, a CEO, or a socialite.

There were times during our travels when I felt as if we had been hired for the day as bit-players for a scene from *Lifestyles of the Rich and Famous*. We dipped in and out of this world of privilege with ambivalent feelings, knowing that it would cease at once for us when Allan stopped being Mr. Ambassador. Americans often incorrectly assumed that my husband was an ambassador because he had money of his own. American administrations habitually appoint rich men with no professional diplomatic experience to comfortable posts such as London, Paris and Rome. At various times during the Reagan administration millionaires without any diplomatic training occupied all these posts. The Reagan administration may have neglected professional diplomats in the State Department more than any other administration, but the practice was in the tradition of American politics. When John F. Kennedy was running for president, one of his rich friends accompanied him on the campaign plane. His only function was to walk Kennedy's dog when the plane landed on the tarmac. A reporter observed this activity for several weeks and finally asked, "Don't you find it demeaning to walk Senator Kennedy's dog?" The man replied, "That's not a dog you're looking at. That's an embassy."

When socialites and corporate executives in California and Texas discovered that Allan had been a public servant for thirty years, he would get uncomprehending stares. Few of the American rich had ever met a long-term public servant except for the nasty ones from the Internal Revenue Service.

Our first taste of the charity ball spoiled my enthusiasm for such events ever after. We attended the Red Cross Ball in Palm Beach, Florida, upon the advice of other foreign ambassadors in Washington. Some of them held this particular event in such high esteem that they made it a yearly pilgrimage.

We had been in Washington six weeks, and this was our first trip outside the capital. It started badly. Rito forgot to put our luggage in the trunk of the car and we discovered its absence only at the airport, to the dismay of our tour guides, if one can describe Baron Walter and Baroness Garnet Von Stockleburg in such a fashion. We were late for the plane, and the luggage contained Allan's white tie and tails as well my two evening gowns – one sewn for me ten years before by a dressmaker in Ottawa and another freshly purchased at a January sale in Washington. The Baron and Baroness delayed the plane's departure and waited impatiently along with the rest of the ambassadors while our driver rushed back to collect the missing luggage.

We arrived at Palm Beach around ten at night and were met by our host and hostess in one of their Rolls-Royces. Each ambassadorial couple was to be kept in a local mansion. Before we could go to sleep we were taken to the Bath and Tennis Club for a Moët and Chandon champagne cocktail party. Moët, I discovered, was the local drink apart from the hard stuff. In the morning we woke up in a large house coloured entirely in white – walls, upholstery, rugs, marble floors, as well as the figurines on the shelf. This was the only colour our hostess, dressed in white, liked. She was ashen-haired, with a very white face. We had made no plans for our first morning, so she kindly offered Allan an activity. "If you want to play polo we can get you a good mount."

The last time Allan saw a horse up close was about fifty years ago in Winnipeg, where it was pulling a milk truck. Allan said, "I just want to walk on the beach."

Our hostess was startled. "Walk on the beach? We never walk on the beach. You'll get cancerous warts. We haven't walked on the beach in five years."

Indeed we later discovered that the real Palm Beachers all had white, pale faces. Only tourists had tans. For those who live permanently in Palm Beach, sun is the enemy – and not only because of the fear of basal-cell carcinomas. Sun endangers the ubiquitous Palm Beach face lift.

She also warned us about tar on the beach. Eventually our hosts drifted off to watch a little morning television and I trudged behind Allan, for whom a wink is not as good as a nod, for a walk on the beach. Our hosts had told us their house was prime Palm Beach property because of its situation between the lake and the sea, and Allan wanted to get a better feel of it.

When we returned from our walk and wandered around the

empty house, I noticed that the white marble floors were covered with black footprints, as if two large dirty dogs had run amok. Except that the prints were human and our feet were covered with tar. My first instinct was to leave immediately for Fort Lauderdale, but Allan wrapped our feet in his dress shirts and we spent the morning scrubbing the tar out with Estée Lauder soap and Kleenex.

I said bitterly to Allan, "If you knew how to play polo like all the other ambassadors, this would never have happened."

There was a lunch at a country club much vaunted by the members because it was restricted – "It's even hard to bring in 'you know who' as guests," confided Mr. Gardiner, who has a long pedigree and owns the famous Gardiner's Island off New York. I wanted to tell him that the Canadian ambassador and his wife were "you know whos," but after all, we were clumped with the other ambassadors and it was only lunch.

The prolonged pre-lunch cocktail hour at the club gave Mr. Gardiner a chance to show me some of the jewellery worn by Palm Beach ladies. He took one woman's hand, held it like a dead fish, and pointed to the emerald on her finger. The woman, desiccated, her face taut from too many face lifts, continued her conversation with someone else while he told me that the emerald was worth over half a million dollars. "This is only her lunch-time jewellery." She withdrew her arm and said, "I don't know why you make a fuss about my emerald. The ruby," she said, showing her other hand, "may be smaller, but it's worth close to a million."

The lunch was unexceptional and long, its tediousness in no way relieved when all our hosts sang "Getting to Know You" to all the ambassadors.

In the evening, at the main event, we and the other ambassadors stood in a reception line and greeted the ball-goers, the women in couture gowns, bejewelled, and the men all wearing medals they never got from fighting in a war. We were escorted to our tables by Marines (the only young men present except for a few neutered walkers, escorts of rich ancient ladies), while the cameras flashed for the shiny sheets, the local society magazines as well as *Town & Country* and *W*. Someone asked me if I had sewn my own dress. I asked the people at my table how they spent their time in Palm Beach.

"We dance," they answered. "We dance at balls, private dinners and at the country clubs. We dance at least five nights a week, but only the foxtrot." Most of the people at our table had taken special Palm Beach foxtrot lessons. Apart from Allan, there was no man present at our table under seventy. I was thankful when a fifty-year-old came over and asked me for a dance. He was, I found out later, the chief of police of Palm Beach and I had committed a *faux pas*. Ladies don't dance with men from other tables at the Red Cross Charity Ball.

The next night Mrs. Sue Whitemore, who had actually married and divorced a Palm Beach policeman but remained a doyenne of Palm Beach, gave an elaborate dinner and dance. Mrs. Whitemore, a generous hostess, dressed in a way that the other Palm Beach hostesses considered eccentric. She wore a net kerchief around her hair and a muumuu-type garment over her ample frame and running shoes. I admired the fact that she held to her own style amidst the Chanels, the St. Laurents and the Galanos. This time I wore my Washington-sale French-designer dress, which didn't look as if I had sewn it myself. But it was velvet with a high neck, the temperature was about 90 degrees and I was sweating, as the dinner was an outside-inside affair in Mrs. Whitemore's elegant hacienda-style house. During dinner I sat next to a gentleman who sold the jewellery to the local ladies, including a woman who introduced herself, if I remember correctly, as Mrs. Shmidlapp. "My name may be Shmidlapp," she said apologetically, "but I haven't anything but pure Irish in my veins." The Bath and Tennis Club had given her the O.K.

The Red Cross Ball in Palm Beach was not just one event, it was a weekend of numbness and boredom, parties without conversation for the overdressed and unemployed. It was the exclusive rite of ageing *rentiers* – coupon clippers – and attracted gold-diggers of both sexes seeking sugar daddies and mummies. I am a strong believer in the capitalist system and have a conservative turn of mind. My weekend at the Red Cross Ball in Palm Beach almost turned me into a Marxist.

For the first two years we went to all the balls we were invited to, including the ambassador ball in Dallas, where our hosts were Herbert Hunt and his wife. One of the famous Hunt brothers who tried to corner the silver market, he was then being sued by the U.S. government and a lot of private folk as well. Herbert Hunt, a small, chubby man, himself drove us around in an old Mercedes sedan. I don't quite know what was wrong with the mechanicals, but gas fumes were backing up into the car's interior. Between coughs Mrs. Hunt pointed out the buildings Herbert owned, saying, "Herbert doesn't like to brag on them himself." He was more disturbed by all the office space that wasn't being rented than by the gas fumes choking us. We sat at his table at the ball; the rest of the group consisted of his employees, who chewed when he chewed, laughed when he laughed and nodded vigorously when he spoke bullishly about his worldwide investments, which seemed to include a large chunk of northern Canada. Mrs. Hunt told me she was going to a white dove party the following day. A white dove party, as I understood it, is a Texas specialty given in honour of sixteen-year-old girls, where all the ladies, young and old, wear white, and at the peak moment a shower of white doves is released over the heads of the guests. I was sorry to miss that. But I had had enough of white in Palm Beach.

There is a third type of travel that many ambassadors undertake in the United States – trips designed to keep in touch with the ethnics or nationals of their home country. The British ambassador talks to English-speaking unions and accompanies the numerous members of the royal family when they come to the United States to play or to sell a British product. The Italian ambassador was always rushing off to attend Italian-American parades and as many events as possible featuring Frank Sinatra. The Irish ambassador was a most desirable commodity in Boston and New York, and the Israeli ambassador was constantly attending Israel bond fundraisers from one end of the country to the other. The

Italian, Greek, German, French and Scandinavian ambassadors and their colleagues were necessary adjuncts for ethnic food festivals in New York, Chicago and Minnesota. But for us there was no ethnic parade or Canadian food festival, no donning of national dress. Canadians disappear too easily into the American woodwork.

We found one major exception: Hollywood. At a party given in our honour by the Canadian film director and producer Norman Jewison in his house in Malibu Beach, we encountered one of the few gatherings of Canadian nationals and ethnics.

In the entertainment business in Los Angeles, the nationalities stick together. The British colony plays cricket and has tea parties, and, to my surprise, the Canadians find sustenance in each other as well. Jewison, who lives part-time in Toronto, had invited many Canadians in the movie industry to meet us – Donald Sutherland, Ted Kotcheff, Alexis Smith, Suzanne Sommers, the late Lorne Greene, many screenwriters and directors, and some of my old high-school chums from Winnipeg, such as Perry Rosemund and Allan Blye, who had made good in the television business.

Norman Jewison seems to be at the centre of the Canadian community in the Hollywood entertainment world. He explained to me, "The movie people are kings. Good films are lasting, T.V. miniseries are transitory. Most people who work in T.V. – no matter how much money they make – actors, producers, directors – are dying to get into the movie business." Yet he was disturbed by the adulation given to film stars. Later, when he was making the film *Moonstruck* with Cher, he was appalled by the public's obsession with her. It was impossible to go anywhere with her without being mobbed by adoring crowds. "After all," he said, "she's not Mother Teresa, she's only a film star."

On this same grand tour among the Canadian ethnics in California, Donald Sutherland gave us a splendid dinner party at Ma Maison (one of those restaurants in Los Angeles with unlisted numbers). Little maple-leaf flags decorated the table. David Steinberg, the comic, a former Winnipegger, was eating at another table in the corner before Donald or his guests arrived. He was fascinated by the flags. "I thought it would be Pierre Trudeau," he said afterwards, "but it was only you."

Donald had told us beforehand that Sean Connery and his wife were going to be members of his party. Sean Connery held a mythic place in our family. My son and husband were fanatics about James Bond movies, but only the ones with Sean Connery playing the lead. Moreover, in Washington we used to give a dinner and movie party once a year or so in honour of George Shultz, who also turned out to have a great liking for James Bond movies, Sean Connery vintage.

So there I was sitting beside Sean Connery with the little Canadian flags in front of us, and I couldn't get him to say a word. But by this time I had sat beside quite a few important men in Washington and had developed some specific techniques. I'd start with, "You look so fit. Do you jog?" Even if there was obvious belly-overhang, the men would usually tell me about their particular fitness and diet routines. In Washington it was always safe to say to a powerful official or journalist, "I agreed with what you said in the newspaper last week." It didn't matter in the least whether I knew what they had said or not. They would repeat it back to me at dinner and tell me who else agreed with them.

I tried the jogging routine with Sean Connery, but his fitness answers lasted about half a minute. More silence. I noticed he had tattoos on his arms and that he spoke with a broad Edinburgh accent. When I commented, he told me that he covered up the tattoos and accent on the screen. More silence. Then almost a glumness. Finally I told him I thought he was such a success on the screen because he had perfect actor's timing. Something clicked and he smiled and said, "Not many people realize that." And then he chatted about his filmmaking for at least a quarter of an hour.

One of the signs of Donald Sutherland's Canadian loyalties was his passion for the Montreal Expos. The Expos were then playing the home team at Candlestick Park in San Francisco, and the Canadian ambassador, sitting in the owners' box, was asked to throw the first ball. Donald Sutherland happened to be in the box at the same time – he travelled with the team whenever he could.

If that became impossible because he was filming on some faraway location, his movie contract included a clause saying he could take time off to listen to the games via long distance, the telephone bill to be paid by the movie company.

On this occasion Allan went down to the dug-out. Donald was watching; the owners were watching; I was watching; the fans in the stadium were watching; the television audience was watching. The billboard lit up with Allan's name. "Throwing out the first ball: Alan [*sic*] Gotlieb, Canadian Ambassador to the U.S." We sang the two national anthems. Allan, wearing an Expos jacket, strode to the pitcher's mound. He did some kind of tricky pitcher wind-up, threw the ball, and it fell ten feet short of the batter. Everyone booed. I was mortified. Nobody in the owners' box said a word. Donald had his eyes shut.

Every four years ambassadors are asked to attend the Democratic and Republican presidential conventions. But they are asked as a group, and only to specific events where protocol is more prominent than the political process. The only way an ambassador can worm his way into places where the real action is taking place is by knowing someone who is a special friend of, or is close to, the candidate. (When writing for the *Washington Post*, I dubbed such people "Close to the Candidate," or simply "Close To's.") We struck it lucky at the Mondale-Ferraro Democratic convention in San Francisco in 1984. Lane Kirkland, head of the AFL-CIO, and his wife, Irena, had become good Washington friends. Lane, who was at the centre of the action at the convention and "close to" Mondale, found himself without a car and accepted the offer of the Canadian ambassador to drive him around. We had a small consulate car – in it was the driver, the four of us, occasionally the Canadian journalist Allan Fotheringham, and Joe and Polly Kraft. Wherever we went, whether to the Moscone Center where the convention was taking place or to the numerous "insider" parties that were part and parcel of the convention, we tumbled out of the car like a gaggle of circus clowns.

The political convention was an extended mob scene, with

journalists, delegates and lobbyists wandering aimlessly through the freebie section (free beer, nachos and hot dogs), never looking at the T.V. monitors that revealed earnest senators giving mid-morning speeches. It was obvious, even to me, that the delegates on the floor of the convention hall had little to do with mainstream America. There were too many activist women, too many special-interest groups demanding that Mondale fill their laundry list. When Geraldine Ferraro's Vice-Presidential appointment was announced, the delegates on the floor exploded with joy and I don't think I heard the word *Mondale* mentioned by the delegates or in the speeches for the next few days. We were sitting in the bleachers with Sol Linowitz, a Democrat, a lawyer and a Washington insider, when Mrs. Ferraro was pronounced the Vice-Presidential candidate. Sol sighed and said, "We have lost the election. Her husband's a lawyer from Queens." Mr. Ferraro's problems were already out on the street. The lawyers knew it, we knew it, but the Mondale people didn't.

Nevertheless, the San Francisco convention was the most amusing political event we attended if only because of the street life. We watched the gay-lesbian parade featuring the Little Sisters of Perpetual Indulgence, a gay male splinter group who dressed as nuns. There was a chic reception at Gumps department store, where I dropped half-eaten sushi into Chinese antique pots, and there were pasta parties for the media in outdoor malls. In contrast, Dallas, where the Republicans held their convention that same year, was deadly. There were no downtown parades in Dallas because there is no downtown. Besides, it was 100 degrees in the shade and there were no surprises – the main event being the deification of Ronald and Nancy Reagan.

At the Democratic convention we attended a party given by Ann Getty, wife of Gordon Getty, heir to Getty Oil, for important Democrats at her *Architectural Digest* (or clone thereof) featured house in Pacific Heights overlooking San Francisco Bay. The guests stood and watched on the small television in Mrs. Getty's spacious marble atrium as Governor Mario Cuomo gave his acclaimed speech about America being a nation divided between the rich and the poor. He spoke of the "shining city on a hill" and of how Americans needed to help those millions of Americans who were not part of the shining city. One thing was clear. None of them were at the Getty party, which was smack in the centre of the "shining city on a hill." The Democratic guests, who were drinking champagne in that curatorial-designed mansion, thought that Governor Cuomo had given the speech of the century. "Dickensian," they said. "He really cares about the poor."

Mrs. Getty had been floating through her house rather absent-mindedly. After the speech someone sat me beside her on the silk sofa. A gentleman had told me the wallpaper was important eighteenth-century chinoiserie. My hostess's glance told me she knew instantly we had nothing in common. While she talked about her forthcoming travels to the people around her, my eyes wandered and I noticed the bowls of peach-coloured roses gathered in huge bunches. Each flower was fully bloomed, yet no one flower was opened more than the one pressing next to it. It was the roses more than any of the objets d'art in the beautiful house that brought to mind Scott Fitzgerald and his famous phrase about the rich being different than you and me. This was the first but not the last time I was to see designer roses.

10/Houseguest Anxiety

SCOTT FITZGERALD'S DESCRIPTION of East Egg and West Egg in *The Great Gatsby* seemed as accurate to us when we visited the Hamptons on Long Island as when he wrote the book. Except that thousands of Gatsbys seemed to have taken over the Hamptons and built elaborate beach houses – to the regret of those who liked the fields of potatoes and tomatoes that had been there before the real estate boom. The Hamptons was and is the playground of the New York rich, super-rich, famous and would-be famous. As well, the Hamptons used to be a cheap place for writers and painters to live and work, winter as well as summer. Now it seems to be the centre for those artists who were smart enough to buy before the potato fields were sold to arbitragers, plastic surgeons and dress designers.

The late Joe Kraft, the columnist, and his artist wife, Polly, owned a modest (relatively speaking) country house in Wainscott, East Hampton, and had asked us to be their guests for a weekend during a couple of summers. Polly had been going to the Hamptons for more than thirty years and could write a thesis on the sociological make-up of the place. From Scott Fitzgerald to Tom Wolfe, luncheon, cocktail and dinner parties are integral to life in the Hamptons.

We discovered that it was a Hampton rule that one can't have houseguests without giving them a party. And one can't have houseguests without taking them to the parties to which one is invited. Which means houseguests are a big responsibility.

I was unaware of all this when we went there the first time. My first inkling of what was in store occurred in Islip, the nearest airport to the Hamptons. While we were waiting for Polly to pick us up at the airport we spotted William Safire, the writer and essayist for the *New York Times*. Safire asked, "Whom are you staying with?" The question was phrased significantly. If we had met him in a different airport he would have asked, "What hotel are you staying at?" or "Where are you staying?" But in the Hamptons it's not chic to stay in hotels. In fact the number of hotel guests in the Hamptons is in reverse ratio to the number of parties going on at any given time.

We also learned that social life begins on the beach. The Krafts belonged to a private beach, and every time Allan and I settled down with our sunblock and books we found ourselves jumping up to be introduced to someone who was or had been famous for something. If it was movie-making, the person was Sidney Lumet or maybe Alan Pakula. If it was banking, it may have been Felix Rohatyn or Walter Wriston, or it might have been aristocratic ladies such as Louisa Kennedy, whose husband had been held hostage in the U.S. Embassy in Iran.

Given our hectic lives in Washington, I was ready for calm, anonymous afternoons on the beach, but this was not the way of the Hamptons. While we were lying and jumping up on the beach, Polly, back at the house, had been twirling and worrying, planning a party in our honour. She had no servants, except that three women, locally known as the Polish Tornado, came a couple of hours once a week to clean her house.

When we arrived from the beach, exhausted from social chitchat, Polly was busy on the telephone, arranging and pruning her party. "I told Mort Zuckerman he couldn't bring a date, I just don't have the room. The Eastmans are bringing Paul McCartney and his wife. And Paul Simon is coming."

Allan asked, "Who's Paul McCartney and Paul Simon?"

"Singers," Polly answered. "I can't talk now, I have to pick up the salmon at this woman's house."

"Opera singers?" Allan asked Joe. He didn't ask me because he knew I was a musical illiterate. Joe explained. Then he described the rest of the guests, many of whom were household names to readers of *Woman's Wear Daily*, *Forbes* magazine and *Variety*. I felt a nervous breakdown coming on. I understood why Polly was a little anxious.

Allan sat next to Paul McCartney, whose wife, Linda, was on his other side. "They always sit together at parties," Polly explained.

When McCartney discovered that Allan was the Canadian ambassador, he asked him, "What does Canada do with lobsters?"

"Actually," Allan said, "we eat them." Then, figuring that McCartney must be a serious environmentalist or something, quickly added, "Canada has strict laws about harvesting lobsters."

McCartney wasn't mollified. He explained. "Linda and I save lobsters after they've been bought by the fish shops and restaurants. We travel everywhere in Britain doing this. Today we drove all over the Hamptons and bought as many live lobsters as we could, picked them right from the tanks in the restaurants and shops. Then we drove them to the nearest beach and released them to their home in the sea."

I wondered if the McCartneys took off the little piece of wood that secures the lobsters' claws as they crawl in the tanks.

When I got back to Washington, I wrote a 'Dear Beverly' column in the *Post* about "having a nervous breakdown in the Hamptons." I was subsequently to undergo a similar experience every time we were to have one of those marvellously "informal" weekends as someone's houseguests in the country.

In Canada, when I was a houseguest, very few of my hosts had a live-in maid. In the morning I would make the bed and help clear the breakfast table, reluctantly. If there was a dinner in our honour I'd wash the lettuce, chop the chives and make a feeble attempt to help with the dishes after the party. My houseguest present would be a bottle of wine or a book, and, since there were no servants, there was never any worry about how much to tip them.

As an ambassadorial couple in the United States we were

occasionally houseguests of people who were used to entertaining regularly and royally although always 'informally'. There were three styles of entertaining in this grander category typified for us by Sunnylands in Palm Springs, the winter home-art gallery of Lenore and Walter Annenberg, where they were frequent hosts of Ronald Reagan; the sprawling turn-of-the-century summer house of *Washington Post* owner-publisher Katharine Graham (usually – and accurately – styled the most powerful woman in America) in Martha's Vineyard; and Mrs. Lamont duPont Copeland's museum-like estate outside Wilmington, Delaware. In their different ways, our hostesses showed us an expansive and diverse American style of entertaining. But as hospitable as our hostesses were, I always suffered from houseguest anxiety.

On these visits there were no beds to make, lettuce to wash or dinner plates to stack. Still, there were other things to worry about. Clothes, for instance. When I went to the Annenbergs I was told it would be California-style, "casual but elegant," no black tie for the men, but probably "a little fancier" for the women. I wasn't quite sure what "a little fancier" for the women might mean. In Canada, when the invitation was black tie, even at Government House, I would often see men dressed up with medals and dinner jackets, while the women wore short silk shirt dresses, with bows tied under the collar. Sometimes I couldn't see myself dressed like that at Sunnylands, even if Allan wasn't supposed to wear a dinner jacket.

On the liberal north shore of the Vineyard, where Kay Graham had her home, we were told the absolute rule was no ties for the men and very casual for the women. But how casual is very casual? At Canadian lakes, very casual is the bottom half of a jogging suit, sandals and your husband's sweater. I didn't see myself dressed like that at the Vineyard.

At the Copeland estate in Delaware, I was told "just ordinary dinner dresses."

So it was to be informal at all three houses. But how informal can it be when each of the six or eight houseguests has a typed sheet of paper in their bedroom with a list of other guests invited for lunches and dinners planned for the weekend?

To be on the safe side I used to take my entire Washington wardrobe, plus scroungings from friends, to all three places. At first I would force Allan to join the guests before me, scan the women and run back to the bedroom, where I was waiting in my underwear, with fashion information. This turned out to be a useless ploy because he was incapable of rational description. "How can I tell?" he'd say, irritated. "One of them is wearing a shiny dress. Hurry up, they're all there."

Casual California elegance, I discovered, included long gowns for the women on Saturday night. Kay Graham's parties were more informal. But still, in the evening guests wore silk pant-suits and cocktail dresses or long designer cotton skirts. Some of the wives of the writers and artists who came for dinner did wear little faculty-wife outfits, similar to what public servants' wives, like me, wore in Ottawa. Mrs. Lamont duPont Copeland entertained many of her relations, and they took pride in wearing new fabrics that were being marketed by Du Pont.

What delighted me the most at these great houses were very different things.

The Annenbergs' contemporary house was designed with an Aztec-influenced roof and surrounded by a golf course with plantings of rare trees and shrubs and waterfalls and streams filled with baby ducks. Most of the guests at the Annenbergs' golfed in the morning, except us. We spent our mornings gawking at his Van Goghs and Impressionist paintings and walking around the golf course avoiding the areas where we might be hit by a ball. Houseguests like us can cause hostess anxiety.

The flowers from Mrs. Lamont Copeland's numerous indoor greenhouses win most of the prizes in the Philadelphia flower show. The Copeland estate was the oldest we had stayed in, and with its fine Federal American furniture was reminiscent of the grand American houses described in Edith Wharton novels. The Victorian conservatory where we had cocktails was filled with rare varieties of orchids, primroses and cineraria grown by her gardeners. Mrs. Copeland had willed her estate and its contents as well as the famous outdoor wild-flower gardens to the state of Delaware. It was winter when we were there, and nobody played golf or tennis. So we drank 1903 brandy and visited the greenhouses, both activities giving me intense pleasure.

Kay Graham's summer house was a comfortable sprawling turn-of-the-century-style bungalow with down-filled furniture covered in white cotton. Behind the house a meandering path followed marshland ponds filled with mallows and other water flowers to the beautiful rocky beach below, where we would take long walks. Kay loved to play tennis and had her own courts. We didn't play tennis, and the first time we were there she worried about what to do with us. A dutiful hostess, she gave up her morning tennis game to drive us around Martha's Vineyard, which we had never seen. Kay explained the difference between Edgartown and the north shore. "In Edgartown they wear ties and plaid pants to cocktail parties, which is taboo on the north shore."

The north shore of Martha's Vineyard is a writer, artist and media colony whose doyenne for a long time was Lillian Hellman. We dutifully noted that William Styron, Arthur Miller, Walter Cronkite, Art Buchwald, Mike Wallace, John Hersey, Robert Brustein, and Henry Gruenwald did not wear ties and plaid pants at the cocktail and dinner and lunch parties. The main subject of gossip on the north shore of the Vineyard the first year we were there was Lillian Hellman's behaviour when she was alive (difficult) and, during our second year, who came or didn't come to her funeral or memorial party. She left money in her will to students who would study classical Marxism. Even on the liberal north shore no one knew if classical Marxists still existed. "Certainly not in Russia or China," Arthur Miller declared.

Allan's houseguest anxiety was always the same; it gripped him the moment he entered each house and stayed with him until he left. There was always a large staff and he suspected that tipping was in order. But who to tip and how much? He would spend most of his time calculating tips in a note book and then rubbing them out every time a new maid or under-butler emerged. The houseguests at the Annenbergs' were for the most part old friends, and often members of the Reagan kitchen cabinet. Allan asked Bill French Smith, Reagan's first Attorney General, who became one of our close friends, about tipping. He shook his head. "We come here all the time and know the staff. I'm not going to tell you what we give them because it's out of your league." Allan made some kind of wild calculation, took up a wad of bills, placed it in the envelope and offered it to Lenore for the staff. She said, "Walter wouldn't want you to do that." But we followed the practice of the other guests and handed the envelope to the butler, while I left another envelope in the bedroom for the maid, even though we knew we were out of our league.

At the Vineyard Allan handed an envelope to Mrs. Graham's social secretary, to be distributed as she saw fit, hoping that its contents would put him somewhere between the piker level and Diamond Jim Brady. At Mrs. Copeland's, his tipping anxiety went into remission because he was able to receive a reassuring and decisive answer from her son-in-law, Bob Duemling, who used to be the Minister (the No. 2) in the American Embassy in Ottawa (now president of the National Building Museum in Washington) and on whose diplomatic experience in such matters Allan felt he could rely.

11/The Rites of Georgetown

"IF YOU WANT to know who Nancy Reagan admires, read *W*," Joe Kraft said.

"What's *W*?" I asked.

This conversation took place at a gathering including Muffie Brandon, then social secretary to Mrs. Reagan, who smiled knowingly but said nothing, Polly Kraft, Gaetana Enders, Evangeline Bruce, the Georgetown hostess with a talent for sociopolitical brunches, and Bob Gray, a prominent Republican lobbyist whose firm had organized President Reagan's inauguration in 1981. If I had asked "What's the *Washington Post*?" their amusement at my naiveté would not have been more spontaneous.

Muffie, or Vangie or Polly or Bob, sent me a copy of *W* the next day. It was a hefty tabloid with thick expensive paper and coloured inserts of models wearing Oscar de la Renta and Adolpho designer clothes. As well, there were black and white snapshots of socialites wearing Oscar de la Renta and Adolpho designer dresses attending parties in New York, Los Angeles and Washington. The black and whites were interesting because of the flattering and not so flattering pictures of people I had actually met during my first nine months in Washington. There was the swan-necked hostess Evangeline Bruce wearing Chanel, caught by the cameras at various functions in New York and Washington. There was Jean French Smith, and Katharine Graham arm in arm with her lanky journalist-socialite daughter, Lally

Weymouth. Marietta Tree, prominent New York socialite, widow of Sir Ronald Tree, was snapped chatting at an opening at the Metropolitan Museum, and Susan Mary Alsop, the Washington hostess and writer, at a book party. Jerry Zipkin, Mrs. Reagan's friend (whom I had heard of but never met), and Nancy Kissinger seemed to show up on every other page. New York names strange to me, like Brooke Astor, Annette Reed, and Jayne Wrightsman, appeared several times in the issue. And, most importantly, Mrs. Reagan was featured attending large fashion events and little dinners in her honour in New York, Los Angeles and Washington.

Then I noticed two long columns, placed side by side in the middle section of the newspaper, titled "In" and "Out." That year Evangeline Bruce, Kay Graham, the Tivoli Gardens in Denmark and hand-sewn sequined evening dresses were "in." I glanced at the "Out" column. Oh, shock and shame. Canada was near the top of the list along with the Moscow government. Did W mean the municipality of Moscow or the politburo? Poor Lee Radziwill and the Stuttgart Ballet were blacklisted with Canada in the "out" column. It appeared that Canada, a land without titles and aristocracy, was simply not chic. I was amused and bewildered. Why should a shallow publication like this be so well read in Washington? I soon realized that many of my new friends in Washington scrutinized it avidly, if secretly, their emotions swaying unsteadily between desire for party gossip, social envy and self-disgust for paying attention to a tabloid that celebrated dressmakers, social climbers, socialites and interior decorators. But the President's wife paid it attention and so why shouldn't they?

None of my friends actually admitted to subscribing to W. But they all knew who was gushed over or trashed in the latest issue. I took out a subscription to W but didn't tell anyone. Would a senator or an ambassador admit to having a subscription to *Penthouse*? As a writer, I told myself, it was necessary to keep tabs on Mrs. Reagan and the rest of the rich and powerful's social life – for the record. But, after seven years, a read through W gave me a sour aftertaste – it wasn't *Penthouse*, but it was a form of social pornography.

W, however, did me a big favour. At the time I had written very little since arriving in Washington. It took me all of six months to write a travel piece of eighteen hundred words about Asolo, Italy, for the *New York Times* Travel section. Subsequently I wrote two short articles for the *Washington Post Magazine* section, one about my disorganized attempts to be an ambassador's wife. Ed Meese, then Counsellor in the White House, told me he loved the piece because he said it described the way his day went too. (Ed Meese was already famous for his bottomless briefcase.) I also wrote about the doldrums of a Washington summer. Other than that my writing efforts were nil.

W gave me an idea for a funny piece about Washington and what it felt like to be representing a country that had been pronounced "out" in a fashionable and influential magazine. I sent it to the *New York Times*, which published it in their op-ed section. Aside from Russell Baker's column, it was the first humour piece printed on that page, I was told, in years. The *New York Times* was said to have a humour detector from which I was the only freelancer to have escaped.

The pictures of Mrs. Reagan and her old and new friends in *W* helped me understand what Joe Kraft had meant when he told me that the Reagan administration was about "social climbing." He didn't mean the President but his adored wife, his lifeline to the world. Whatever Nancy wanted, Nancy got. Mrs. Reagan was a *W* person, and the people who interested her were featured there. A *W* person has to have money, social connections and wear designer clothes. A *W* person is not necessarily a Republican. Mrs. Reagan's desire to be friendly with those who were not exclusively from the ideological right of the Republican Party, or even from the Republican Party, helped, at times, to swing the early Reagan administration somewhat away from its ultra-right stance. She was encouraged in this by the political pragmatists in the White House and cabinet. Mrs. Reagan, not unnaturally, was more interested in her husband's image than in policy matters.

Apart from her desire for social status, "making Ron look good" was her prime goal. To achieve this, she reached out beyond her husband's initial constituency and this gesture was warmly welcomed by the Georgetown and New York hostesses – many of whom were in the W set, including Democratic hostesses in Washington ignored by the Carter administration. When I arrived, the Georgetown set was craving to go to the Reagan White House and be a friend of Nancy – or at least be "in" with the winners.

What does Georgetown mean in the context of power in Washington? Why did the phrase "Georgetown hostess" still have some kind of resonance during our years in Washington, although many of the most interesting and useful parties we attended had nothing to do with Georgetown, the site, or the people?

Georgetown is a low-lying swampy area near the Potomac formerly occupied by working-class blacks. After the Second World War the narrow, three-storey, nearly indistinguishable brick houses, often sharing a wall, were gentrified, and eventually the working class was forced out by the high costs of real estate. After the gentrification, powerful political names moved to Georgetown: millionaire statesman Averell Harriman; journalist Joseph Alsop; Dean Acheson, Truman's brilliant Secretary of State (who was born in Canada and whose parents were Canadian); Philip Graham, owner of the *Washington Post*; Ben Bradlee, then editor of *Newsweek*; Senator John F. Kennedy and his wife, Jacqueline; the Krafts; Paul Nitze, the defense expert and policy planner; and columnist Walter Lippmann. Many of these were part of the group of "Wise Men" – for example, Dean Acheson, Paul Nitze, Averell Harriman – the small band of exceptionally influential individuals chosen as aides and advisers by President Truman and by General George Marshall, whose goal was the reconstruction of Europe and whose shining achievement was the Marshall Plan.

During the decades of the Cold War and the Vietnam War, small political dinner parties became the hallmark of the Georgetown set. To be a member of the Georgetown set didn't mean you had to own a house on site – it was enough to be seen frequently at their parties. Conversation and ideas flowed easily between the men of power and the men of the press. Henry Brandon, Washington correspondent of the *Sunday Times* of London, and his wife, Muffie, who lived at first in Cleveland Park, moved eventually to Georgetown, a hop, skip and a jump away from Ambassador Averell Harriman and his wife, Pamela, while Joseph and Stewart Alsop, immensely influential syndicated columnists, were only blocks away from Dean Acheson. Notwithstanding the rivalries and the fall-outs, they all gathered at unpretentious dinners in Georgetown when the United States was the foremost power on earth to plan and cogitate upon the destinies of America and the rest of the world. In their heyday, during the pre-Watergate era, political columnists were far more trusted by high officials than in years to come. A shared wish for long-term intelligent policies and mutual respect outweighed the desire for a minor scoop or the need for a favourable sound bite from a policy maker. James "Scotty" Reston, who was Washington bureau chief of the *New York Times*, described to me the time he went to Dean Acheson's office when he was Secretary of State and was shown a top-secret memorandum. Reston said he would as soon have exposed his sex life in the *Times* as publish the contents of what Acheson showed him. After Watergate, Vietnam and the advent of television, that trust was barely a memory.

The "Golden Years," the Kennedy Years, had a profound effect on Georgetown. It was the first time the East Coast establishment, Hollywood, the intelligentsia, artists and the press were brought together to be entertained, informed and manipulated by an administration in Washington. Being "in" in Washington was taken to its most rarefied level by the Kennedys. Thirty years later I would still hear those in Washington who were part of Camelot sigh, "You can't imagine what those times were like." Talleyrand could not have sounded so nostalgic when he talked of the sweetness of life before the Revolution.

Ben Bradlee became a close friend of Jack Kennedy. Muffie Brandon was Joan Kennedy's confidante. Columnist Joe Kraft admired and was close to Robert Kennedy. Art Buchwald was (and is) Ethel Kennedy's friend. The aristocratic David Bruce, accompanied by Evangeline, was posted as ambassador to Paris and London by President Kennedy. Philip Graham, then publisher of the *Washington Post* and husband of Katharine Graham, was one of the first to urge Jack Kennedy to run for President. Robert McNamara was Kennedy's Secretary of Defense, and all four Kennedys, Jack, Jackie, Bobby and Ethel, would go to Tom and Joan Braden's or Joe and Susan Mary Alsop's or the other houses I have mentioned for little Georgetown dinners. Many of the friends, mentors and often bewitched admirers of the Kennedy clan were powerful members of the press who have remained in Washington to the present day.

These Kennedy and Johnson Democrats, permanent Washingtonians, are no longer close to the policy makers, but are still secure in their social cachet. By now I was coming to understand better what, many years ago, a previous Canadian ambassador to Washington, the diarist Charles Ritchie, had told me about Georgetown during the Kennedy years: it was, he said, a community of "ins" and "outs," and if you wanted political influence and social cachet, it was a good idea to be part of the "ins." Ritchie disliked his years in Washington because of this frat house mentality.

When I was writing my "Dear Beverly" columns for the *Washington Post*, we were asked by George Stevens, Jr., director of the American Film Institute and a friend of the Kennedys, to the première of a documentary film he made about his famous father, George Stevens, who directed *Shane* and many other American film classics. Meg Greenfield, editor of the Editorial and op-ed pages of the *Washington Post*, was also one of the guests. She took one look at the crowd, which included Ethel Kennedy, Pamela Harriman, Art Buchwald, the Bradlees, Evangeline Bruce, Susan Mary Alsop, Robert McNamara, and Sargent Shriver, Kennedy's brother-in-law, and said to me, "These are the 'ins' of the 'outs.' You ought to do a column about them."

I never wrote the column but I understood what she meant.

The "Golden Days" of Georgetown may never have been the same after the Kennedys, but they established the Georgetown set, and the name became part of the socio-political vernacular. The rites of Georgetown continued, with additions from each new administration. Jack Valenti, who was in Lyndon B. Johnson's White House (and is now the president of the Motion Picture Association); foreign policy stars Henry Kissinger, Larry Eagleburger and General Brent Scowcroft from the Nixon and Ford administrations; and, from the Reagan administration, White House aides Richard Darman and Michael Deaver, Secretary of State George Shultz and Secretary of Defense Caspar Weinberger (the last two not newcomers to Washington, having served in previous administrations), were all warmly welcomed by the Georgetown set. The additions were sometimes temporary, sometimes permanent, depending, at least in part, on their political fortunes.

Notwithstanding the appeal of Georgetown to some, it has been the custom of the Hill Folk – senators and congressmen – to keep themselves to themselves, and few descend from the Mountain to dine in Georgetown or anywhere else, except for the sake of an old friendship or for specific political reasons, such as to attend a fundraiser in their honour, given by Democrat Pamela Harriman, for example, or Republican Robert Gray, or a party given by Kay Graham or an important political columnist. The Hill Folk would come down for parties given anywhere in Washington by the upper media. When the *McLaughlin Group*, a hyperactive talk show popular during the Reagan years, or the *Today* show gave themselves birthday parties, the reclusive warlords of the Senate and Congress – such as Senators Lloyd Bentsen, Bill Bradley, Robert Dole and Russell Long, Speaker Tip O'Neill and Democratic whip Tom Foley – would pay their respects in front of the television cameras, snack on Virginia ham and sweet biscuits, and even stand and listen to a toast or two. When ABC gave a birthday party in honour of the David Brinkley Show, the room was packed wall-to-wall with senators, congressmen, White House people and cabinet secretaries. At the *McLaughlin* party at the Ritz-Carlton, while many heavy-hitters from the Hill were mixing with the leading members of the Republican cabinet and the White House, the klieg lights suddenly went on, the multitude of cameras and booms swung towards the door and a large cluster formed. Allan asked a senator, "Is it the President?" "No," was the reply, "he's in California." "Then is it the Vice President?" "No, he's supposed to be out of town." So who could it be? Several hundred eyes looked towards the door to see who could be so singled out among this potent group. It was Sam Donaldson, then White House correspondent for ABC, dropping in for a biscuit as well. Sam Donaldson was famous for his loud voice and aggressive interviewing manner towards President Reagan. "Mr. President," he'd yell, "Walter Mondale says you're intellectually lazy and you're forgetful. He says you're providing 'leadership by amnesia.' Do you agree?"

Apart from the President, or the Vice President, only a media prince, a star of television, could attract such interest from a political crowd or from his own creatures, the cameras, some, of course, belonging to ABC. A party given by half a dozen of the chief executives of America's largest corporations, even if hosted together, could never attract a political crowd equal to the sort of crowd a media prince could draw on any average day in Washington.

The Hill Folk followed a well-defined social pattern. They liked their own company best. But when they did decide to descend from the mountain they were most particular about the hosts of the parties they attended. If you saw a senator at a Georgetown or any other party, the host usually had something to do with the media. The media – particularly the *Post*, the *New York Times*, the *Wall Street Journal*, the television networks and weekly journals – are major powers in Washington, certainly as powerful as any administration, and definitely more permanent.

It was therefore not surprising that for many years the most powerful hostess in Georgetown – and Washington – was and remains Katharine Graham, publisher of the *Washington Post*. Katharine Graham, a tall, stately woman who speaks in the clenched-mouth tones of the upper-class East Coast boarding school, is the daughter of Eugene Meyer, the late owner of the *Washington Post*. Katharine Graham came to be publisher in spite of her father and because of tragic personal events. Eugene Meyer had left the majority of the newspaper shares not to his daughter, but to his son-in-law, Philip Graham, who was, according to all accounts, brilliant but mentally unstable. He eventually shot himself and Katharine Graham took control of the *Washington Post*. Until then she had had little to do with the newspaper. I remember her saying about that period in her life, "I stayed at home with my four children and did car pools and volunteer work." When she took over her husband's job, after what must have been a bitter and horrifying experience, she hired Ben Bradlee of *Newsweek* as her editor. I heard her describe how difficult it was for her at first. "When things got really tough, I tried not to show any weakness in front of the staff. But as soon as they left my office, I would go in the bathroom and have a good cry."

Katharine Graham now stands at the core of the old Georgetown community, all members in their own way acknowledging her presence and her primacy. Most of the group were women, with one major exception.

One of Mrs. Graham's oldest friends was Joseph Alsop, former columnist and a curmudgeonly mentor to the Georgetown set. He would peer over his spectacles and harrumph, pronounce and confront, his high cheekbones pink from indignation or a libation. A great walker, we often would see his short, compact body slightly bent over, stick in hand, making his way from the National Gallery to his Georgetown home, pausing here and there to chat with babies in their strollers and complimenting the parents "on your splendid-looking infant." Joe Alsop was by no means a cheery Santa figure, but babies and small children brought out his softer side. Alsop, with his late brother Stewart, wrote a highly influential syndicated column during the Eisenhower, Kennedy and Nixon periods. I recall one evening when Joe, a Vietnam hawk among the doves of Georgetown, an admirer of Henry Kissinger, and by then long retired, predicted correctly, to the dismay and disbelief of his liberal Georgetown friends, that Reagan would last two terms.

Like most of Georgetown, Joe Alsop would never have asked a Canadian ambassador to dinner unless there was a common old-school tie, and possibly not even then. Sir Nicholas Henderson, the British ambassador to the U.S. at the time of our arrival, invited us to a small lunch in honour of the British scholar, Sir Isaiah Berlin, along with Larry Eagleburger and his wife, Marlene, Mrs. Katherine Darman (blue-stocking wife of Richard, the clever White House strategist who became director of the Bureau of the Budget in the Bush administration), Joe Alsop and ourselves. The favourable piece about me in the Style section of the *Post* had recently appeared, and we had given a couple of dinners that some of Joe Alsop's friends had attended. They apparently had passed the word that we "gave a good party." Whatever the reason, Joe Alsop decided that Canada might well become "in" and asked us to come for dinner the following week.

As well as being a celebrated journalist and art historian, Joe was a self-admitted snob who liked "cosy" small dinners with guests who were distinguished by their political power. He designated two of his best friends, Kay Graham and Meg Greenfield, Mrs. Powerful and Miss Awesome respectively. Joe was not averse to ancestor worship, and a good many people without political power at his table came from "old money," although he wasn't all that snobbish about new money either. His dinners were ritualistic, and many of his social dictums have been followed faithfully by Georgetown. Joe Alsop's law of *placement*, which appeared to be practised in many private homes in Washington, was that an ambassador must sit on the right of the hostess and the "wife of" on the right of the host. According to these rites, which approximate the seating protocol in the State Department at official functions, Allan, or the senior ambassador present (the one who has been longest in Washington), would always take precedence over somebody richer, more interesting or more powerful. He would always have to sit to the right of the hostess instead of someone else she might prefer. In Georgetown the celebrity might be someone such as Rex Harrison, Harold Pinter, or his wife, Antonia Fraser (Anglophilia is ripe in Georgetown), the novelist Larry McMurtry, or Henry Kissinger. That's why Georgetown mulls things over when inviting an ambassador and "wife of," or, worse, two ambassadorial couples for dinner.

The hosts don't want bores on their right and left when instead they could have an unofficial but witty Gore Vidal or an unofficial nouveau billionaire from New York beside them.

Nervously, feeling as if I had just fallen off a turnip truck outside my home town of Winnipeg (a city not known for dwellers of long pedigree), I noticed that the rooms were filled with portraits of Alsop's Roosevelt ancestors. On entering the dining room in the basement of his typical three-level George-town house, he pointed out one particular portrait, saying, "That was my pansy uncle. I loved him dearly." Before dinner he sat himself down in his special chair, with a little footstool for his feet, urged me to sit beside him, and pressed vodka (his drink), "not too terrible Spanish champagne" or whisky upon us. His maid, Gemma, who had been with him for many years, and as I learned later was occasionally on speaking terms with him, passed what I came to call the Georgetown hors d'oeuvre, caramelized bacon.

Joe Alsop was born into an upper-class milieu in Connecticut where "the word *guilt* did not exist": he happily described himself to me "as a perfect shit." Hence he had no qualms about dominating the women on either side of him with reminiscences of times past, occasionally fascinating, sometimes less so, including descriptions of luncheons with his Roosevelt aunts, or with Franklin at the White House, or of his experiences in a Japanese prison camp in Hong Kong when he was a correspondent during the war. He was not above a little bullying, and one interrupted him at peril.

After dessert, his maid placed a humungous *café au lait* in front of him before the others were served (his guests were provided with regular-sized cups). Later I learned this was a signal that a general conversation might now take place and that any turning from left to right should cease. Unusually for Washington, there were never any toasts, because he disapproved of them.

What followed was often the most brilliant talk in Washington, the cleverness and learning of the guests almost always being challenged or surpassed by a host who had an unrivalled knowledge of the political history of Washington in modern times. No one ever sat at Joe Alsop's table without learning something about American history or without being astonished by the power of his intellect and domineering personality. Nevertheless, I often felt ill at ease during these dinners, especially when he had an old friend present. It was like eavesdropping in the middle of a long, secret and sometimes unintelligible conversation about people I knew only by name – W people or those with formidable reputations or ancient lineage, be they from Connecticut, Paris or Venice.

About a year after our arrival in Washington we were asked to Joan and Tom Braden's for dinner on a snowy night. Joan was a tiny woman who chewed tobacco and adored political men and beautiful clothes. She knew Jack and Robert Kennedy, Nelson Rockefeller and Henry Kissinger. Robert McNamara remains her longtime friend. It would appear from her public statements that not all her friendships with these men were platonic. She often wore gowns made by St. Laurent, Bill Blass or Oscar de la Renta. "I really can't afford them," she'd say, "but I like to indulge myself." She, like so many others in Washington and New York, would frequently get her clothes at cost from the designer showrooms in New York.

Being newcomers, we didn't realize that few people go out to parties in Washington during a snowfall except Canadians, a strange breed who discovered the utility of snow tires. The Shultzes, who had the Secret Service with four-wheel drives to look after them, managed to get there, as did Joe Alsop, carried in by bearers, Warren and Teenie Zimmerman, his close relatives, who had lived in Moscow and knew about snow. The rest of the guests, Washingtonians and Californians, were afraid to back out of their driveways or had bumped into cars as they drove home from work. The telephone kept ringing with cancellations, and our hostess, who did not live in Georgetown but was part of its history and ethos, was distressed because she had set tables with place cards and flowers for thirty-two. Twenty-three people did not show up. The Bradens, the Shultzes, the Zimmermans, Joe Alsop and ourselves sat around one table in the dark room, lit only by scented candlesticks surrounded by empty, elaborately arranged tables that remained fully dressed in case others managed to conquer the hazards of snow. The presence of the Secret Service men in the hall and the nervousness of the hostess, the Zimmermans (he was a State Department official dining with the big boss) as well as myself, heightened the feeling of an unnatural evening.

Whatever the reason, my husband decided to break the tension by being provocative. The argument had nothing to do with U.S.-Canada relations. It seemed to have focussed on the American will, or lack thereof, to lead the world. Allan was like a terrier going after a bulldog. He worried and barked and danced around George Shultz, but Shultz didn't show his throat or even retreat. Neither man gave ground all evening. (No matter what one said to George Shultz, his face remained as impassive as an Easter Island statue.) I knew ambassadors were not supposed to have fierce philosophical arguments with the Secretary of State. Nobody else spoke except Joe Alsop, who snapped regularly at Allan, agreeing wholeheartedly with George Shultz. Warren Zimmerman kept quiet.

Our host Tom Braden, author of *Eight Is Enough*, was a taciturn man with a pugnacious manner shown to advantage on a CNN television talk show, which he then co-anchored. Tom represented the liberal democrat voice in Washington. He was also known to give eccentric toasts. While his wife would listen anxiously, he'd rise, hold up his glass and drawl, "Joan didn't tell me why we're giving this party. I barely know the guest of honour and, since this is the first time I've met his wife, I can't say much about her." End of toast. He of course never gave a toast like that to George Shultz. But he did tell me that evening that he wished Allan would shut up. As we left, Joan wondered out loud if she would ever get George Shultz to come to dinner again. In Washington there are a hundred and fifty ambassadors and only one Secretary of State. So we knew where her priorities lay. Anyway, I was pretty unhappy when I got home and figured that Allan wasn't going to last long in his job. I was sure George Shultz had gone directly to the State Department at midnight in the storm and wired Ottawa to get rid of their obnoxious ambassador.

I tossed and turned all night while Allan snored. I had been uneasy during my whole first year in this city, wondering what I or even Allan was allowed to say in his official and my unofficial capacity. We had met hundreds of people, but I had one close friend. We were too busy making contacts to have friends. During the night I felt my loneliness more than at any time in Washington. I rose at six the next morning and remembered what Harry Truman said. "If you want a friend in Washington, buy a dog." I opened the *Washington Post* and saw an ad for a breed I had never heard of, the Tibetan terrier. An hour later I called Polly Kraft, my only close friend; we went out to Virginia and I bought Sweet Pea.

George Shultz didn't ask Ottawa to fire Allan. We became quite good friends and I believe he came more frequently to our embassy for dinner than to any other embassy. So much for worrying about your husband's arguments. That evening, which began so inauspiciously, had turned out well. I now had another friend, Sweet Pea, who became my comfort blanket when worse things happened. And the Bradens even asked us back to dinner.

The most desired invitation in Georgetown was to Katharine Graham's house. There was generally only one topic of conversation in Washington, politics, and the guests at Katharine Graham's parties were those who made political news – the latest National Security Adviser or Secretary of State or newly elected senator. She was the quintessential political hostess. Even the Georgetown haters, reverse snobs, Hill hermits, right-wing Republicans who despised the news reporting of the left-leaning *Post*, cabinet secretaries and acquaintances who had their names and reputations hung out to dry on Katharine Graham's pages would not hesitate to attend her parties if invited.

The *Post*, never a fan of the Reagan administration, was especially harsh during the Iran-Contra episode. One night at the home of another Georgetown hostess, during dinner at the height of the crisis in 1986, Walter Pincus, the *Post*'s defense writer, covering developments for the newspaper along with Bob Woodward of Watergate fame, predicted that George Shultz and Caspar Weinberger would be forced out of office within a month and that Reagan would have to leave the Presidency by July. Many of those writing gave the impression that they wanted to see the President destroyed, and this animus was as evident in the pages of the *Post* as in other major papers. But politics is politics. Keep your friends close and hug your enemies closer. When Katharine Graham's children gave her a huge seventieth birthday party a year later in June 1987, both Reagans attended, sat through the speeches until almost midnight, and the President gave a toast. He described how Katharine Graham, knowing that he was absent for several days from the White House when they had just arrived in Washington, had called Nancy and asked her for dinner just in case she was lonely. The President did not make a speech about Katharine Graham and her newspaper. It was her personal gesture that had meant something to the Reagans – his little toast was an attempt to disassociate Katharine Graham from politics, power and the *Post*. To the surprise of many, Mrs. Reagan and Mrs. Graham became good friends towards the end of the Reagan administration – Mrs. Reagan did not hold Mrs. Graham personally responsible for what was written in the *Post* about the administration. Mrs. Graham, I think, appreciated Mrs. Reagan treating her not only as the personification of a powerful newspaper but as a human being.

Even so, at the beginning of Art Buchwald's speech, during the birthday dinner, the audience roared with nervous laughter when he yelled at the guests, "Hypocrites. You all came here out of fear." Buchwald, an old friend of Katharine Graham as well as of Ben Bradlee, knows of fear and loathing amidst the Potomac swamps.

Katharine Graham, in her Georgetown house, one of the few with a large front lawn and a circular driveway, was always an attentive, hardworking hostess. Even though there might have been sixty or more at her parties, she had a sense of duty unlike some other grand hostesses, and always tried to have a word of welcome with each of her guests. At the dinners we attended, aside from the political men and women, her guests included old friends, family, members of her board, her editors Ben Bradlee and Meg Greenfield, and always a few writers from her newspaper or *Newsweek* magazine, as well as those who wrote for rival newspapers or commented on television. There would occasionally be a spattering of *W* people from New York and those she approved of from former administrations. Her guests would mill about engaging in intense conversation in her red drawing room for an extended cocktail hour until her French chef decided that dinner was ready. The traditional Washington round tables would have been set up, eight to ten guests at each; four very substantial courses (rather more than usual at private parties in Washington) would be passed around on large platters, and coffee would be served at the tables. Katharine Graham's house was run like a small but significant embassy in Washington. But it was far more important than any embassy. It was the engine room of the *Washington Post.*

Evangeline Bruce, "wife of" the universally respected American ambassador to the U.K., France, Germany and China, the late David Bruce, maintained a wide network of international connections, mostly British. Evangeline, about five foot eleven with an elegant swan neck and often photographed and eulogized in *W*, tended to speak in whispered tones and was considered a fashion example rather than a fashion victim. Fond of eloquence, she placed literacy over power in her choice of guests. Her social hallmark was her large Sunday brunch, although she would give small lunches and dinners from time to time. Concentrating less on American political figures than Katharine Graham, Evangeline would often give a brunch in honour of a British literary lion such as Edna O'Brien or Harold Pinter, or of royalty, such as Princess Margaret, or British aristocracy, such as the Duchess of Devonshire, whom she entertained often. The Georgetown set, always highly Anglophile, rarely had difficulty attracting to such events members of the administration or some senators such as the liberal Mac Mathias from Maryland, John Warner from Virginia (ex-husband and still friend of Elizabeth Taylor) and the extraordinarily wealthy John Heinz from Pennsylvania. (Joe Alsop used to say that "the best Senators don't dine out" – which, in the main, was true.)

Evangeline Bruce's brunches were floating, casual affairs, with no chairs, few introductions and no precise arrival or departure time so long as it was between one and three. She was a good friend of the famous British writer Anthony Powell, author of *At Lady Molly's*, one of the novels in his "Dance to the Music of Time" series. Lady Molly used to be married to a marchioness and had to preside over rigidly formal parties. As soon as her husband died, she rebelled from this formula and was soon known for her unstructured parties with the most surprising mix of people. To me there seemed to be an element of Lady Molly at Evangeline Bruce's brunches. She had been a gifted diplomatic wife who once had to abide by the rules of protocol. But when her diplomatic duties ceased, she was able to cut the formalities and do a Lady Molly. One could stay for five minutes or two hours. There was a wide diversity of guests as well as the regulars. Among the cruising journalists, one might bump into Caspar Weinberger or Michael Deaver or other top officials. One might see Henry Mitchell, the gardening expert from the *Post*, hanging around the shrimp bowl, or George Shultz talking to her caterer (a Russian aristocrat) by the oyster bar, or Harold Pinter in the garden. At one such brunch Pinter informed me (although he hadn't a clue whom he was talking to) that he was going to Turkey in order to protest their practice of imprisoning people for political purposes. I asked Mr. Pinter, "Don't the Soviet Union, Romania and Czechoslovakia go in for that kind of thing as well?"

"Have you," he said, bitterly, "received any Czech toes in the mail?" I replied negatively. "Well, I have received Turkish toes," and he stalked off.

Unlike Anthony Powell's character, Evangeline Bruce was fastidious about her house. Guests discreetly took note of the delicate yellow silk curtains in the dining room, the fur throws in the green room downstairs, her Aubusson rug and the unusual and sometimes spectacular arrangements of plants and shrubs on her tables. At one Sunday brunch, Joe Alsop, one of her oldest friends, settled down with a cup of coffee on a settee. "Joe," she breathed, "don't sit there. You'll spill the coffee. Go upstairs and drink it by the oysters." Joe, usually not one to take orders about where to drink his coffee, rose obediently and went upstairs to finish his cup safely, but with only the oysters for company. The food at her brunches was elegantly served but fashionably spare. A large smoked salmon usually sat in front of a window facing her garden where she had primroses or pansies planted outside for the occasion. A maid would pass around very thin egg and curried chicken sandwiches, crusts off, and, always, caramelized bacon.

Other Georgetown dinner parties – of the type often given by the Bradlees and the Krafts – would be stand-up or sit-on-the-floor or sofa affairs. A year after our arrival Sally Quinn invited us to a stand-up buffet in honour of television producer Norman Lear and his wife, Frances. Later Frances divorced her husband and started *Lear's*, a magazine for older women (like me) with photographs reminiscent of those Oil of Olay *"Can you guess* how old I am?" ads. Norman Lear was the financial political force behind People for the American Way, a controversial organization that spearheaded the campaigns against Robert Bork, President Reagan's candidate for the position of Supreme Court Justice. Those present at Sally and Ben's party included her best friend, the writer Nora Ephron, along with Sally's favourites in the *Washington Post*. There were few political people, which was generally true of Bradlee parties during the Reagan adminis-tration. I had just written a humorous piece about being an ambassador's wife in the *Post* magazine section and had to come alone to the party because Allan was out of town. Sally, blonde, pretty, much younger than Ben Bradlee, was called the Madame Nu of the Style section because of the reputed influence she had on the newspaper through her husband. She congratulated me "on being so brave to come by yourself," observed my behaviour during the evening and told me that I "was doing very well at her party" and that some of her guests seemed to like my article. I was being sized up to see if I fitted into the Bradlee group from the *Washington Post*. I don't think I made it.

Although we never did lose the feeling of being strangers at Court we did attend some of the ceremonies. A lot of hostesses gave lively, small dinners in the Georgetown style. None surpassed Susan Mary Alsop, Joe's divorced wife, whose fine Georgetown home was a few blocks from his. I had read Susan Mary Alsop's books long before I met her. In Ottawa I had read *Letters to Marietta*, an account of her time in Paris after the Second World War as the young wife of an American diplomat, Bill Pattison, written to her best friend, Marietta Tree. Susan Mary Alsop had been a friend of Lady Diana Cooper and the mistress of Duff Cooper (although this was never revealed in her book) and had been close to Nancy Mitford. Because of Susan Mary's books, she was the only nonpolitical person I had heard of and wanted to meet before I came to Washington. I was introduced to this frail and elegantly dressed woman, wearing bloomers by Balmain, at one of Polly Kraft's parties. Susan Mary, despite a series of delicate eye operations, was working on her latest book, *Dance of the Congress of Vienna*. Her entertainment style consisted of blending extraordinary politeness, courtesy and attentiveness to all of her guests with a talent for mixing the academic and political worlds with foreign aristocracy.

During our first year in Washington, shortly after we had met, she invited us to a black-tie dinner. The day of the event she called me up at five in the afternoon and said, "You're it. I'm giving you an early-warning signal so you can be prepared. You're sitting on Henry's right." "Henry" was Henry Kissinger. I had an awful three or four hours thinking how to "be prepared." I even picked up his memoirs and started reading them, but soon realized what a futile act that was.

At dinner he seemed anxious about possible Jewish criticism of a speech he was going to make concerning Israel. I said, "You shouldn't worry about them. They think you're king of the Jews."

He said, "You know, Madame Ambassador," paying attention to me for the first time, "I think you may have a point there."

That evening gave us further insight into Canada's standing in Washington. The French ambassador and his wife, the Verniez-Palliezes, also attended the dinner. At one point Susan Mary rose and toasted Henry Kissinger. Allan, realizing he was the senior ambassador present (by a couple of weeks), knew that he would have to say a few words. It was that kind of dinner. As he rose, a Georgetown woman pulled him down and hissed, "Let the French ambassador speak," horrified that a Canadian would take the floor when a Frenchman was available. Allan, confused, sat down, and the French ambassador rose and gave a flowery tribute to Dr. Kissinger. The lady who had pulled Allan down so suddenly realized that she, an arbiter of protocol, had done him wrong. As well, she had disliked the French ambassador's toast. "Get up," she said to Allan, "Henry deserves a better toast than that." This social and political devotion to France and Britain was symptomatic not merely of Georgetown but of all of Washington, the Reagan administration included.

Equally adept as political hosts were Rowland Evans, a dapper man from a blueblood Philadelphia background, and his wife, Katherine, then editor of the *Washington Monthly*. Rowland was a hardworking journalist and co-author of the widely syndicated Evans and Novak column. Evenings spent in Rowland and Kay Evans's Georgetown solarium, with my shoes slipped off under the table feeling the warmed tiles beneath my soles, were enlivened by Roly's boundless curiosity, capacity for friendship, sense of humour, civility and direct, sometimes brutally direct, approach. "Well, is your husband going to be fired because of this Deaver business?" he'd ask, half joking, half working journalist gathering information. Immediately his wife (Polly Kraft's cousin), who had radar ears, would yell, even if she was sitting at another table, "Roly!" Her "Roly" warnings would punctuate the conversation during the evening. Rowland Evans would respond with an innocent and feigned "sorry to be misunderstood" look and then proceed with the inquisition.

Through Susan Mary Alsop we were introduced to David and Susan Brinkley, who knew everyone in Georgetown (but did not live there). The Brinkleys served delicious food because Susan was the chef – an anomaly in catered Washington. David Brinkley, who knew everyone and remembered everything, lacked some recognizable features so endemic in the upper media. David Brinkley didn't have wandering-eye trouble – that is, he never looked over your shoulder to see who were the most important people in the room – very reassuring to a newcomer like myself. He'd concentrate on his conversation with you and not make you worry that you were taking him away from someone more newsworthy at the party. Brinkley believed that being a tinker, tailor or Indian chief was just as high a calling as being a television commentator. (I'm not sure if congressmen, however, came into the tinker tailor category.) Unlike some others in his profession, Brinkley did not believe that television or press pundits had cornered the market in moral judgement or political wisdom. "We have to sell soap," he used to say. "And don't you forget it." Once I asked him if there was any future in the print media, given the enormous role television plays in interpreting and selecting the news. "I don't know if people in the future will read the *New York Times* or the *Washington Post*. But those papers have to exist – if only for television. The networks couldn't last a day without them," he said sardonically. "They do our research."

Jim Lehrer, of the *MacNeil/Lehrer NewsHour*, was also devoid of press pomposity. He could often be seen standing in a corner talking to the "wife of" an ex-administration official (a "used-to-be-close-to," a "has-been," a "nobody" in the terminology of crueltown Washington) about some subject such as dog training. His interest would never flag. A subtle, humorous man, he appeared to relish everyone's conversation. Jim and Kate Lehrer, not certified members of the Georgetown set, were nevertheless much-desired guests. In Washington, where information was always at a premium, the *MacNeil/Lehrer* report became a kind of teaching device for senators and congressmen. Many would tape the show and watch it late at night so that they would know its contents next day.

Others who were of the Georgetown set, without necessarily owning real estate in the area, were several of Washington's greatest humorists – Art Buchwald and his wife, Ann; the politically astute lawyer Robert Strauss and wife, Helen; the wittiest senator of our time, Alan Simpson and wife, Ann; as well as *New Yorker* correspondent Elizabeth Drew and her husband, David; broadcaster Andrea Mitchell; chairman of the Federal Reserve Board, Alan Greenspan; Reagan's in-house biographer, Edmund Morris, and his wife, Sylvia, Clare Boothe Luce's biographer; and the civilized and erudite labour leader Lane Kirkland and his wife, Irena, who became, along with Susan and David Brinkley, our close friends.

What I hadn't realized when we first came to Washington was that many of the Reaganites were curious about the Georgetown set. And the Georgetown set, fed up with being ignored by the Carter administration, wanted in turn to meet members of the new team, even though many of them were life-long Democrats with political views that seemed to have fossilized during the fifties and sixties like flies embedded in old Kennedy amber. Somehow we found ourselves in the unique position of being able to introduce many members of the Reagan administration to the Georgetown crowd. Each side revealed to us their curiosity about the other and complained to us about the coldness of the other. Georgetown, especially the press component, had two major grievances: the lack of invitations to White House dinners, and, quite frequently, "to hell with him, he doesn't return his phone calls." I heard this said several times about the highly sought-after Michael Deaver, and I believe it was one of the reasons the press went after him with such a vengeance when he later got into trouble. The Reaganites came to be flattered by the attention of the Georgetown set, while the Georgetown set, in turn, came to be flattered by the company of the new administration. We came to be neutral observers of this compelling engagement between liberal Georgetown and conservative Reaganites, an engagement that was always valued and constantly cultivated but was marked and marred by scoops, scandals, political antagonisms and the need to sell soap – to use David Brinkley's phrase.

Our embassy thus became kind of a no-man's-land in the early Reagan years where the Georgetown set, the media and members of the current and former administrations would meet. The presence of the media would attract senators and congressmen to our dinners. This of course helped Allan enormously in his work, because at these events he was able to corner an elusive official or legislator (one who never returned his calls) and focus their attention upon Canada's problems, even on a topic as obscure to them as the value of stumpage rights. The presence of formidable Washington columnists and broadcasters added greatly to the liveliness of the conversation, as well as to the exchange of gossip and information, while acting as a magnet for all sorts of important players in the Washington political game. Into the unique brew of social Washington with all its political and snobbish components, a Canadian ingredient was thus added, even if only in the form of an occasionally Canadian shake – or shingle.

One early example of our commingling parties was the dinner we gave in honour of Ed Meese, old and close friend of the President, who was then the White House counsellor. We placed Lane Kirkland and Ed Meese at the same table. Later both men told me that they had never met each other before. Meese was hardly a union man but seem gratified that he had at last met the head of the AFL-CIO. Obviously, Lane was not a fan of Meese but was bemused by his seating.

Many men who disagree on most issues profoundly and publicly are not averse to getting to know a little about their adversary in person. As I discovered, however, that was not always true of their wives. After a few years in Washington we had a large "arms control" dinner and invited, among others, Paul Nitze, who was Reagan's arms-control czar, along with Paul Warnke, who had the same position in the Carter administration. I had seated Mrs. Warnke on the left of Paul Nitze. Each time Paul Nitze made a statement about the Soviet Union, Mrs. Warnke contradicted him. Paul Nitze appeared oblivious, but the conversation was heated, almost acerbic. As the guests were leaving, Mrs. Warnke came up to me and said, "When I saw that you put me next to Paul Nitze on your seating plan, I was going to walk out. Do you know that during a congressional hearing, he called my husband a traitor?" Naturally I didn't know anything of the sort and was embarrassed and nonplussed. "Anyway," she said, "my husband told me to calm down, take a big scotch and soda and not let Paul Nitze get my goat. I'm glad I didn't walk out." So was I.

Although we gave many large parties during our seven years, I think the parties we liked best and which I know our guests enjoyed most were those small ones around a circular table I had had built out of plywood specifically to seat fourteen people. These dinners were very much in the Georgetown style, especially as practised in Joe Alsop's basement dining room. Our small dinners, usually arranged at the last moment to make them as informal as possible, were designed for holding a single conversation among a mixture of politicians, columnists, historians and others, regardless of profession, political stripe or ideology. The sole criterion for an invitation was a capacity to be provocative. I simply hated stuffy parties, and I believed that the reason we got so many strong and independent-minded people to come was that they knew they were going to be stimulated intellectually even if it meant risking anger and hot debate. At one such small dinner three members of the Carter cabinet happened to be in attendance – Carter's National Security Adviser, Zbigniew Brzezinski, his special Trade Representative Robert Strauss, and his Secretary of Energy Jim Schlesinger. Schlesinger, who, along with Brzezinski, was strongly supporting George Bush for President, showed Robert Strauss a letter with which Dukakis was associated reflecting a weak stance on defense on Dukakis's part. Strauss, a leading Democrat, was going strongly with Dukakis, although he had not been Strauss's initial choice. Strauss knew about the paper and didn't like it much, but he liked it even less when Schlesinger displayed it and asked Strauss to comment. Strauss threw the paper aside and it just missed the head of Jim Lehrer who was coming in the front door. Richard Thornburgh, the newly appointed Attorney General after Ed Meese, had just arrived in Washington and was also present. I wonder if he thought this was usual Washington behaviour. Tension at an embassy always makes for a memorable party even if it means that the host is insulted. Robert Strauss was very close to many members of Congress, including Robert Dole, leader of the Republican Senate, and Jim Wright, the controversial Democratic leader of the House, who had been accused of conducting his own foreign policy in Central America. At one point during the meal, Allan said, drawing on his experience with Congress during the U.S.-Canada Free Trade negotiations, "I believe that the United States is now being governed by two executive branches instead of one. I even believe Congress has tipped the balance and is definitely more powerful than the Presidency." This statement irritated Strauss, who turned to Allan and said, "Gotlieb, you talk like a fool." There was dead silence around the table, and I felt like blowing up at Robert Strauss, who had become a good friend of ours, for insulting my husband in our embassy. Instead I apologized for not serving him potato pancakes, which was his favourite dish at our table. The tension gave way that night to one of the best discussions of the upcoming political contest between Bush and Dukakis that we, and possibly our guests, had heard in Washington.

The exuberance of the Reagan administration waned, of course, during the last couple of years of their long reign. The Georgetown set, the Potomac permanents, became blasé and just a little bored with the old gang. Those from the Reagan administration, wounded by the Iran-Contra affair (some of them fatally) and tired of the endless "sleaze" allegations against them, withdrew more and more into themselves. They were going back to California, they were stale news, transients, soon to be powerless, soon to be "used-to-be's."

The Georgetown set was already beginning to bubble over the Bush-Dukakis contest. Polls were taken at every party, and Dukakis usually won – for a time. The Reagan people would sometimes be invited and the Georgetown set would make gracious but slightly absent murmurs of goodwill to the soon-to-be-departing ones. Soon Georgetown was eagerly looking forward to Bush, the likely winner.

Although many of the hostesses of Georgetown were getting on in years and their social cachet was slowly fading towards the end of our time in Washington, I was aware of no new ones rising up to replace them. But Georgetown parties will always be part of the political scene as long as Kay Graham remains a force in Washington. The network of people who gave political parties in Georgetown during my years in Washington were her friends or long-time acquaintances. And Georgetown dinners are certainly continuing with the new Bush team. Among them are many on our old guest lists, such as deputy secretary of State Larry Eagleburger, National Security Adviser Brent Scowcroft, Director of the Budget Richard Darman, and Boyden Gray, the White House Legal Adviser. And so it may always be. For the hidden message of the Georgetown set is, "We'll be here when you're gone. We'll be here when the parties start again."

12/"La Malcontenta"

AFTER AN INITIAL couple of years of on-the-job training I had learned how to be a hostess, a hotel manager and a saleswoman. I went out to dinner or entertained at the Residence almost every night and wore more evening dresses in a month than I had during the twenty-nine years of my marriage. My life was filled with social, political and promotional activity. So why did Allan tease me about being "La Malcontenta"?

La Malcontenta was the unhappy wife of a seventeenth-century Venetian nobleman who, dismayed by his wife's worldly behaviour in Venice, had her exiled to a lonely Palladian villa among the reedy marshes of the Brenta Canal. Removed from her Venetian life of parties and pleasures, she eventually died of boredom. In sympathy the locals named her villa La Malcontenta. My situation was precisely the opposite to that of the Venetian lady. I was La Malcontenta because our social duties exhausted me and I found no time or energy to write.

This would not have been a serious excuse for a better writer. Trollope wrote more than fifty novels and invented the British Post Office. Robertson Davies was a newspaper publisher, then a professor, and wrote his plays and novels in what time he had to spare. Barbara Pym worked full-time in an African Information Centre and wrote her novels in the evenings. Only I (in the words of Lyndon Johnson) could not walk and chew gum at the same time. In Washington, the only writing I had done was some travel pieces for the *New York Times*, a couple of articles for the *Washington Post Magazine* and an aborted attempt at a book about influential women in Canada, an absurd thing to try from our post in Washington.

Eventually, as the newness and strangeness of my life wore off, a routine settled in and my writer's itch began to scratch. But our program was as heavy as ever and Allan was dubious about me taking on a writing project. Although he was the ambassador, I was always the one complaining of fatigue. He propelled himself energetically through the day, which often started with him briefing businessmen or officials at breakfast meetings, then speaking at lunch and lobbying various congressmen and administration officials. In the evening he was scrupulous about showing up at receptions and always looked forward to the dinners that we gave or to which we were invited. He burned with a two-hundred-watt bulb and I burned with a sixty. My mother used to say, "You never had much energy even when you were a little girl. You'd get so cranky towards the end of the afternoon I'd have to put you in a room by yourself." In Washington, if I saw too many people, I still got cranky and the whites of my eyes turned green.

Allan's job was substantive. I was involved only with the froth – necessary though it was to his work. I wanted to do something of my own. Allan, realizing the "froth" was not going to end until we left Washington, said, "Why don't you try and enjoy yourself?"

I was truly La Malcontenta because I never did learn to enjoy myself at certain kinds of Washington parties, particularly the big ones. A kind of social competition takes place in Washington, which can be soul-destroying. What surprised me was that so many serious-minded and intelligent people in Washington as well as New York, people with talent and humour, would get miffed, hurt and even depressed if they were not invited to what they considered "in" parties. This affected not only the socialites but the media as well. Journalists and columnists were notorious for the way they treated private parties, including the ones they give themselves, as opportunities for networking, not for enjoyment.

In 1983 Sandra Gwyn, the Canadian writer, gave me a book of the hilarious "Dear Bill" letters from a fictional Denis Thatcher, husband of Margaret Thatcher. A few weeks after I read it, it occurred to me that I might attempt a similar epistolary book about Washington.

I wrote my first "Dear Beverly" letter and sent it off to an agent in New York, thinking I would publish a book of such letters after I left. Coincidentally, I had lunch with Meg Greenfield, the Editorial Page editor of the *Washington Post*, the day after I sent off my first letter.

Meg, a small, reticent, round-faced woman, an observer rather than a talker, has created what is probably one of the most interesting and varied editorial pages in North America. She has published writers as politically diverse as George Will, Michael Kinsley, Charles Krautheimer and Dave Broder, as well as Norman Podhoretz, Evans and Novak, Richard Cohen, Mark Shields, Henry Kissinger and Jeane Kirkpatrick. Her pages offered a wider range of opinion than the rather predictable editorial pages of the *New York Times*, the *Post*'s closest rival.

Meg is a middle-of-the-road liberal with an old-fashioned respect for tradition. If you rang her at the *Post*, her secretary responded, "Miss Greenfield's office." I learned not to put "Ms." Greenfield on her place card at dinner. Although, along with the majority of writers in the *Washington Post*, her leanings were probably towards the Democrats, she cast a doubtful eye on the excesses of the left of that party, whether those of Jesse Jackson or of the more strident affirmative-action movements. Many Republicans who complained regularly about the partisan reporting of the *Washington Post* and *New York Times* told me that Meg Greenfield was an editorial-page editor who was capable of seeing their point of view.

About a year before our lunch Meg had noticed a short piece I had written for the *New York Times* op-ed section about "Canada not being chic." She had asked me then if I could write something like that for her. So much time had gone by that I thought she had forgotten all about the conversation. Just as we were finishing Meg's usual menu choice at the Jockey Club (iced tea, consommé, seafood salad – dressing on the side), she asked me if I had any writing to show her. Diffidently, I sent her the letter, which I thought too frivolous for her highly political pages. But she seemed to like it and asked me to do another. She liked the second too, and we agreed that I would write two letters a month for the *Post*. The next week two extra-long letters appeared within a few days of each other, occupying a large portion of the op-ed pages. Meg even had the letters outlined in a curved-back frame.

In this manner I became a member of the Washington media.

They say that Washington has more lawyers, psychiatrists and journalists per capita than any other city in the world. Columnists, editors and television commentators belong to the "upper media," a phrase I invented in my columns. The stars of the upper media living in Washington included George Will, Ben Bradlee, Meg Greenfield, William Safire, David Brinkley, Sam Donaldson, Leslie Stahl (of CBS), Andrea Mitchell (of NBC), Pat Buchanan, Tom Braden (of CNN), Jim Lehrer (of PBS), Johnny Apple of the *New York Times*, John McLaughlin, Scotty Reston, Arnaud de Borchgrave (editor of the second newspaper in Washington, the *Washington Times*) and the late Joe Kraft.

Less glamorous than the upper media, but very useful for the administration and Congress, are the regional working media. No congressman from Arkansas or Ohio would ever neglect the local newspaper's Washington correspondent or the local cable television producer. In fact, the Gridiron, Washington's most influential roast – an evening that is supposed to relieve any little tensions that may have come up between the Powerful Press and the Powerful Jobs – is organized by the working media.

The rules of the Gridiron are sacrosanct.

1) Individuals are asked, not couples.
2) The men wear white tie and tails.
3) Everyone is flattered to be asked except the President and the *really* Powerful Jobs, who would rather be at home.
4) The hosts and guests sit at long narrow tables and are given a copious amount of food and drink.

5) After dinner reporters dressed as turnips and *Saturday Night Live* coneheads get up on stage and sing sarcastic lyrics about their guests to tunes like "Hello, Dolly."

6) Everyone looks at the President to see how he's taking it.

The Gridiron is a potent forum for changing "perceptions," a favourite word of the so-called morality-watchers or ethics press. At the 1983 Gridiron dinner, Nancy Reagan made a surprise appearance on the stage. She was dressed in rags, sang "I'm Second-Hand Rose" and smashed a teacup on the floor. Until that moment Nancy Reagan had been "Fancy Nancy" in the press and was presented to the public as a woman interested only in buying new china for the White House and borrowing designer clothes. The reporters roared at her self-mockery and began to report her activities in a kinder light. Her standing in the polls went from the cellar to the penthouse and stayed there, despite the Iran-Contra affair and despite the astrology, until she and President Reagan left the White House. Nancy Reagan's stunning "Second-Hand Rose" act was one of Michael Deaver's many successful ideas for setting the most appealing stage for the President and his wife.

I think I was the only ambassador's wife to be invited to the Gridiron. And the only reason I was invited was because I had stopped being merely "wife of" and had become a writer.

The third, murkier, media category in Washington includes a swarm of freelancers, hatchet girls, hacks, desperadoes and paparazzi who would sell their underpants to Lyndon LaRouche in order to get a piece or picture published in anything from *People* magazine to the *Post* as well as the many Washington magazines – *Regardies* is a prime example – that rely excessively on dubious anonymous quotes.

The fourth media category comprises foreign correspondents. They are generally not appreciated in Washington. Neither the administration nor Congress will bother with them, for the simple reason that foreign T.V. and newspapers can't deliver votes or local publicity. In most instances their countries are not on the

American power-players' agenda. One Canadian correspondent from Quebec's biggest French-language newspaper, *La Presse*, was successful in getting interviews from American politicians only when he wore an identity card saying LA PRESS, which looked just like L.A. PRESS to a busy candidate at an American political convention. The Canadian correspondent thought he had hit the jackpot when Jesse Jackson stopped to talk to him. But Jackson looked closer at his identity card and asked him who he represented. When the correspondent told the truth, Jackson turned his back and walked away. Jackson's behaviour on that occasion was typical of most American politicians towards the foreign media.

Shortly after Brian Mulroney became Prime Minister, the Canadian columnist Allan Fotheringham was posted to Washington by his newspaper and magazine publishers. Fotheringham, whom I had known for a long time, asked me to lunch shortly after his arrival and intimated that he would like to be included in the more glamorous dinners and receptions we were planning to hold. He hearkened back to our old friendship and also told me that he had become a "close to" the Mulroneys and often lunched with Mila. Allan had just been re-appointed to Washington by the new Prime Minister but we barely knew the Mulroneys. The emphasis Fotheringham put on his relationship with the Mulroneys made me feel uncomfortable. I sensed a certain intimidation in Fotheringham's name-dropping.

Ruefully I realised that we would be damned if we didn't invite him and damned if we did. I included him in many of our parties, knowing full well I would regret my decision later on, hoping in the meantime that Fotheringham's best side, his sense of fun, would come to the fore.

Fotheringham used us as a conduit to meet prominent Americans – fair game because of the difficulty foreign journalists have in getting to know American politicians. What was not fair game was describing nasty personal tidbits about us to the female reporters he dated. Two of his girlfriends in particular wrote mean articles about us, although they scarcely knew us, replete with pejorative anonymous quotes – which to me sounded a lot like Fotheringham.

He was successful in gaining entrée to our embassy, but less so to the American media. I never saw his by-line in U.S. newspapers. A high-up deep throat in the *Washington Post* mentioned that Fotheringham had been peppering the paper with unasked-for columns, but that they were too anti-American and anti-Reagan to be published in that newspaper. Needless to say, the *Washington Post* was hardly a pro-Reagan or conservative newspaper.

It was clear as time went on that Fotheringham was unhappy in the U.S. and never understood or wanted to understand the American system. On the whole he disliked Americans and this showed in his writing.

In Canada Fotheringham was a big fish; in the U.S. it was hard for him to see himself reduced to minnow size.

Specialists in public relations have described the *Washington Post* op-ed section as some of the most expensive newspaper real estate in the world. Meg Greenfield called it the "Vatican" and the rest of the newspaper, Ben Bradlee's kingdom, "Italy." Suddenly I was being printed in her section, and there were plenty in the journalistic clergy inside and out of Washington who were not happy with the idea of an ambassador's wife taking up writing space in the "Vatican."

A year earlier, when I had written a couple of travel pieces for the *New York Times*, some newsmen in Canada had thought it terrible that "the ambassador's wife" was doing "piece-work." Perhaps they should be included with those who believe an ambassador's wife should stick to what she's supposed to know best: being dignified. When I attended a ladies' luncheon shortly after my letters began to appear, a woman on my left said, "Don't you think it's undignified for an ambassador's wife to make fun of herself and her husband in a newspaper?" I was nonplussed but, encouraged by sympathetic laughter around the table, I said truthfully, "I was a writer long before I became a dignified ambassador's wife. Being a writer comes more naturally to me than being dignified."

She wasn't the only person who told me I shouldn't make fun of myself, given my exalted if temporary status. But the people who wrote to me about my columns liked the idea of me poking fun at diplomatic or political stuffiness and pretension. In many people's minds dignity connotes stuffiness. Stuffiness is a characteristic I dislike in others. Why was it necessary for me to be stuffy just because I had become an ambassador's wife for the first time in my life?

Of course there were repercussions – in Washington and in Ottawa – even though the only real-life characters I made fun of in my column were my husband, "Mr. Ambassador," and myself. The "Dear Beverly" letters were intended to be humorous social commentary on the way human beings react to temporary power and temporary status. My characters who were clothed in fiction included such figures as Popsie Tribble, the Washington socialite; Sonny Goldstone, the Gilded Bachelor and Social Asset; Baron Spitte, the Dusty diplomat; Senator Pod; and Congressman Otterbach.

Here's how I once introduced Popsie Tribble, the woman who loves to put me down, explaining her social manifesto:

Popsie Tribble dropped by looking marvellous in a suit designed for her by Oscar and gave me a few tips about how I should behave. It was kind of her to take the time, since she has a pretty busy schedule being such a well-known socialite. . . .

"In Washington," she said, lighting up a Balkan Sorbranie, "parties aren't supposed to be fun for ambassadors' wives. Remember that you're sitting next to a job, not a person. Sondra, you have to charm the Powerful Job."

"Aside from the President, who do I have to be nice to?" I asked.

"Anyone who has a Job-That-Influences-Government-Policies. . . "

"What about rich people?"

"Powerful Jobs are more important than money in Washington, but money can't hurt."

Popsie's rich, so I think she was being straight with me. She was planning a party, and I asked her if she would seat me next to a Powerful Job who was warm and witty. Popsie said, "Any Powerful Job who is warm and witty sits by me.". . .

"Should I be nicer to the men than the women?" I asked.

"Well, I wouldn't snub Elizabeth Dole or Justice Sandra Day O'Connor or wives of Powerful Jobs, especially the second wives. Second wives," Popsie repeated, "have more influence because they are younger."

She was one up on me again. She's on her second husband and I'm still with Mr. Ambassador. I'm not sure if Popsie is younger than me, but I let that one go.

The "Shuttle Huddle" piece I wrote about going from Washington to New York on Eastern Airlines seemed to tickle the wife of the Vice President, Barbara Bush, who wrote me a complimentary note about it.

On normal plane trips, Beverly, the rules of social behaviour are cut and dried. Don't make eye contact, keep your skirts drawn in, and place your carry-on luggage on the seat beside you so a stranger won't sit down.

These rules are more embarrassing to follow on the shuttle, even though we all make the attempt. You see, Beverly, except for the odd tourist like you, everyone on the shuttle knows each other.

There's Lionel Portant, world-famous columnist and T.V. commentator, who broke bread at our Residence two days before, with his head buried in the *New York Times*, avoiding eye contact with Mr. Ambassador. Melvin Thistle, Jr., from State is pretending to sleep standing up because Joe Promisall, the world's most expensive lobbyist, talking anxiously on the pay phone, might hang up and talk to him. Joe Promisall used to have Thistle's job in a past administration, and, who knows, might get it again in the next.

Beverly, Powerful Jobs become Profitable Jobs when Powerful Jobs leave government. Profitable Jobs are more sociable, unless they suffer from "decompression," a Washington codeword for an emotional state caused by loss of power.

In the bleakness of Shuttle Gate 18, decompressing former Mr. Secretaries who used to fly on government planes to New York now have to press their bodies against people whose phone calls they never returned.

Washingtonians were sure that they knew the identities of the characters. In fact the Swedish ambassador, Count Willie Wachmeister, told me that he was certain he was Baron Spitte. Not true. Others told me they were sure that Lionel Portant was Joe Kraft. (This came especially from his rival columnists.) Not true either. My characters were based on the absurd characteristics of all ambassadors, journalists, politicians. And Popsie Tribble, the Great Destabilizer, was my personification of W.

Because of Allan's position, I carefully stayed away from partisan politics and ground no political axes. So my columns fell between two stools. For some people they were too discreet, and that was one of the reasons they eventually ceased. Early on, a freelancer, one of those who had been desperate to get an invitation to our embassy, wrote a parody of my columns, complaining bitterly that there was nothing to read because I didn't dish out spicy Georgetown gossip. Official Ottawa, on the other hand, thought my columns were indiscreet. The External Affairs Department haughtily told Allan that they had not given me permission to write in the *Washington Post*. (As if I were an employee of External Affairs.) As further warning they told him that an ambassador's wife in Singapore or Thailand had wanted to write a column in the local newspaper about, if I remember correctly, nature walks in Central Asia. She had been forbidden to do so by the Department. Later, Michele Landsberg was to write a weekly column in the Toronto *Globe and Mail* that was highly critical of the United States and its policies, while her husband was ambassador to the UN. Perhaps my unpolemical pieces paved the way for her. Most ridiculous of all, the officials sent a memorandum to the Minister of External Affairs, Allan MacEachen, telling him that the Canadian ambassador was guilty of conflict of interest because his wife was obviously planning to use confidential information not available to the public to make her columns interesting. But the nastiest reaction of the External Affairs Department was a libellous, anonymously written, anti-Semitic parody of one of my "Dear Beverly" letters that circulated throughout the ministry and was passed on to the press. It described Allan eating corned-beef sandwiches in North Winnipeg (the Jewish section) with Ed Schreyer, then Governor-General of Canada, and plotting with two Canadian advisers of Pierre Trudeau, Michael Pitfield and Jim Coutts, to find ways to make the Canadian government more pro-Israel. It libelled Allan by accusing him of forcing the External Affairs Department to buy my books at a huge cost. When it appeared in the press, there was nothing much we could do about it. What was sickening was that mature Foreign Service officers were proud of this hateful and malicious piece and that there were more than a few Canadian diplomats who wondered why we objected to a little "fun."

Questions were also asked in the Canadian Parliament about my columns, although nobody had read them at the time. I was compared to another ambassador's wife who was alleged to have had something to do with a dope transaction.

Allan was amused. As ambassador he felt the benefit of my column immediately. Senators and officials in the administration gave him speedier appointments – many out of sheer curiosity. His "recognition factor" increased enormously. Not a bad thing when there are a hundred and fifty other ambassadors in the Washington herd.

"If they're going to fire me over your column," Allan decided, "then let them. It would be a wonderful way to go."

The reaction to my columns in the hothouse of Washington was more complex. There's barely a Washington job that won't get a wife into trouble if a righteous meddler from the press or leakers on the other side of the political fence decide to use a distorting magnifying glass. I learned that these people are often sanctimonious pseudo-feminists who are the first to give lip-service to equal rights. Although many wives of public officials work in Washington, you never know what an "investigative reporter" can dig up and misrepresent if you're in the public eye.

Antoinette Hatfield, a senator's wife, selling real estate; Michael Deaver's wife, Carolyn, working for a public relations firm; Ursula Meese; Betty Wright, wife of the Speaker of the House; Mrs. Newt Gingrich, wife of the Republican leader of Congress – all received nasty, distorted and overblown publicity about their jobs.

All the press has to say is that the wife is earning money because her husband pulled strings – an accusation almost impossible to deny in Washington. Everything is connected in Washington and everyone has heard of everyone else. Amongst the Congress, the staffers, the lobbyists, the lawyers and the press, every individual has his own little sphere of influence. They all intersect or interconnect and there's nobody you will not meet if you live in Washington long enough. The most fatuous criticism I heard about my writing was that I was being published in the *Washington Post* because we had entertained Meg Greenfield and Katharine Graham. As if those two powerful women weren't flooded with embassy invitations. This comment was a specialty of the cheap-shot media, including some of the Canadian press who had no idea how social life in Washington operates.

Many political wives agreed with me about their negative status in Washington. A former congressional wife, Arvonne Fraser, a senior fellow at the Humphrey Institute of Public Affairs at the University of Minnesota, said it well: "I soon learned that, in the capital, congressional wives – wives of all public officials – are to be above suspicion but always suspect. We are not individuals but extensions of our husbands. I remember the day we convened the Nameless Sisterhood, a group of Washington wives. Each woman was asked to introduce herself without mentioning the name of a male relative. The group took its name when the press heard about us and the first question asked was 'Who are their husbands?' " When a man has a high profile, there is often resentment when the "wife of" achieves some kind of prominence as well. "Isn't it enough," people thought, "to be an ambassador's wife?"

Two categories of women were unhappy with my dual role. On the whole, diplomats' wives in Washington, especially ambassadors' wives, do not work. More than a few of them felt I was making fun of them, or at least was getting too big for my boots. The other group of women were journalists themselves. It just wasn't fair, my having it all. My most vicious criticism came from female journalists whom I scarcely knew.

Some of the upper media, the Lionel Portants, may have been amused by my columns. But the working media and journalists who had been rejected by the *Post* tended to resent an ambassador's wife occupying so much of the op-ed page – even though I had been a writer long before I became an ambassador's wife. Washington is a leaky, gossipy city, and I was told – *sotto voce* – that Ben Bradlee and his wife, Sally Quinn, were unhappy about me writing for the *Post*. They couldn't do much about it in the short run because the op-ed section was ruled by Meg Greenfield. As my good fortune increased, so did my enemies.

Happily, the majority in Washington seemed to enjoy my columns. I received complimentary letters from the Pentagon, the Senate, the State Department, lawyers, lobbyists and "wives of" every profession. All of a sudden I was a celebrity. My signature on credit cards was instantly recognized by people working at airline counters, dress shops and doctors' offices. And they were all anxious to give me ideas for my next column. It seemed a lot of Washingtonians thought the city took itself too seriously. At receptions strangers would come up to me, shake my hand and say, "I love your column. I just wish it would appear more often," and political and business organizations, book clubs, churches and women's groups asked me to speak about Washington life in the fast lane.

Jesse Helms, one of the most controversial senators in Congress – an extreme right-winger – was famous for holding up the appointments of American ambassadors and State Department officials. Being close to a "left-winger" like Henry Kissinger was enough to bring on Helms's disapproval. Ambassadors from other countries were not high on the list of Helms's priorities either. Nevertheless, when Premier Peter Lougheed of Alberta visited Washington he wanted to call on Helms, given that the senator was chairman of the Senate's powerful Agriculture Committee.

Allan accompanied him to the senator's office. At first Helms, who in person has a courtly Southern manner, didn't seem to pay too much attention to Peter Lougheed's careful exposition of the agricultural problems that had brought him to see the senator. The Premier grew more and more ill-at-ease as the senator glared at my husband. Finally Helms interrupted the Premier.

"The gentleman with you. Are you the Canadian ambassador?"

"Yes," my husband replied, very nervously.

"You are, then, the ambassador from Canada to the United States? Here in Washington?"

"Yes I am," Allan replied, even more nervously.

"Oh, so then you're 'husband of,' " Helms said with a smile. "My wife and I are great admirers of your wife's columns. We'd like to meet her."

Allan invited him to come for dinner at the Residence. Helms shook his head, thought a bit, then said, "I never go to embassy parties, but this time I might make an exception."

Shortly afterwards he showed up for dinner, to the astonishment of many of our American guests who had had their difficulties with him in the Senate.

The government's concern about my column offending the Americans ceased during Brian Mulroney's first visit to Washington as Leader of the Opposition. Barbara Bush, who was then wife of the Vice President, invited Mila Mulroney, Noreen Stevens, wife of Sinclair Stevens, and myself for tea at the Vice President's Victorian residence in the Naval Observatory. As we were chatting, George Bush, the most unpretentious and informal Powerful Job in Washington, popped in, wearing his jogging shorts, for a quick hello to the ladies. I remember Barbara Bush saying, "Don't you think he looks pretty cute for his age?" During the conversation, George Bush addressed me by my first name – "Hi, Sondra" – and told the company, "We're all crazy about her columns." A member of his staff may have primed him or perhaps it was a spontaneous remark. It was a terrific boost to my morale and I was grateful. After that visit I heard no criticism from official Canada.

I had been writing my letters in the *Post* for three years when

Meg told me she wanted me to write without the letter format or fictional characters. She wanted real names, more controversial subjects and less disguise. This was late in 1986. The Iran-Contra affair had just become news, and the administration was in turmoil. Trying to be constructive, she suggested a topic: "When the laughing stopped in the Reagan administration." I knew that one column of that ilk would have got us back to Ottawa sooner than we wanted. I knew I couldn't put real names, especially politically prominent names, in my columns unless I mentioned the person favourably. What if Allan had diplomatic business with him? It was only fiction that gave me any freedom to make a point. Since the *Post* wouldn't take my fictional format any longer, I could see only one way out of the quandary. I stopped writing for the *Post*. We were then receiving a lot of bad publicity in the *Washington Post* Style section, part of Ben Bradlee's "Italy," because of the "slap flap" and the Michael Deaver affair. I wondered if somehow Ben Bradlee and Sally Quinn's opinion had finally prevailed.

13/The Day of the Slap–
Wednesday, March 19, 1986

I DID NOT wake up that morning with an easy mind. My anxieties, generally free-floating, this time were focussed specifically on the day ahead.

We were having 225 people for dinner that night in honour of Prime Minister Mulroney and his wife – the largest dinner party we had ever had at the Embassy Residence.

The night before there had been a White House dinner for the Mulroneys and that was when Mrs. Reagan and the chief of protocol, Lucky Roosevelt, ticked me off because Allan and I were late.

The written scenario went thus. We were to stop at the Madison Hotel to greet the Mulroneys, then rush on ahead with Lucky Roosevelt to the White House, where the Reagans would be waiting in a private reception room upstairs to welcome the Mulroneys formally and offer them a quiet drink. We were supposed to be part of the small greeting committee that included the President, the Secretary of State, the Vice President, Mrs. Roosevelt and their spouses. One thing was written in stone: following ancient protocol (which seems to go back to the Greeks and the Romans), Allan and I had to be in place before the Mulroneys arrived. However, as soon as we arrived at the Madison Hotel Brian Mulroney pulled Allan into a room and shut the door. Lucky Roosevelt and I were left standing in the hall. After several minutes, Lucky began to fret.

"Let's go. We can't keep Mrs. Reagan waiting."

I didn't answer because I hadn't a clue what to do. Lucky became overwrought. "Allan is keeping Mrs. Reagan waiting. We have to go." At that point I protested.

"What can he do? He's with the Prime Minister. Why don't you go to the White House yourself?" I suggested naively.

Lucky was furious, because her job was to accompany the ambassador and his wife and introduce them to the President. "Go in the bedroom and get Allan," she suggested.

Even if the hotel was on fire there was no way I would open that door and interrupt the conversation between the Prime Minister and Allan. I had been trained as a good public servant's wife.

"You interrupt them," I said edgily. "Go on, open that door." Of course she didn't dare, but her face was dark.

Finally the door opened and the two of them reappeared. Even then they continued to talk. Somehow Lucky pulled Allan away and we drove to the White House, with Lucky uttering from time to time, "Mrs. Reagan's going to be very upset."

I had seen the First Lady only at public events and during coffee that morning. The formality of the White House, with military aides and security guards at every corner, can be very intimidating. For some reason Lucky dropped behind to talk to Allan, and I entered the upstairs reception room ahead of them. Mrs. Reagan stood at the doorway and said, "You're late. Where have you been? You've kept everyone waiting." I felt as if I was a member of her under-staff instead of a guest. Then she held out a pen and said, "Sign the book."

I could have done with a slightly warmer welcome. Worse was to come. The dinner was of course black tie and I had worn an evening dress. So I couldn't carry my reading glasses with me and couldn't see the precise line to which she had pointed. I scrawled my name I know not where. Mrs. Reagan peered at my signature.

"You've signed in the wrong place."

Before I could throw myself down the stairs or out the window, Allan walked in, took the proffered pen from the First

Lady and signed the book on the right line. The President was standing in the background and Lucky and her husband, Archie, who is a grandson of Theodore Roosevelt, stood in a huddle with the Reagans while Allan and I sat by ourselves on a silk sofa. Neither the President nor Mrs. Reagan spoke to us. Eventually the Shultzes walked in, followed by the Bushes. Mrs. Reagan left the Roosevelts and talked animatedly to George Shultz.

Mrs. Bush surveyed the room, saw the lonely couple on the sofa and sat down and tried to put us at our ease. "Don't be nervous. Why don't you have a glass of wine? This is a place to relax before dinner." Then she went on chatting about the visit, how much she liked Mila, Canada and ourselves.

Barbara Bush has become famous for her social grace and warmth, and those who had known her for many years often said she would make the perfect presidential wife. But these qualities were deliberately kept hidden from the public during the Reagan era. At no point during her eight years as wife of the Vice President did she ever upstage Nancy Reagan. Her volunteer work in Washington at shelters and soup kitchens, at Sasha Bruce House and at Martha's Table, were deliberately kept from the press so as not to get in the way of Mrs. Reagan's publicity. Once I watched a celebrated female broadcaster interview her on television while she was still the wife of the Vice President. "People say there is a big difference between you and Mrs. Reagan. Can you describe it?"

This was a tough question. The inner circles knew there was no love lost between the two women and obviously the interviewer wanted to trap Mrs. Bush.

"Yes," Mrs. Bush answered, "there is a big difference. Nancy's a size 4 and I'm a size 14."

At dinner I had the good fortune to sit beside George Bush, a man devoid of pomposity. By now I was used to chatting up stuffy senators, cabinet secretaries and self-important media stars. But I knew it was not necessary to chat up George Bush. Like his wife, he felt it was his duty to put one at ease. He had a way of seeming to take you into his confidence, and even of asking your opinion, that was rare and flattering, especially to a Washington "wife of." I never understood why the media gave him that "preppy" stand-offish image during the Presidential election.

After the White House dinner I went home to bed, but not to sleep. I was worried about the dinner we were giving the next day. If I had known what was going to happen, I wouldn't have got out of bed.

I had bought a red dress for the occasion and it was too tight. So I decided not to eat until dinner time, which, in retrospect, was one of the stupidest mistakes I made in my life.

A hundred and fifty names had been added within the last two weeks by the Prime Minister's Office, and the formal seating with place cards had become a major and unfinished task. Acceptances and cancellations were still in play.

A tent, which had been erected a few days before to accommodate the guests, appeared to be unsteady. Hurricane winds had been predicted for the day of the Prime Minister's dinner, and I could hear and see the tent's flaps blowing underneath my window as if it wanted to fly away with Dorothy to Oz.

There had also been some minor platform trouble, which I hoped would not bother us further. A specially built wooden platform – the dining room floor for the Prime Minister's dinner – had been built inside the tent and over the drained swimming pool. Without the platform only 125 people could be accommodated for dinner.

During the weekend Allan, myself, Donald Macdonald and his wife, Ruth, weekend guests from Toronto, had tested the platform for sturdiness.

"Why do I hear a sloshing?" Don asked.

"The floor is moving," Ruth announced.

Indeed the platform was sliding around like a water raft – our weight had caused it to shift from under the tent and we were gently sailing into the neighbours' hedge.

"But it's supposed to hold 225 guests plus the waiters and the dinner tables," I said in a panicky voice as we jumped off between a myrtle bush and a blue spruce.

Allan, angry, called the maintenance man, Glen Bullard. "Someone has launched the dining room floor. There seems to be a lake underneath."

By the time Glen arrived, we were beginning to bail. A nameless person had turned on the outside water system so the workmen could use the bathrooms in the bath house and had then forgotten to turn it off. The swimming pool had filled up, flowed over and sent the platform sliding to the bottom of the garden.

After five years these little difficulties should never have given me undue anxiety. I did, however, want everything to be perfect and the build-up of excitement, busyness and tension before and during the visit, along with my foolish day of starvation, was the instrument of my self-created disaster.

The visit of Prime Minister Mulroney was the first official visit of a Canadian Prime Minister since 1977, when Prime Minister Trudeau had visited President Carter. Trudeau had come to Washington a couple of times while we were there, but they had been "working visits," which entailed very little pomp or protocol. Unlike Pierre Trudeau and Ronald Reagan, Brian Mulroney and the President had taken to each other, and American goodwill towards Mulroney was extraordinarily high. We realized that our dinner in honour of Mulroney would have to be the grandest of the parties of our four and a half years in Washington.

When Trudeau came on his working visit and Brian Mulroney came as Leader of the Opposition, we had given beautiful dinners for about seventy to eighty people on the patio near the same amphibious swimming pool.

There was a big difference between Trudeau's style in Washington and that of Brian Mulroney. The earlier dinner for Mulroney had been in 1984. John Turner, who was about to replace Pierre Trudeau as Prime Minister, was on top of the polls when the Leader of the Opposition, Brian Mulroney, decided to visit President Reagan. It was a strategic political decision to strengthen his image and gain experience before the imminent federal election.

We had not met the Mulroneys before, but Allan, as the

Canadian Ambassador, properly asked if he could give a dinner in the Mulroneys' honour. Mulroney's people told us he would like to accept but he had only one night available. We discovered, alas, that it happened to be the same night as the President's Annual Congressional Fishfry at the White House. We were told that all the cabinet and chief White House aides, the 535 members of Congress and their top aides were on the President's invitation list. And we thought from experience that a visit by any country's opposition leader – especially one behind in the polls – would interest political and social Washington about as much as prune juice excites a Pomeranian.

Despite the negative entrail readings by everyone including Michael Deaver, the gods were with us. Eighty people turned up for a balmy dinner on the garden terrace and around the pool. Hill Folk, members of the Reagan cabinet's Supreme Court, the haute media all turned their noses away from the frying fish at the White House and came to meet the Mulroneys. Unlike Pierre Trudeau, Brian Mulroney needed no introductions, although he had met few, if any, of the guests before. He felt completely at ease with political Americans while Trudeau was interested in the stars, not in the senators and congressmen, the politicians who grind the wheels.

Mulroney acted as though he knew virtually every member of the guest list. He was fascinated by their histories and difficulties, quizzed them about their constituencies, asked Ben Bradlee and others about their relationship with the Kennedys and seemed to know everything about everybody. Mulroney genuinely liked Americans and understood their system. Trudeau was a sorcerer. He could attract those to whom he was indifferent or positively disliked. Mulroney lacked the magnetic aura but his enthusiasm for Americans and their style was warmly appreciated by them.

Now, in 1986, this grander dinner for Mulroney was to be in March, too cold for an outside dinner in Washington, and we realized that we would need a tent, something we had avoided during the other visits. I never knew a tent without a problem. They are either stifling or freezing, the acoustics are bad, they leak, they flap, the lighting is poor, you can't see what you're eating and so might end up spilling something on your best dress and not know about it until you reach the light and someone else points out how sloppy you have been.

Still, tent or no tent, life would have been manageable if all those new names hadn't come dribbling in. Instead of eighty people as we would have wished, we found ourselves planning a party for 100, then 125, then 150 people. We thought about having it in a hotel, but hotel dinners are undistinguished and cost a fortune, and we did happen to have a wonderful domestic staff and the best chef in Washington, Christian Le Pièce. The suggestions for names continued to dribble in every day and I watched as the numbers finally jumped to 225.

At the very last moment the Prime Minister's Office added a number of Canadian businessmen to a lunch that Secretary of State George Shultz was giving at the State Department, and we were told that the businessmen would be highly insulted if we didn't accommodate them as well. The more guests one adds to a party, the more difficult it becomes to leave people out. Once people know there's a truly big party taking place, no one can think of a good reason why they shouldn't be invited. Anyone who has given a big wedding knows that to their chagrin. My parents had five hundred Winnipeggers to my wedding thirty-five years ago and to this day my mother claims that certain folk in Winnipeg always give her a dirty look because she never invited them. Not everyone is as sensitive as my mother, of course, but I have inherited her guilty uneasiness about leaving people out when I have a party. In Washington we were on the receiving end of the blame and bitter feelings of the uninvited.

As usual, Allan and I supervised the seating since we believed a good part of our success was our instinct for putting compatible people together. Many ambassadors and their wives leave the seating to staff who cannot possibly know the characteristics and preferences of their guests. I have been to embassy parties where the ambassador and his wife have no idea who many of their guests might be and care not a whit whether they are happy with their dinner companions. Washingtonians had told us many horror stories about their seating at other embassies and how they vowed never to return. So seating the right people together had become my specialty. I have sat strangers side by side who eventually married – for example, Reagan's deputy secretary of State John Whitehead and broadcaster Nancy Dickerson – and I know that a number of people benefited politically, socially, and some I think financially, because they sat next to the right person at our embassy. I felt that I knew how to make a table happy. I realized too late during the planning of the Mulroney dinner that taking a personal interest in the seating, with the numbers increasing every day and with changes and cancellations being made several times a day, was beyond my capacity and was overwhelming our staff. We had never seated 225 people before and we had never had a party where there were so many other compelling duties.

During the weekend of the drifting platform there had been constant meetings, telegrams and phone calls between Allan and the White House, Allan and the State Department and Allan and the Prime Minister's Office. We had both been busy every night that week. We had met the Mulroneys at the airport on Sunday night and between Monday and Wednesday there had been the dinner at the White House, a lunch at the State Department given by the Secretary of State, visits with Mila Mulroney to the Children's Hospital, lunch with Mrs. Bush and morning coffee with Mrs. Reagan, among other events. The Embassy Residence was in turmoil and there were constant decisions to be made about "crowd flow," placement of dinner tables, flowers, microphones, speeches and menu changes.

President Reagan never attended and Vice President Bush rarely attended the "return hospitality" dinners offered by embassies after the state dinner at the White House. So it was a coup when we were told that the Vice President was willing to accept our invitation, although it would only be for coffee because of a previous speech commitment in Pennsylvania. Knowing this, we realized that the time of the party had to be moved up. Then the Vice President's schedule changed once more and his staff thought he might come in for the cocktail hour – so we moved the time of the party back. Then to our satisfaction we heard that he would come to the whole dinner, but would arrive late. So we changed the time of the party yet again. The ever-changing schedule of the Vice President added to the uncertainties of our planning, but our primary emotion was delight that the Bushes were coming. The security had to be very tight, and on the day of the dinner the Secret Service came with their dogs, who sniffed the house from top to bottom for bombs while the staff, ourselves and especially our Tibetan terrier waited outside. Two frogmen descended under the platform over the swimming pool to make sure that we wouldn't all be blown up during dessert.

According to media myth and what many people who weren't there believed, I slapped my social secretary, Connie Connor, that night in front of the Prime Minister, Vice President Bush, Barbara Bush and all the famous people at our party. Strangers believed my behaviour caused a scandal at the dinner and that the guests were shocked. People also believed I had been photographed in the act of the slap and told me they had seen the photograph in papers published around the continent and beyond.

None of this was true. No more true than other bizarre tales that were to appear in the weeks to follow, such as that Allan was having an affair with Connie, I was drunk, or that Connie had insulted me. All that was false. Much has been written about perceptions and reality. I found out that people don't want to know the difference. I found out that once a rumour is published in the newspapers, heard on television or spread through word of mouth, everyone believes it. I learned that once a thing is said or written it may as well have happened. Denial is worse than useless – it just gives the story "legs" or adds more ink to the tale and becomes supplementary fodder for the never-ending hunger of the media for gossip and speculation.

Here is what happened. By eight o'clock on the evening of our dinner I was still running around on an empty stomach. I was edgy, testy, nervy and famished. As my children will testify, my nature turns nasty at the end of a day when I try a starvation diet, especially if I haven't slept well the night before. They roll their eyes and say, "She's got the sundowners," and keep out of my way. If I'm sensible I have a snack and lie down. That day I wasn't sensible.

So when people ask, "What really happened? What was the secret behind the slap?" I know there was no secret. The whole thing was so silly that I can hardly believe it myself.

Most of the guests had arrived and had gone through into the drawing room and into the tent far from the front door. There was no reception line. The Prime Minister's staff told us that he disliked reception lines and preferred to work the room himself. As well, he was suffering from an ear infection of some kind and wanted as little strain as possible.

In a sense the party had not really started because the Bushes had not yet arrived. There were a few photographers, a couple of chauffeurs and some Secret Service men standing in front of the house waiting for the Vice President to drive up. Every two minutes the men with the wires coming out of their ears would report that his car would be coming round the corner momentarily, then suddenly they would retract their statement. "There's been a delay; another four minutes." Then we'd witness a little dispute among themselves. "Well, Bud, I'd make it 2020." "No, Mac, my info says 2030." I guess they were all wired to a different source. The on-again, off-again arrival created a bit of tension. Allan and I were standing in the front hall waiting to greet the Bushes.

Connie Connor was outside standing on the front driveway. There were no guests in the driveway or in the hallway where we were standing.

My red dress fitted reasonably well because I was hungry enough to be able to suck my empty stomach in. My figure may have been imperceptibly better, but my temper wasn't. While we were waiting for the Bushes to arrive, Allan told me to find out if there had been any last-minute changes in the seating. I stepped outside into the dark and Connie told me that there had been four or five cancellations that afternoon and the seating would have to be rearranged yet again. That's when I slapped her. It wasn't her fault. The media wrote that I got upset because Connie mentioned that Richard Darman, who was then deputy secretary of the Treasury, had cancelled in the afternoon. I have no recollection of Connie mentioning his name. I do remember that I just couldn't bear the thought of fussing with those tables at such a late moment, perhaps seconds before the arrival of the Vice President. I would probably have slapped one of the strange chauffeurs if he had been closer to me than Connie. Connie, upset, ran around the back of the house and into the kitchen. Tearful, I ran into the front hall, paused, told Allan what I had done and went into the kitchen. I embraced Connie in the midst of the platters of food and the uncomprehending, very busy kitchen staff and asked her to forgive me. I think she said, "Forget it, Mrs. Gotlieb. We're all overexcited today. It's nothing."

This happened within a time-frame of several minutes, maybe less. There were no guests present or near us during the incident, let alone the Vice President, Mrs. Bush or the Mulroneys. I apologized instantly. Nobody took a photograph of me slapping Connie. We believed the incident to be over and both of us stepped out of the kitchen, which was closed to the press, into the front hall. Connie took her place outside and I stood in the doorway with Allan. A few minutes later the Bushes arrived and we welcomed them to the embassy. The Mulroneys were deep inside the crowd talking to people in the drawing room. The photographers got their photo ops of the Vice President and his wife entering the Residence, and then they joined the Mulroneys and the rest of the guests who had been filing in around them. Then a photographer asked me if I would mind him taking a picture with Connie. Of course I agreed, not knowing that someone had witnessed the slap. Juliet O'Neill of Canadian Press (who was not a guest) had already begun to spread the word to her colleagues in the press. Juliet broke the story, but I don't think she witnessed the incident. Her first account in the newspapers said I was "reported" to have slapped Connie. If she had witnessed it, I think she would have said "I saw" instead.

Such was my innocence that night that until about midnight I believed everything had gone smoothly. Allan did too. In fact it was an almost perfect party. The Prime Minister and the Vice

President had given short but funny speeches. As everyone filed out, they told us the evening had been an unqualified success.

Then Allan, myself and Bruce Phillips, the Minister for Public Affairs at the embassy, sat down in the library for a drink, a post-mortem and a glance at the early morning edition of the *Washington Post*. Connie had just left in an excellent mood. We were pleased with the effusive account of our party in the *Post*. The social reporter who had been present at the beginning of the evening knew nothing about a slap. This was confirmed by Katharine Graham in a phone call to me a couple of days later. We were all feeling terrific when the phone rang in the library. Allan picked it up. It was Fred Doucet, the Prime Minister's senior policy adviser who led the Prime Minister's Office in the preparations for the visit. He told Allan a story was going around in the Canadian press that I had slapped Connie. He said, "The Prime Minister wants to know if it is true." Allan said, "Yes."

We didn't know then that we were about to be engulfed in a tidal wave of poisonous abuse and denigration from the media. The following morning Juliet O'Neill spread word of the slap to all the other Canadian reporters.

The Prime Minister's advisers expected that the press were going to question the Prime Minister, who, of course, had no personal knowledge about what happened. It was the custom of the ambassador and his wife to accompany the Prime Minister at the departure ceremonies at the airport. Fred Doucet told Allan that if I came along it would create a frenzy among the media. That was my first inkling of what was to come.

14/The Ride Down
the Rollercoaster . . .

THE MORNING AFTER the dinner, Allan told me that he feared we were in for a bumpy ride. Nevertheless, I don't think even he realized there would be such a savage and concerted attempt to push both of us off the rollercoaster in the next year. Juliet O'Neill (egged on by Allan Fotheringham) had filed her story and got her scoop; her slap story was already front page across the Canadian papers. The American papers learned about the incident from the Canadian Press wire service report.

The *Washington Post* got its story out only on Friday, two days after the event. This was particularly annoying for them because their publisher, Katharine Graham, their two senior editors, Meg Greenfield and Ben Bradlee, and Ben's reporter wife, Sally Quinn, were all guests at the "slap flap" party, as it was soon to be called. A *Washington Post* reporter and photographer had also been ensconced in the front hall to cover anything unusual. Nobody at the *Post*, from publisher to editors-in-chief to the working staff, had left our house thinking anything unusual had happened. Perhaps that's one of the reasons why the *Post* repeated the story with some rococo embellishments well after the news had died down.

My schedule for the days immediately after the dinner was filled with long-standing public functions, including speaking to the Women's Democratic Club, an appearance on a panel at the National Press Club and co-hosting a black-tie dinner given by the Bank of Montreal in honour of the Montreal Symphony at the Kennedy Center. I had also been invited to the Gridiron, the annual roast given by the American press, which is attended by the President, his wife, most of the cabinet, members of the House of Representatives, the Senate and, of course, the print and television media.

It would have been best if I had been previously scheduled to go on a little vacation somewhere to the north of Temiskaming, Ontario, instead of having to make public appearances every day after the slap incident.

But it didn't occur to Allan or myself that there would be such a frenzy over a spontaneous incident where no one was hurt, which was a private matter between two individuals virtually without witnesses, and following which an apology had been immediately tendered and accepted. There simply wasn't any secret or other angle to the story.

The only event I cancelled was my appearance on the panel at the Press Club. Bruce Phillips, the top press officer at the embassy, had told Allan he'd better give me a big kiss before I went on the panel, because it would be the last time he'd see me alive.

On the second day after the dinner, virtually every newspaper in both Canada and the U.S., including the *Washington Post*, gave me star billing, as did the *International Herald Tribune* and a number of British newspapers. My name was already known as a journalist to some newspaper readers, but now I had become notorious. That same evening I had to look forward to the symphony dinner at the Kennedy Center and an onslaught of cameras. If only I had won the Oscar.

Earlier that day, Barbara Bush, who along with her husband had been our American guest of honour at the Mulroney dinner, picked up the *Washington Post* and read how I had made a disgrace of myself at the party she had attended. She was furious at the press report and called the embassy right away and asked to speak to me. Allan took her call. Her sympathy, her anger at the media and her tales of how she suffered from misrepresentation in the press (she was almost crucified because a reporter was alleged

to have overheard her say "witch" or "bitch" in a private
conversation about Geraldine Ferraro) helped sustain me through
the worst times. Her words were so forthright, so sensible and so
warm that I will remember her gesture for the rest of my life. It
says much of her heart and character that (a) she rang me up and
(b) she didn't wait to see which way the wind was blowing.

I had given many speeches before, but the attention I received
from the salivating press and from the sympathetic and packed
audience at the Women's Democratic Club was unparalleled. The
organizers of the luncheon managed to control the number of
reporters, and Peatsy Hollings, the wife of Senator Ernest
Hollings from North Carolina, introduced me with elegance and
style in her Nawth Carolina drawl. A savvy woman who had
recently been supporting her husband in his campaign for the
Presidential nomination, she told me to answer only written
questions from the floor. Somehow I got through my speech,
answered questions about the slap, and said, "I was devastated."
(Those immortal words were repeated around the world.)

Everyone was giving me advice. At a *New York Times*
pre-Gridiron reception, Meg Greenfield, my editor, and Sydney
Gruson of the *New York Times*, advised me to write a "Dear
Beverly" column – a light-hearted and self-deprecatory one – in
the *Washington Post* about the incident. They felt it could help
deflect the mounting press speculation and abusive stories. The
Canadian Embassy, the Prime Minister's Office and Bruce Phillips's office asserted that the less I said about it, the sooner it
would go away. Bob Strauss told Allan that the story ought to die
down because it had nowhere to go. Warren Phillips, publisher of
the *Wall Street Journal*, whom we had lunch with in New York
the following week, echoed the Canadian advice, saying, "Don't
talk to the press, don't write about it in the press. You'll only give
the story legs."

To this day I'm not sure if I did the right thing by refraining
from saying or writing anything about the slap until now. Would I
have stopped or slowed down the endless articles about me and
Allan if I had gone public? Or would I have only created more
gossipy "news"?

Not only was I in a daze about the press reaction. The press consistently and continually described the slap flap as a "diplomatic incident" causing "continental reverberations." I came to regard this as a wild left-handed compliment, giving me a grossly distorted importance in the world of international relations. There was no "diplomatic incident." The U.S. State Department, reacting only because of the press, relayed a White House message to the Prime Minister's Office saying that they were not the least concerned. And I know that many prominent Americans called the Prime Minister to reassure him that no one in the American Congress or administration regarded the incident as other than a private one and that there were certainly no diplomatic reverberations. The Leader of the Opposition, John Turner, never brought the matter up in Parliament and, when asked about it on a television show, dismissed it in the most understanding fashion.

An important discovery on our part and a welcome by-product of the bad publicity I was getting was the sympathy I received from so many public figures who felt they had been victimized one time or another in the press. The most sympathetic and encouraging individuals were often the most well known, as in the case of Barbara Bush. I learned that one has to go through the phenomenon of the media feeding-frenzy to know what it's like. I would get calls from wives of American political figures telling me about their beastly headlines, which everyone had forgotten except themselves.

My husband and I received a lot of hate mail, some of it anti-Semitic and some of it threatening violence. But piles of encouraging notes poured in, virtually all with the same message: "Don't let the bastards get you down." Barbara Walters, Ethel Kennedy, Sargent Shriver, Senator Alan Simpson, the columnist George Will among so many others – all wrote or spoke to me personally to let me know they were on my side in my ordeal with the media.

This sustained me through the worst. Those who were truly nasty were a couple of ambassadors' wives who perhaps had been previously envious of my profile in Washington and some members of the social press who had never met me or barely knew me but who used to call to be asked to our embassy as a guest.

Perhaps the slap story would have died down if Michael Deaver's troubles had not become a leitmotif in our lives during the following year. Michael Deaver had been a friend and close confidant of President and Mrs. Reagan for over twenty years. A public-relations wizard, he had been assistant to the President in the White House during his first term but had left the White House at the beginning of Reagan's second term to set up his own public-relations firm.

Shortly after Michael Deaver left the U.S. government, Allan, on behalf of the Canadian government, signed a one-year contract with Deaver to get his advice on how to ameliorate the "being-taken-for-granted-image" that Canada had long had in the United States. The Canadian Government believed that with trade protectionism on the rise, being taken for granted was not a good thing. Hiring a public-relations expert is normal practice in Washington. It is virtually impossible for foreign and domestic industries as well as for most foreign countries not to need public-relations firms and lobbyists to combat hostile legislation and slanted imagery created by other public-relations experts and lobbyists. Japan, for example, spends many millions of dollars annually on public-relations and lobbying firms.

Then came the bombshell. The *Washington Post* published a page-one story accusing Canadian officials of cutting a deal with Deaver while he was still in the White House. The implication seemed to be that Allan had enticed Deaver, while still in the White House, into supporting Canada's acid-rain position by bribing him with this contract to take effect when he left the White House.

It was an appalling lie and, by implication, a slur on Allan's integrity. But no matter how much the story was denied by Allan, the embassy and the Prime Minister's Office, it was picked up and repeated in the Canadian press. Once a thing is written and gossiped about, it is difficult to erase the suspicion from people's minds. Why the *Washington Post* chose to feature the lie so prominently was puzzling.

About the same time John Dingell, one of the most powerful congressmen, asked Allan to appear before his committee investigating Michael Deaver's lobbying activities. He knew that foreign ambassadors do not appear before American congressional committees. But it made for interesting headlines.

Dingell's investigation led to the allegation that Deaver had perjured himself, and the committee recommended that he be investigated for perjury and for violation of the government's ethics rules.

Whitney North Seymour, Jr., a tall, white-haired patrician-looking Republican, was chosen as the independent prosecutor responsible for investigating Michael Deaver. It was being said by many in Washington that the man acted as if he had some sort of grudge against Deaver, with whom, it was believed, he had crossed swords before. He convened a grand jury, which in turn recommended prosecuting Deaver for perjury on several counts, including lying about his role in the White House concerning acid rain. The grand jury made no charges about violating conflict-of-interest rules. (Many American legal experts call the grand-jury system licence to prosecute because of the prosecutor's overwhelming influence with the jury; the defendant is not even allowed, in many jurisdictions, to have his lawyer in the court room.)

Allan knew nothing of independent prosecutors or of Michael Deaver's alleged illegal activities. But Mr. Seymour, in his investigations, seemed to love mentioning our names to the press. Even I was supposed to have some sort of secret knowledge of Michael Deaver's business affairs. This I apparently learned at a lunch involving us and the Deavers at Christmas time at the Jockey Club while Deaver was still an aide to Ronald Reagan.

Our involvement in the investigation began in April, one month after the slap incident. And, to make our lives even more exciting, a crisis emerged at the very same time in the Free Trade negotiations between Canada and the U.S. in the powerful Senate Finance Committee.

In October 1985, Prime Minister Mulroney had proposed a Free Trade agreement, which President Reagan had accepted. But there could be no negotiations unless Congress authorized the administration to conduct them. And the authority had to come from the twenty members of the Democrat-controlled Senate Finance Committee. The administration was unaware that there might be a problem in the Senate (not an unusual happening during the Reagan years). It was Senator Patrick Moynihan, the pro-Free Trade Democratic senator from New York, who tipped off Allan, with a late-evening telephone call, that trouble was brewing. Although it was supposed to be the responsibility of the administration to pilot its own bill through the Senate, power was so dissipated in the second Reagan government that the embassy realized it could not rely on the administration for information about what was going on in the corridors of the Senate. The Senate blamed the President for the U.S. trade deficit and was angry at the Reagan administration for being "soft" on Japan's unfair trading practices. Even I was hearing plenty from congress-men about the "level playing field." A large number of senators, even if they were not intrinsically against the Free Trade agree-ment, decided to get even, and if possible extract concessions against Japan and the Europeans, by not co-operating with the President on the U.S.-Canada Free Trade pact.

The administration kept insisting there wouldn't be a problem, but Allan and his embassy colleagues had better sources of information. They realized they would have to become heavily involved in the management and tactics of getting the bill passed and not merely rely upon the U.S. government. Both classic diplomatic efforts and some unorthodox methods would be needed.

Among senators who were refusing to vote for the negotiations was a pro-Free Trader from a sunny state, Senator Matsunaga of Hawaii, who told Allan that he had nothing against free trade between the U.S. and Canada – far from it – but he had promised his vote to Senator Russell Long of Louisiana, the legendary Democratic chairman of the committee. Russell Long believed, along with a number of his Democratic colleagues, that the

Reagan administration was being hopelessly wimpy in dealing with the unfair traders from across the seas. The fact that the Canada-U.S. Free Trade pact would get sideswiped seemed of little concern to him, although, as he told my husband, he certainly had nothing against Canada.

During an embassy staff brainstorming session, someone remembered what had happened to Mexico when it voted in favour of the Zionism-is-Racism resolution at the United Nations. Outraged Jewish tourists stopped vacationing in Mexico, hotels emptied, and the Mexican tourist industry had forced the government to soften their anti-Zionist stance – or so it was believed at the time.

So what has this got to do with Canada?

Canadians spend a lot of time and money in the warm state of the senator concerned. Needless to say, most of these Canadian vacationers had never heard of Free Trade. Until the election of 1988 it was not a well-known or emotional issue in Canada. But my husband and the embassy strategists knew that the senator was unaware of what might motivate Canadians to dramatic gestures. A call was made to the state governor through a Canadian official who knew him well. The idea was that the official would speculate that Canadian tourists might get into a huff and refuse to continue to take their vacations in the state if the senator didn't vote the right way on the Free Trade issue. I don't know exactly what he said or if he reminded the governor of what happened in Mexico. But the governor called the senator. The senator switched his vote (with a little help from the President) and the 10-10 vote meant that the Senate authorized the fast-track negotiations.

As a result of his efforts Allan was criticized mightily by the Canadian press for allowing the American Senate to come to such a close vote. Despite the slap, despite the Michael Deaver affair, Allan was apparently still seen by the Canadian press as having greater powers over the Senate than the President of the United States.

As if the *Post* story about the slap flap and the second story about Allan and Michael Deaver were not enough, a third appeared shortly after the Free Trade near-fiasco. An article featured in the *Washington Post* Style section damned us with a headline, "A Big Chill for Canada." The story was a pot-pourri of anonymous quotes and old press clippings, a mixture of praise about our impact in Washington and criticism about the slap and the Deaver connection. And the headline, which implied that we had become pariahs, was repeated in many Canadian and U.S. newspapers.

Despite the media mythmakers, the opposite of a chill from the North was taking place. Prominent people in New York, Los Angeles and Washington whom we scarcely knew sent us invitations to balls, dinners and "little lunches." Perhaps my notoriety piqued their curiosity and instead of being shunned we became objects of their fascination. My reaction to this sort of attention was ambiguous, but I tried to take it at face value. Also, everyone who ever came before to our embassy continued to come, except those we refused to invite. I was especially amused to note that those who wrote about the lack of entertainment at the Canadian embassy in the following two years were writers who had never been on our list and who remained off it.

Not long after the last story appeared in the *Post*, Katharine Graham and Bob Strauss told us they wanted to give a party in our honour. The party – a black-tie dinner – was to take place in Mrs. Graham's Georgetown home and she asked me for a list of people we would like her to invite.

This was a gesture of goodwill by the proprietor of a newspaper some of whose staff appeared to be conducting a smear campaign against us. Perhaps it was her way of saying that they had gone too far in their coverage. Later we were told that the acceptance rate for the party was one of the highest in Washington and that many of the seventy or so guests made a special effort to attend to show their solidarity with us. Mrs. Graham's parties are never written up in her newspaper. But this time she deliberately had the guest list placed in the Style section as a signal to her media minions. From then on nasty stories about the Gotliebs virtually ceased in the *Post*.

Michael Deaver's investigation dragged on for two years. The independent prosecutor kept trying to force Allan to testify at the trial. But the Canadian government refused to allow this because of the principle of diplomatic immunity and to avoid getting drawn into a nasty domestic political affair. It would have been better for Allan, personally, if he could have testified, to clear his name once and for all in public. But Canada did not wish to create a precedent and the U.S. authorities unanimously supported Canada in its right to make this decision. Unfortunately the media kept referring to the decision to claim diplomatic immunity as Allan's decision and not that of the Canadian government.

It took many months before Michael Deaver's ordeal was over. The judge found him guilty, not of illegal lobbying, but of perjury. Michael had perjured himself to the grand jury about certain perfectly legal activities.

By August the worst was over for us, or so we believed. We went on vacation to Brittany and returned refreshed to Washington in September.

If we thought we had gone through the most difficult period in our lives, it was trifling compared to our next ordeal. Shortly after we returned to Washington, my son-in-law, Keith Ham, a lawyer in Toronto, called Allan and told him that Rebecca, our eldest daughter, had been diagnosed as having advanced cancer of the ovaries. She had gone into hospital for some routine tests and the ultrasound had revealed disturbing abnormalities. We flew immediately to Toronto and discovered that the doctors were not in agreement with the initial diagnosis, although they all felt something was seriously wrong. Rebecca was in hospital waiting for the doctors to operate. We were in a state of disbelief but we found Rebecca and Keith in a courageous and positive state of mind. After an agonizing wait, a return to Washington, and then back to Toronto, an operation did take place. Rebecca did not have cancer of the ovaries. She had a sarcoma around the portal vein. We barely knew what a sarcoma was and had never heard of the portal vein. None of the doctors in Toronto had ever seen a sarcoma around a portal vein. One of the surgeons said he found one example in a German medical text that had occurred some forty years before. The portal vein feeds blood to the liver, pancreas, bile duct and all the organs around the stomach. Because the sarcoma had closed off the blood supply from the portal vein, Rebecca's body had compensated in a singular manner by growing a multitude of supplementary veins to keep her blood supply flowing.

This vast tangle of veins, which was keeping her alive, prevented surgical access. There was fear that she might bleed to death on the operating table. After many weeks of indecision, the Toronto doctors believed that the most complicated operation was in order involving, among many other things, a possible liver transplant. They believed that the surgeon Dr. Thomas Starzl in Pittsburgh, who invented the liver transplant and who was one of the world's great surgeons specializing in this area of the body, was the only one who could even make an attempt at eradicating the tumour.

It's hard to believe that Rebecca continued working at her law office and that we went back to Washington to continue our life as best we could during this period. In November we joined Rebecca and her husband at the hospital in Pittsburgh. Dr. Starzl began the operation at 10:00 P.M. We waited in a small hotel near the hospital, by the telephone. At four in the morning Dr. Starzl appeared and sat down beside us in the motel lobby. His words were not encouraging. He told us that the network of veins that her body had produced was so engorged that it was impossible for him to reach the liver or the portal vein. He had managed to build a bypass or shunt and had removed a portion of the sarcoma for a more precise biopsy.

After a week in the liver transplant ward Rebecca returned to Washington with us and our son-in-law to recuperate from the massive surgery. During this sad period we continued with embassy business and official entertainment while Rebecca and Keith returned to Toronto to explore other possibilities, such as radiation or chemotherapy.

About a month after the operation in Pittsburgh, Dr. Starzl called Allan and told him that the pathology report was hopeful. He said that once the action of the shunt reduced the hypertension in her venous system, he wanted to operate again. So as not to raise hopes unnecessarily, he did not contact Rebecca or her doctors in Toronto. Months passed by after that single phone call. The Toronto surgeons continued to believe that she was inoperable and could not make up their minds about treatment.

This was a terrible period for Rebecca, who was working daily in her law office. Few of her friends and acquaintances knew that she was ill. It was her desire to keep life as normal as possible.

Given her desire for privacy, we were all upset when Sally Quinn, who was promoting a sexy novel about reporters in Washington, announced on network Canadian television that Rebecca was suffering from a tragic illness. Sally's public statement apparently made Allan Fotheringham feel he had licence to mention my daughter's illness, which he then did in a dramatic manner in his syndicated column. Sally's television statement and Allan's column resulted in Rebecca receiving morbid and painful phone calls to her office and home from people she hadn't seen or heard from in years. She felt – with reason – that her privacy had been grossly invaded.

Finally in March, because of the extreme rarity of her case and the lack of consensus among doctors, Rebecca's oncologist in Toronto advised her to get a third opinion at the National Cancer Institute in Washington. She left her office for a day, flew to Washington and consulted with Dr. Steven Rosenberg and his team of radiologists and chemotherapists. They told her that her best hope was surgery and that Dr. Starzl was the only man who could "create" the operation for her. They called him directly and he immediately agreed to operate upon her in May. That one hopeful phone call in November, which then seemed like a dream, was beginning to take on some kind of reality.

Dr. Starzl warned Rebecca that he could not operate if the shunt was not working. Our anxiety was greatly increased when last-minute doubt was expressed in the Toronto General Hospital that the shunt was functioning. We all went to Pittsburgh, Rebecca, Keith, and my son, Marc, with fear in our hearts. An angiogram revealed that the shunt was functioning. But we still hadn't heard from Dr. Starzl. We finally met him in a small lobby in the motel near the hospital – the site of all our previous consultations with him. This time the lobby was filled with conventioneers. He placed his hands on Rebecca's waist and said he would give it another try. He explained that the operation would last from twelve to fourteen hours if it was to be successful. "If it's less than four, that means nothing can be done."

The night before the operation we all went out and toured Pittsburgh.

Rebecca's operation lasted about twelve hours, and Dr. Starzl came down to the waiting room and told us he believed that a cure had been effected. He had removed the sarcoma and in the process redesigned much of her vascular system.

Although her recovery was not easy, Rebecca insisted on leaving the hospital after a week. She lay in the back of the car with five drainage bottles hanging out of her abdomen, while I sat beside my son, who drove the car back to Washington. The car phone rang. It was Allan, who had flown back, warning me to be on my guard when I returned to the Residence. The persistent independent prosecutor was trying to subpoena him and me to compel us to testify at Michael Deaver's trial. When Rebecca heard that she rose up from the back seat, bottles and all, and said angrily, "They can't do that, it's illegal."

I knew then that she was going to be all right. I almost thanked Whitney North Seymour, Jr. for providing some comic relief.

Almost four years have passed since that ghastly ordeal began for Rebecca, and she is well and flourishing.

15/... And Up Again

DURING THE LAST year our Washington rollercoaster chugged its way towards the top again. Allan was immersed in the Free Trade negotiations between our two countries and actually saw the fruits of his labours (a rare thing in diplomacy) – the passing of the laws to implement the U.S.-Canada Free Trade Agreement in the U.S. Congress in the autumn of 1988.

The turbulence and drama of the Canadian election later that fall, with its single issue of the Free Trade Agreement, added to the excitement. As the Canadian debate, with its stridency and anti-American overtones, spilled over onto prime-time American television, we had to accustom ourselves to the unique situation where Canada was the centre of political attention in Washington – a delightful experience for us, even in these circumstances. We were overjoyed when Canadians, who had never thought about the Free Trade Agreement six months before, listened to the arguments and voted for the future – rejecting the distortions emerging from some of the opposition, the media doomsters and obscurantists who lived for the most part in the rich city state of Toronto.

Allan also had the satisfaction of seeing the completion of one of the most beautiful buildings in the capital, the Canadian Embassy. It too had a rollercoaster ride. At first the new Mulroney government decided to shelve or postpone the project partly for financial reasons and partly, I suppose because the architect, Arthur Erickson, was regarded as a close friend of Pierre Trudeau and it was Trudeau and his cabinet who had selected him. After the most intense lobbying on Allan's part directly to the Prime Minister and Joe Clark (he even got George Shultz to lobby Clark), Prime Minister Mulroney directly intervened and ordered the embassy to move ahead, and now Arthur Erickson's magnificent building embellishes the Pennsylvania Avenue Mall. Allan was convinced that Erickson's visionary construction, sitting on a site described by Senator Howard Baker as the best piece of real estate in the U.S., would enhance our reputation among the millions of Americans who file past that spot each year, and thus help to wipe out that country-cousin image. At a final farewell reception we gave at the new embassy the day before we left Washington in January 1989, hundreds of Americans told us how excited they were to have such a magnificent building so close to Capitol Hill. Several weeks before, a museum official in Washington who supervises architectural visits to buildings and monuments had told us that the tour in greatest demand was that of the new Canadian embassy.

Allan was the chief cheerleader for the project and its constant champion amidst endless bureaucratic battles and intrigues, but, like Moses, he never got into the Promised Land. The embassy was officially opened two months after we left and he never was able to use the magnificent ambassador's office.

We also witnessed the rollercoaster ride of George Bush in the Presidential election. In June 1988, President Reagan held a dinner at the White House in honour of Prime Minister Mulroney, which the Bushes attended. Bush, in the middle of the Presidential campaign, was some fourteen points behind Michael Dukakis in the most recent poll. Exhausted, the Bushes had flown in specially from the hustings to be at the dinner. Bush was taking a terrible beating in the press. *Newsweek* put him on the cover with "Wimp Factor" printed over his face. "Bush speak" was featured nightly on Johnny Carson, David Letterman and in the newspapers. (A waitress offered Bush a cup of coffee in a working man's diner and he said, "Just a splash." He had previously announced that he was in "deep doodoo" for some now-forgotten political sin.) This "Bush speak" was supposed to be ruinous to his image. The American public was supposed to be seeing him for what he really was – an effete Eastern Establishment type who could never fit in with good old boys, rednecks, hard hats, real Americans.

Vice President George Bush couldn't do anything right. Even being Vice President was a mistake, since Vice Presidents hardly ever get elected President.

"A.B.B.," the Republicans yelled. "Anybody but Bush."

This was the atmosphere surrounding the Bushes when they attended the White House dinner in honour of the Mulroneys.

The Reagans were late and the guests who were invited to the upstairs reception room to greet the Mulroneys were kept waiting downstairs until the Bushes ignored the restraining officials and told us to follow them upstairs. Mrs. Reagan and Mrs. Bush exchanged a few words and then Mrs. Bush, who looked tired, spoke to me.

"I'm angry with myself," she said. "I've put on fifteen pounds."

I murmured something about the difficulty of regulating diet on the campaign trail.

"I don't put on weight then," she said. "It's when I get home. I get so frustrated I raid the refrigerator at three in the morning."

Anyone who's ever had a weight problem has to find that remark endearing.

There was a large pre-dinner cocktail party downstairs at the White House with the usual sprinkling of Mrs. Reagan's *W* and *Suzy* friends, the people who appear in the social columns of the New York daily tabloids. I had just had a back operation and was uncomfortable on my feet, so I decided to sit down at my designated seat in the empty dining room. Just as I was beginning to feel like a sore thumb, sitting alone in the White House dining room, George Bush walked in and took his seat wearily in his place, which happened to be next to me.

When I had sat beside George Bush previously he had always been the most attentive and least pompous of dinner companions, in a town where self-importance and rank are paramount. But this was election year and here was a Presidential candidate in trouble, stuck beside a foreign "wife of" who had no power to raise campaign funds or deliver a single vote – who was totally devoid of political or financial influence. Given this situation, most men and women with connections and power in most centres of the world would have excused themselves and gone off to gossip or deal with someone of importance – at least until all the guests had been seated.

Just then, Jim Baker, then Secretary of Treasury, who was later to become Bush's campaign manager and subsequently his Secretary of State, also wandered into the still empty dining room. Obviously they had quite a few things of interest to discuss. Baker, from afar, gestured to Bush to come over. "Let's talk," he said. I knew Bush and Baker were old friends as well as political allies. The Vice President had just finished telling me how close he felt to Baker, how much he admired him and that he hadn't seen him for a while. Nevertheless, George Bush refused to budge.

"No, no, I'm not going to leave Sondra by herself. I'm going to stick with her." (It astonished me that he even remembered my name. How many hands had he shaken that summer?)

And there he sat, chatting about everything except campaign politics until the end of dinner. He discussed the guests, turned up his nose towards the Social X-rays, the jet setters, the *Suzy* and *W* people at the dinner, and told me how much he adored his sister, Nancy Ellis, who had been invited for the first time to a White House dinner.

Among people of power and influence civility is one of the rarest qualities. I don't know how history will remember George Bush, but I shall remember him as that rarity – a gentleman.

After more than seven years my worries about the domestic perils of embassy life had disappeared. I had the perfect chef, housekeeper and staff. We knew most of the political and media people in Washington, and putting together guests lists was no longer a chore. In fact it had become highly enjoyable giving dinners for small groups of interesting people at our specially constructed round table for fourteen. I had come to specialize in organizing last-minute "salons," mixing a wide cross-section of people from different backgrounds – political, media, academic, business and the arts. This was the kind of party I liked best and I believe my guests enjoyed the most.

I used to hear jaded Washingtonians complain that Washington was provincial, lacking New York's money and London's culture. There is money enough in Washington, except that too much conspicuous display is dangerous in a political town. But the centre of what is still the most powerful country in the world naturally attracts those with new ideas who in turn create intellectual energy and electricity, and that is the Washington I adore. For me it was a privilege to be there and observe.

Most people have a reason for coming to Washington – for a couple of days, for a couple of years or for a political term. Those who come for a political term often stay in Washington for the rest of their lives even though their political party has lost and their position is gone. These people become lobbyists, media types, think-tank specialists or lawyer-lobbyists. Every lawyer in Washington, willy nilly, becomes a lobbyist if his work has something to do with the government. Potomac fever is a highly communicable disease, especially among those who have tasted power. All this results in a mix of committed and involved people that is probably unique in the world. There was always something unexpected happening – good, bad or ridiculous – but never dull. Serge Diaghilev, the Russian ballet impresario, said that Paris in the twenties was a city where he could safely say, "Etonne-moi – Astonish me." Washington, in the political and human sense, though much less so in the arts, has a high astonishment factor. Few cities, other than London and New York (and now *perhaps* Moscow), can make such a boast.

For me, the most enjoyable aspect of being an ambassador's wife was being able to take advantage of the human resources on my doorstep. It was a privilege to be able to summon the best and the brightest to your table. There was the continual discussion of grand events, for example listening to Zbigniew Brzezinski, Brent Scowcroft and Richard Burt discussing the future of Germany and Eastern Europe. Or receiving political analysis and gossip from the insiders. Or being able to meet John Updike, Larry

McMurtry and Glenda Jackson along with historians, artists and Pulitzer Prize-winners. Any ambassador has the ability to entertain in Washington. It just takes a little imagination to put a few diverse guests together.

One evening not long before we left Washington we had a dinner in honour of Christopher Plummer and Glenda Jackson, who were performing in *Macbeth*. I had been warned that Miss Jackson was a classic left-wing British Labourite and looked upon the CIA as a tool of the devil. My other guests included Bill Webster, director of the CIA and an admirer of Miss Jackson's acting. I decided to seat them together. When I told Glenda Jackson about her dinner partner, her eyes widened and she said, "Well, you won't mind if I say exactly what I think."

After dinner I asked both of them how it went. "I sort of liked him," she said. "Not at all what I expected." Webster rolled his eyes and said Miss Jackson was "lively."

During my last years in Washington I relaxed and enjoyed myself. But for Allan the representational duties became tedious and anti-climactic once the Free Trade negotiations were over. And apart from the small salon-type dinners, I knew I couldn't face standing in one more reception line for all the bankers, the bakers, the ballerinas and the U.S. congressmen who had filed through our doors.

It was time to leave and one fact was certain in our minds. We didn't want another embassy. We had had the privilege of being at the most interesting post in the world at one of the most important times in U.S.-Canadian history and for longer than any other Canadian ambassadorial couple in Washington. So we knew that when the Reagan administration was over, it was time for us to go. Even though the Bush administration, which some Democratic cynics have dubbed Reagan III, contained many people we knew well and who had become our friends, our taste for diplomatic life was sated.

Although there is new administration, Washington still works the same way. As Robert Strauss said to me when I returned on a visit six months after we left Washington, "Some faces may change, but Washington stays the same."

He meant that there are permanent power-players in Washington, including the warlords of the Senate and the House of Representatives and the princes and princesses of the media. Anyone who is a member of these institutions has a catbird seat in Powertown and usually keeps his perch, no matter who is President.

In the current scene there are many "crossovers" – those who played a substantive role in the Reagan administration and continue to do so in the Bush era. Secretary of Treasury Nicholas Brady, Attorney General Richard Thornburgh, Chairman of the Federal Reserve Board Alan Greenspan, as well as Jim Baker, formerly Secretary of Treasury in the Reagan administration and now Secretary of State, are prominent socially in the Bush administration. Greenspan entertains with his close friend, Andrea Mitchell, NBC's congressional correspondent, in Andrea's renovated Victorian house off Chain Bridge Road.

"Remember, the Reagans were Californians and strangers to Washington. The Bushes have been here since 1960. He was a congressman from Texas, head of the CIA, head of the Republican National Committee, as well as being Vice President for eight years. They don't have to court anyone. They know everybody."

This is what everyone said during my visit in mid-1989. The style of entertaining at the White House has changed. It is more informal and politically purposeful. "George Bush loves doing business in a social setting," one White House staff member was reported as saying. Washingtonians are amazed at how much entertaining is taking place in the family quarters upstairs.

I know from my own personal experience in the Reagan era that it was Mrs. Reagan, not the President, who controlled the White House invitation list, and she controlled it absolutely. Her choices had social rather than political motivations. President Reagan let his wife make the decisions about who was coming for dinner.

Barbara Bush, however, calls her husband "Perle Mesta" Bush because of his social tinkering and spontaneous last-minute dinners and parties.

But elsewhere little seems to have changed. On my return visit,

I went to Katharine Graham's birthday party at her Georgetown house with its circular driveway and sweeping lawn. It was for me almost a Proustian party – it seemed that everyone who had been influential during the present and past administrations was there, passing from the red drawing room into the tent set up by the swimming pool to accommodate the huge crowd. It was a typically humid and airless June day, and the power-players in Washington, from old faces like Senator Kennedy to new faces like John Sununu, Chief of Staff of the Bush White House, had come to pay their respects. The Californians had left with President Reagan, just as the Georgians had left with Jimmy Carter, yet the bustle was the same. So many people I had seen hundreds of times before were animatedly discussing the scandal, the deal, the policy, the political celebrity of the week. The wheels were turning, the electricity was on full power. The lords of Congress and the Senate circled and muttered and glanced and assessed the damage the new administration might inflict upon their plans. Those in the Bush administration revelled in their new powerful role. And those in the media watched, waited and wondered where they'd find their new story.

Washington is not a city. It is a compact organism. It lives on itself. I will miss it more than I can say.

INDEX